VERMITECHNOLOGY, FARM AND FERETILIZER

ENV BOOKS SERIES

VERMITECHNOLOGY, FARM AND FERETILIZER

Editors

Dr. Ashok K. Rathoure

Director
Biohm Consultare Pvt. Ltd.
Surat (Gujarat)
(India)

Dr. Pawan Kumar 'Bharti'

Society for Environment, Health Awareness of Nutrition & Toxicology (SEHAT)
B-225/5D, Top Floor, Subhash Gali, Road No. 7, Block B
Ashok Nagar, Shahdara, Delhi - 110 093
(India)

&

Dr. Jaswant Ray

Society for Environment, Health, Awareness of Nutrition & Toxicology (SEHAT)
F-119, Pandav Nagar
Meerut (UP)
(India)

DPH

DISCOVERY PUBLISHING HOUSE PVT. LTD.
INDIA

Published by:
Namit Wasan
DISCOVERY PUBLISHING HOUSE PVT. LTD.
4383/4B, Ansari Road, Darya Ganj
New Delhi-110 002 (India)
Phone : +91-11-23279245; 23253475; 43596065
E-mail : discoverybooksindia@gmail.com
discoverypublishinghouse@gmail.com
namitwasan9@gmail.com
web : www.discoverypublishinggroup.com

***First Edition:* 2020**

ISBN: 978-93-88854-38-2

Vermitechnology, Farm and Fertilizer

Printed at:
Infinity Imaging Systems
Delhi

M.S. Swaminathan Research Foundation

M.S. Swaminathan
Founder Chairman
Ex-Member of Parliament (Rajya Sabha)

Foreword

I am very glad to know that a several books are being edited under the aegis of ENVBOOKS series, Delhi, India on various sub-themes of Agriculture and environment like:

'Cultivation Techniques for Agriculture Crops'
'Air Pollution and Control'
'Seed and Food Storage Technologies'
'Heavy Metals and Impacts on Plants'
'Climate Change and Agriculture Production'
'Scientific Writing and Research Methodology'
'Laboratory Management'
'Statistical Tools in Science'
'Advances in Chemistry and Chemical Sciences'
'Irrigation techniques in Crop management' 'Waste Management Practices'
'Vermitechnology, Farm and Fertilizers'
'Animal Science and Pest Control'
'Recent Research in Biochemistry and Molecular Biology'
'Water Management and Sustainability'
'Soil Quality and Agriculture'

I am very happy to learn that a number of editors and authors from different institutions and university of different nations are involved in editing these books. The books are the compendium of screened-in manuscripts received from different countries like UK, Canada, Egypt, Nigeria, Ghana, Ethiopia, China, South Africa, Japan, Guyana, PNG, Nepal, South America, and various parts of India. I am feeling delighted in writing forward to these books and congratulate to Dr. Pawan Kumar Bharti, Editor-in-Chief and founder of ENVBOOKS series and of course his team for their tenacity and hard work in compiling these valuable compendiums.

I hope these books will be beneficial for academician, researchers, industrialist, policy makers and students as study material and will work as reference for further research work.

M.S. Swaminathan

Preface

In recent years, disposal of organic wastes from various sources like domestic, agriculture and industrial has caused serious environmental hazards and economic problems. Burning of organic wastes contributes tremendously to environmental pollution thus, leading to polluted air, water and land. This process also releases large amounts of carbon dioxide in the atmosphere, a main contributor to global warming together with dust particles. Burning also destroys the soil organic matter content, kills the microbial population and affects the physical properties of the soil. It has been demonstrated that earthworms can process household garbage, city refuse, sewage sludge and waste from paper, wood and food industries. In tropical and subtropical conditions Eudrilus eugeniae and Perionyx excavatus are the best vermicomposting earthworms for organic solid waste management. The use of earthworms in composting process decreases the time of stabilisation of the waste and produces an efficient bio-product, i.e., vermicompost.

Organic farming system is gaining increased attention for its emphasis on food quality and soil health. Vermicompost and vermiculture associated with other biological inputs have been actually used to grow vegetables and other crops successfully and have been found to be economical and productive. In this regard, recycling of organic waste is feasible to produce useful organic manure for agricultural application. Compost is becoming an important aspect in the quest to increase productivity of food in an environmentally friendly way. Compost is becoming an important aspect in the quest to increase productivity of food in an environmentally friendly way. Vermicomposting offers a solution to tonnes of organic agro-wastes that are being burned by farmers and to recycle and reuse these refuse to promote our agricultural development in more efficient, economical and environmentally friendly manner. Both the sugar and rice industries burn their wastes thereby, contributing tremendously to environmental pollution thus, leading to polluted air, water and land. This process also releases large amounts of carbon dioxide in the atmosphere, a main contributor to global warming together with dust particles. Burning also destroys the soil organic matter content, kills the microbial population and affects the physical properties of the soil.

The present book updates the subject content on Earthworm, Vermitechnology, Farm mechanization and details, farming system, bio-fertilizers, bio-composting, eco-friendly approach in agriculture, remediation of soil, biological actions in Farming, organic farming, soil health improvement and bio-fertilizers.

Thanks are due to publisher and contributors from various institutions and universities.

The book will be helpful for the researchers, academia working in the field of Vermitechnology, Farm and farming system, bio-fertilizers, remediation of soil, organic farming, soil health improvement and bio-fertilizers.

–Editors

(envbooks@gmail.com)

Contents

Section III: Fertilizer

Introduction

The disposal and management of solid wastes is a technical and ecological challenge throughout the globe because of their quantities and heterogeneous nature. Vermicomposting is one of the most ecologically and economically sound technologies for handling the biodegradable organic fraction of solid wastes. A large variety of such wastes of plant and animal origins can be gainfully vermicomposted at different scales varying from a household bin to a city level. Vermicompost also has excellent manurial properties as a soil conditioner and fertilizer, being a source of nitrogen, phosphorus, potassium, and other nutrients for plants. These virtues make vermicomposting a good option for processing the enormous quantities of biodegradable organic solid wastes that are generated in huge quantities.

Vermicompost is a rich organic medium consisting of nutrients, plant growth promoting substances, and beneficial micro organisms necessary for plant growth. It is made from agricultural waste and the use of earthworms. By using a layered process over a period of time, an organic medium is derived that reduces the need for large amounts of pesticides and even fertilizers.

Agriculture/Organic waste varies but is quite accessible. Types include dried grass, manure and other animal waste, leaf matter, kitchen waste, leaves and flowers after the extraction of oil, fruit/vegetable rind, pulp and other similar waste. crop remains, seed husk, bagasse and many others.

Vermicompost (vermi-compost, vermiculture) is the product of the composting process using various species of worms, usually red wigglers, white worms, and other earthworms, to create a mixture of decomposing vegetable or food waste, bedding materials, and vermicast. Vermicast (also called worm castings, worm humus, worm manure, or worm feces) is the end-product of the breakdown of organic matter by earthworms. These castings have been shown to contain reduced levels of contaminants and a higher saturation of nutrients than the organic materials before vermicomposting.

Vermicompost contains water-soluble nutrients and is an excellent, nutrient-rich organic fertilizer and soil conditioner. It is used in farming and small scale sustainable, organic farming.

Vermicomposting can also be applied for treatment of sewage. A variation of the process is vermifiltration (or vermidigestion) which is used to remove organic matter, pathogens and oxygen demand from wastewater or directly from blackwater of flush toilets.

In recent years, disposal of organic wastes from various sources like domestic, agriculture and industrial has caused serious environmental hazardsand economic problems. Burning of organic wastes contributes tremendously to environmental pollution thus, leading to polluted air, water and land. This process also releases large amounts of carbon dioxide in the atmosphere, a main contributor to global warming together with dust particles. Burning also destroys the soil organic matter content, kills the microbial population and affects the physical properties of the soil. It hasbeen demonstrated that earthworms can process household garbage, city refuse, sewage sludge and waste from paper, wood and food industries (Kale *et al.*,1982). In tropical and subtropical conditions Eudrilus eugeniae and Perionyx excavatus are the best vermicomposting earthworms for organic solid waste management (Kale, 1998). The use of earthworms in composting process decreases the time of stabilisation of the waste and produces an efficient bio-product, i.e., vermicompost.

Organic farming system is gaining increased attention for its emphasis on food quality and soil health. Vermicompost and vermiculture associated with other biological inputs have been actually used to grow vegetables and othercrops successfully and have been found to be economical and productive (Ansari and Ismail, 2008; Ansari and Jaikishun, 2011). In this regard, recycling of organic waste is feasible to produce useful organic manure for agricultural application. Compost is becoming an important aspect in thequest to increase productivity of food in an environmentally friendly way.Compost is becoming an important aspect in the quest to increase productivity of food in an environmentally friendly way. Vermicomposting offers a solution to tonnes of organic agro-wastes that are being burned by farmers and to recycle and reuse these refuse to promote our agricultural development in more efficient, economical and environmentally friendly manner. Both the sugar andrice industries burn their wastes thereby, contributing tremendously to environmental pollution thus, leading to polluted air, water and land. This process also releases large amounts of carbon dioxide in the atmosphere, a main contributor to global warming together with dust particles. Burning also destroys the soil organic matter content, kills the microbial population and affects the physical properties of the soil.

Farm and Farming

A farm is an area of land that is devoted primarily to agricultural processes with the primary objective of producing food and other crops; it is the basic facility in food production. The name is used for specialised units such as arable farms, vegetable farms, fruit farms, dairy, pig and poultry farms, and land used for the production of natural fibres, biofuel and other commodities. It includes ranches, feedlots, orchards, plantations and estates, small holdings and hobby farms, and includes the farmhouse and agricultural buildings as well as the land. In modern times the term has been extended so as to include such industrial operations as wind farms and fish farms, both of which can operate on land or sea.

Farming originated independently in different parts of the world, as hunter gatherer societies transitioned to food production rather than, food capture. It may have started about 12,000 years ago with the domestication of livestock in the Fertile Crescent in western Asia, soon to be followed by the cultivation of crops. Modern units tend to specialise in the crops or livestock best suited to the region, with their finished products being sold for the retail market or for further processing, with farm products being traded around the world.

Modern farms in developed countries are highly mechanized. In the United States, livestock may be raised on range land and finished in feedlots and the mechanization of crop production has brought about a great decrease in the number of agricultural workers needed. In Europe, traditional family farms are giving way to larger production units. In Australia, some farms are very large because the land is unable to support a high stocking density of livestock because of climatic conditions. In less developed countries, small farms are the norm, and the majority of rural residents are subsistence farmers, feeding their families and selling any surplus products in the local market.

Fertilizers

A fertilizer is any material of natural or synthetic origin (other than liming materials) that is applied to soil or to plant tissues to supply one or more plant nutrients essential to the growth of plants. Many sources of fertilizer exist, both natural and industrially produced.

Fertilizers enhance the growth of plants. This goal is met in two ways, the traditional one being additives that provide nutrients. The second mode by which some fertilizers act is to enhance the effectiveness of the soil by modifying its water retention and aeration.

Fertilizers typically provide, in varying proportions:

Three main macronutrients:

- Nitrogen (N): leaf growth

- Phosphorus (P): Development of roots, flowers, seeds, fruit;
- Potassium (K): Strong stem growth, movement of water in plants, promotion of flowering and fruiting;

Three secondary macronutrients:

Calcium (Ca), magnesium (Mg), and sulfur (S);

Micronutrients

Copper (Cu), iron (Fe), manganese (Mn), molybdenum (Mo), zinc (Zn), boron (B). Of occasional significance are silicon (Si), cobalt (Co), and vanadium (V).

The nutrients required for healthy plant life are classified according to the elements, but the elements are not used as fertilizers. Instead compounds containing these elements are the basis of fertilizers. The macro-nutrients are consumed in larger quantities and are present in plant tissue in quantities from 0.15% to 6.0% on a dry matter (DM) (0% moisture) basis. Plants are made up of four main elements: hydrogen, oxygen, carbon, and nitrogen. Carbon, hydrogen and oxygen are widely available as water and carbon dioxide. Although nitrogen makes up most of the atmosphere, it is in a form that is unavailable to plants. Nitrogen is the most important fertilizer since nitrogen is present in proteins, DNA and other components (e.g., chlorophyll). To be nutritious to plants, nitrogen must be made available in a "fixed" form. Only some bacteria and their host plants (notably legumes) can fix atmospheric nitrogen (N2) by converting it to ammonia. Phosphate is required for the production of DNA and ATP, the main energy carrier in cells, as well as certain lipids.

Micronutrients are consumed in smaller quantities and are present in plant tissue on the order of parts-per-million (ppm), ranging from 0.15 to 400 ppm DM, or less than 0.04% DM. These elements are often present at the active sites of enzymes that carry out the plant's metabolism. Because these elements enable catalysts (enzymes) their impact far exceeds their weight percentage.

Organic Fertilizers

Organic fertilizers are fertilizers derived from animal matter, animal excreta (manure), human excreta, and vegetable matter (e.g. compost and crop residues). Naturally occurring organic fertilizers include animal wastes from meat processing, peat, manure, slurry, and guano.

In contrast, the majority of fertilizers used in commercial farming are extracted from minerals (e.g., phosphate rock) or produced industrially (e.g., ammonia). Organic agriculture, a system of farming, allows for certain fertilizers and amendments and disallows others;

The main organic fertilizers are, peat, animal wastes (often from slaughter houses), plant wastes from agriculture, and treated sewage sludge.

REFERENCES

https://technology4agri.wordpress.com/2013/02/12/vermitechnology-an-introuction/

https://www.sciencedirect.com/science/article/pii/B9780444636645000058

http://www.globalsciencebooks.info/Online/GSBOnline/images/2010/DSDP_4(SI1)/DSDP_4(SI1)22-47o.pdf

https://en.wikipedia.org/wiki/Vermicompost

https://pdfs.semanticscholar.org/44c3/437daabd421112468ab1c79bc1bc69c4bd9b.pdf

https://en.wikipedia.org/wiki/Farm

https://en.wikipedia.org/wiki/Fertilizer

https://en.wikipedia.org/wiki/Organic_fertilizer

Kale, R.D. (1998). Earthworm Cinderella of Organic Farming. Prism Book Pvt Ltd, Bangalore, India. 88 pp.

Kale, R.D., Bano, K. and Krishnamoorthy, R.V. (1982). Potential of Perionyxexcavatus for utilising organic wastes. Pedobiologia., 23 : 419-425

Ansari, A.A. and Ismail, S.A. (2008). Reclamation of sodic soils through Vermitechnology. Pakistan Journal of Agricultural Research, Volume 21, Number (1-4): 92-97.

Ansari, A.A. and Sukhraj, K. (2010). Effect of Vermiwash and Vermicompost on Soil Parameters and Productivity of Okra (Abelmoschus esculentus) in Guyana. Pakistan Journal of Agricultural Research, Volume 23 Number (3-4): 137-142.

Ansari, A.A. and Jaikishun, S. (2011). Vermicomposting of Sugarcane Bagasse and Rice Straw and its Impact on the Cultivation of Phaseolus Vulgaris L. in Guyana, South America.

Journal of Agricultural Technology 7(2): 225-234.

Section I: Vermitechnology

Pages: 3-15

Vermitechnology, Farm and Fertilizer

Edited by: Dr. Ashok K. Rathoure; Dr. Pawan Kumar 'Bharti' and Dr. Jaswant Ray

ISBN: 978-93-88854-38-2

Edition: **2020**

Published by: **Discovery Publishing House Pvt. Ltd., New Delhi (India)**

1

Earthworms and Environmental Pollutants - A View

Kalaiselvi*, P., S.Mahimairaja, S. Paul Sebastian
E. Parameswari, V. Davamani, K. Suganya and R. Poornima

INTRODUCTION

Earthworms play a vital role in soil formation, principally by engulfing organic matter, disintegrating and mixing it intimately with soil mineral particles. They also play an important role in soil macrofauna. The bioaccumulation ability of earthworms is essential for a bio-monitoring organism. Bio-monitoring method would be appropriate to evaluate metal toxicity, because of its sensitivity and availability for unknown metabolites. Recently, earthworms act as a bio-monitor organism for soil pollutants, since it plays a vital role in the soil macrofauna biomass. The species *Eiseniafetida* is most commonly used in ecotoxicology, and is recognized as a useful bio-monitor for testing the chemical toxicity. In this review, we describe the effect of organic and inorganic pollutant on earthworms and the use of earthworms as biomarker.

POLLUTANT

A toxic chemical or pollutant is defined as a substance introduced to the environment by human activity that has a deleterious effect on biological organisms (Moriasty, 1983).

Pollutants are classified into two categories based on their chemical nature:

Department of Environmental Sciences, Tamil Nadu Agricultural University, Coimbatore, (India)

1. Inorganic pollutants (Heavy metals)
2. Organic pollutants (Pesticides)

Effect of Inorganic Pollutants

Among the different forms of pollutants the inorganic form of the pollutants includes heavy metals. Heavy metals are important contaminants in agricultural and non-agricultural soils. Bioaccumulation of heavy metals in earthworms has been studied in many different environments including.

1. Mine spoil tips
2. Land contaminated by the emissions from metal smelting or refining works
3. Land exposed to motor vehicle emissions
4. Municipal waste sites
5. Agricultural soils contaminated with metals applied to the soil as pesticides
6. Land exposed to contaminated sediments dredged from rivers
7. Sewage waste water
8. Sewage sludge

Residues of chemicals can bioaccumulate in earthworms and may be distributed by them to the tissues of animals in higher tropic levels within the food webs. A chemical accumulated in the tissues of the earthworms to be related more accurately to the concentration of the contaminant present in the soil. So they have been used to measure the level of contamination of soils due to heavy metals and long lived organic chemicals (Marquenie and Simmers, 1988).

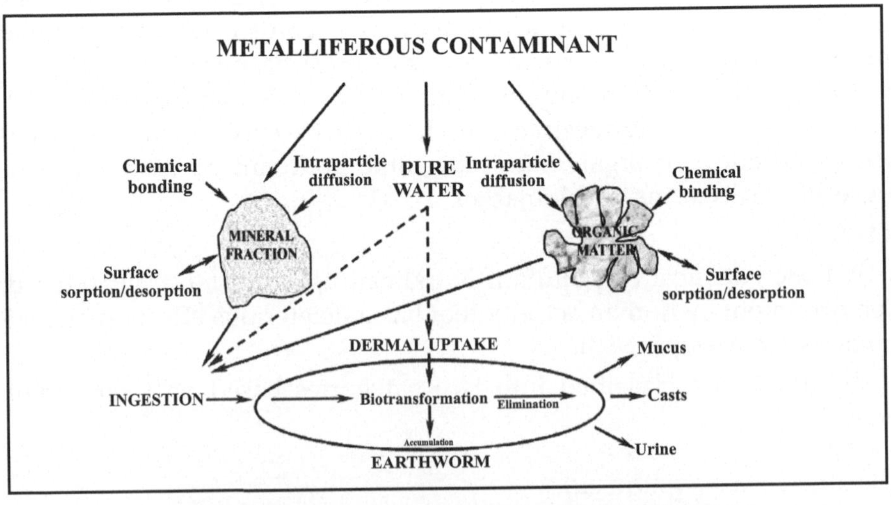

Fig. 1.1. Processes involved in the interactions between metalliferous contaminants, soil and earthworms

Life-History Patterns in Metal-Exposed Earthworm Populations

Spurgeon *et al.* (1999) assessed the growth and development of F1 *Lumbricusrubellus*bred from reference and one metal-exposed smelter populations in soils from both sites. In the clean soil, faster growth maturation was found at selected time intervals for the smelter worms. This result is in agreement with life-cycle models, which indicate that polluted-site populations will be adapted for faster growth, earlier maturation and increased reproductive effort. Life-history adaptation is not, however, the only explanation for the differences in maturation rates found. During the exposures, mortality of smelter worms was higher than for the reference strain. This resulted in a reduction in the density of the smelter strain. In earthworms, both growth rate and maturation time are known to be density dependent. Thus it is probable that density-mediated responses of growth and development, rather than adaptation, are primarily responsible for the observed life-history.

The effects of metal contaminants on the population density and species composition of earthworms were studied by spurgeon *et al.* (1996) at 22 sites around a primary smelting works situated at Avonmouth, southwest England. All worms were absent from six sites within 1 km of the factory and numbers were also reduced significantly at an additional four sites 2 km from the plant. Total earthworm density was found to be inversely related to concentrations of metals in soils. Some species of earthworms were found to be more 'sensitive' to metals and were absent from sites where more 'tolerant' species persisted. For example, *Lumbricusrubellus, Lurnbricuscastaneus*and*Lumbricusterrestris*were all present at sites close to the smelter where *Aporrectodearosea, Aporrectodeacaliginosa* and *Allolobophorachlorotica* were absent. The first three 'tolerant' species have more active calcium secretion glands in their gut than the three 'sensitive' worms. Calcium is known to be involved in the sequestration and elimination of various metals through the chlorogogenous tissue.

Effect of Organic Pollutants

Effects of Toxic Chemicals on Earthworms

Earthworms are exposed to chemicals in a variety of ways. When land is treated with pesticides to control soil inhabiting pests, the chemicals are usually mixed thoroughly into the soil so that the pest comes into maximum contact with the pesticide. A wide range of non pest organisms such as earthworms are also exposed to the chemicals. Residues of chemicals can bioaccumulate in earthworm and may be distributed by them to the tissues of animals in higher trophic levels within the food web. The first compounds to be investigated for bioaccumulation into earthworms were the organochlorine insecticides (Fanelli *et al.*, 1980).

Responses of Earthworms to Toxic Chemicals

Acute Toxicity

Acute toxicity is usually the first criterion used in assessing the susceptibility of earthworms.

Chronic Toxicity

Many sublethal chronic toxicity symptoms of earthworms exposed to chemicals have been recorded some of which are serious and short term others of which are minor but involve long-term effects on the earthworms and their functions.

- Malformation
- Effects on activity
- Effects on nervous and physiological functions
- Effects on growth
- Effects on reproduction

Uptake and Metabolism of Chemicals by Earthworms

Uptake

❖ Organochlorine

One of the first reports on the uptake of chemicals into earthworms was by Barker (1985). He found large residues of DDT and its break down products in the tissues of earthworms taken from soil.

Loss toxic	:	HCH, DDT, Aldin, Dieldrin
Moderately toxic	:	Endosultan, Isobenzan
Extremely toxic	:	Chlordane

❖ Organophosphate insecticide

Most OP are not very toxic. Edwards *et al.* (1968) reported that earthworms from plots treated with the organophosphorus insecticide, chlorfenvinphos, did not contain appreciable quantities of this insecticide or its metabolites. But phorate was foundto be extremely toxic.

❖ Carbamate insecticide

The soluble insecticides such as aldicarb can be bioconcentrated very rapidly into earthworm tissues in large amounts when this is applied to flooded soils. It can be concentrated only as the parent compound, but not as metabolites. All carbamate insecticides are highly toxic.

❖ Pyrethroids

Pyrethroids synthetic and natural are found to be non toxic.

- Fungicides

  Most of the fungicides are non toxic.

- Herbicides

  Very few herbicides directly toxic to earthworms. They have indirect effects due to their influence on weeds as a source of supply of organic matter on which earthworms feed in soil.

  Moderate effects : Atrazine, simazine, dinoseb

Metabolism

The microorganisms living in the earthworm gut can breakdown DDT to DDE (Edwards *et al.*, 1971). Aldrin to dieldrin, Heptachlor to Heptachlor epoxide (Chio and Sanborn, 1976).

There is much less evidence of the role of earthworms in metabolizing organophosphate insecticides. Thompson (1970) reported that earthworms could metabolize fensultothion to its sulfone. Parathion was slowly converted to paraoxon which was then rapidly hydrolyzed to diethyl hydrogen phosphate (Steersen, 1979).

Table 1.1
Relative toxicities of some common pesticides to earthworms

PESTICIDE	TOXICITY LEVEL
I. Vermicides	
Ammonium sulfate	Very toxic on acid soils only
Mowrah meal	Toxic with low environmental hazard
II. Fumigants	
Chloropicrin	Very toxic at normal rates
Methyl bromide	Very toxic at normal rates
Metham sodium	Very toxic at normal rates
Dichloropropane/Dichloropropene	Very toxic at normal rates
III. Insecticides & Acaracides	
Organochlorines:	
Chlordane	Very toxic, used for earthworm control
Toxaphene	Very toxic, used for earthworm control
Heptachlor	Very toxic, used for earthworm control
Aldrin	Toxic at high rates only
Dieldrin	Toxic at high rates only
Endrin	Variable toxicity at does rate
Isobenzan	Variable toxicity
Organophosphates:	
Ethoprop	Very toxic at normal rates
Fensulfothion	Very toxic to some species
Phorate	Very toxic at normal rates
Fonofos	Moderately toxic at normal rates
Karathion	Moderately toxic

(Table Contd...)

PESTICIDE	TOXICITY LEVEL
Methyl parathion	Moderately toxic
Thiomazin	Moderately toxic
Isofos	Slightly toxic at normal rates
Disulfoton	Slightly toxic at normal rates
Fenamiphos	Slightly toxic at normal rates
Chlorpyrifos	Relatively non-toxic at normal rates
Isofenphos	Relatively non-toxic
Malathion	Relatively non-toxic
Menazon	Relatively non-toxic
Phosalone	Relatively non-toxic
Terbufos	Relatively non-toxic
Trichlorfon	Relatively non-toxic
Carbamates:	
Aldicarb	Very toxic at normal rates
Bufencarb	Very toxic at normal rates
Carbaryl	Very toxic, used for earthworm control
Carbofuran	Very toxic
Dithiocarbamate	Highly toxic at normal dose rates
Methomyl	Highly toxic at normal dose rates
Oxamyl	Highly toxic at normal dose rates
Tirpate	Highly toxic at normal dose rates
IV. Fungicides	
Benomyl	Very toxic at normal rates
Carbenzadim	Very toxic at normal rates
Thiophanate methyl	Very toxic at normal rates
V. Herbicides All are relatively non-toxic at normal rates but some may be toxic at rates used to completely suppress plant growth.	

EARTHWORM AS BIOMARKERS

Recently the use of biomarkers to estimate either exposure effects of chemicals have received considerable attention (Fassi *et al.*,1994). A biological response to, or toxic effect of, an environmental chemical and chemicals called biomarkers. The major reasons for the current interest in biomarkers are the limitations of the classical approach to environmental toxicology. In the classical approach the chemical concentration present in the ambient environment is related to adverse organism effects such as mortality, reproduction and growth. But under various environmental conditions the availability of the toxicant may differ, so it is difficult to extrapolate laboratory toxicity data to field conditions. The biomarkers quantifies only the bioactive fraction of the pollutants. They also integrate exposure or effects of complex pollution and can be applicable under both laboratory and field conditions (Weeks, 1996).

DNA Alterations

DNA single strand breakage was also found in earthworms following exposure to chemicals. Chemicals may also cause DNA adducts. A dose – response relationship between pollutant and strand breakage frequency has been observed (Salagonic *et al.,* 1996).

Metallothionein and other Metal – Binding Proteins

Heavy metals entering earthworms may be bound in various fraction within the organism. One way of binding and detoxifying heavy metals in the tissues is by binding the metals to metallothionein (MT) and other metal – binding proteins(MBP).

Cholinesterase (ChE)

In earthworms, the inhibition of ChE by chemical compounds was observed.

Other Enzymatic Responses

Cytochrome p-450 / MFO

This is one of the most important enzyme systems involved in the oxidation of endogenous and exogenous compounds in the Cytochrome p-450 dependent monooxygenase or mixed function oxidase system. This system was induced by a range of xenobiotic compounds (Livingstone,1990).

Glutathione S-transferase (GST)

This is a biotransformation enzyme that play an impotant role in binding or conjugating lipophilic molecules with an electrophonic atom. This is also induced by the chemical pollutants on exposure (Stenersen *et al.,*1987).

Peroxidases

The exposure of chemicals reduces the activity of GP_X (glutathione peroxidase) activity.

Catalases

Catalases are hematin – containing enzymes that facilitate the removal of water. They are localized in the peroxisomes of the cells and are involved in fatty acid metabolism. The metal pollutants reduces the catalase activity.

Lysosomal Membrane Integrity

Lysosomes are a morphologically heterogenous group of membrane – bound subcellular organelles, which contain other substances acid hydrolases. The function of lysosomes in the cell is to catabolize organelles and macromolecules. Changes in Lysosomal membrane stability are thought to be a general measure of stress (Huggettet *et al.,* 1992). The membrane stability decreases in response to stress, and the membrane permeability increases.

Immunological Responses

In earthworm, the immune system is located in the coelom, consisting of coelomic fluid and coleomocytes. They are sensitive to foreign material. There are variety of different immunological responses have been measured in the nonspecific immune system, specific cell- mediated immune defence and humoral – mediated defence (Venables *et al.*, 1992).

Sperm Quality Responses

In earthworms, the number and the integrity of sperm have been studied. Earthworms exposed to the insecticides and metals the number of sperm cells in the testis and seminal vesicles decreased.

Neurological Responses

Measuring the velocity of nerve impulse,in addition to measuring ChE activity may assess neurotoxic effect. Changes in velocity of impulse medial (MGF) and lateral giant nerve fibers (LGF) have been measured (Drewes and lingamneni,1992) to assess the effect of pollutants. Changes in neural impulse velocity have mainly been studied in earthworms exposed to organic pollutants, observed a reduction of the velocity of MGF and LGF.

Behavioral Responses

Behavioral responses in connection with exposure to chemicals enable organisms to avoid intoxication. General behavioural responses observed are whole – body spasms and tight coiling, followed by partial relaxation, may be seen following exposure to various pesticide or some hazardous waste site soils (Stenersen *et al.*,1973).

Earthworms for Environmental Biomonitoring

The impact of toxic and hazardous materials on the soil environment have multiplied in recent years and there has been an increased effort to find methods of evaluating these effects. Most current methods have assessed these impacts primarily in terms of human health (Callahan, 1988). There is an equally important need to assess the long term toxic impacts of chemicals on the terrestrial environment and its dynamic process.

Earthworms are excellent bioindicators of the relative health of soil ecosystems (Kuhle, 1983). Earthworm possess several qualities needed in animals used for biomonitoring of terrestrial systems. They are large, numerous, easy to sample and easily identified. They are widely distributed and relatively immobile, they are in full contact with the substrate and they consume large volumes of this substrate. Not only earthworms killed by toxic chemicals, and their growth rates, reproduction and behaviour affected, they also accumulate some chemicals into their tissues at levels higher than the medium in which they live. So that low levels of contamination of soil can be detected by monitoring number of earthworms and the residues they contain.

Langdon *et al.* (2001) reported that mature or immature *L. rubellus* collected from contaminated mine spoil at Devon Great consols showed yellowing in the posterior region of the body. This is the first report of yellow pigmentation of this kind in earthworms. The pigmentation may provide a useful indicator of exposure to soil contamination. The distinctive yellow coloration could provide a simple, non-destructive indicator of earthworms exposure to soil contamination that may be of value in assessment of soil health.

Determination of Lead Accumulation in the Earthworm

Canbek *et al.* (2005) conducted a study on *Lumbricusterrestris* in order to determine the level of vehicle derived lead contamination on living. *L. terrestris.* The average lead concentration of the earthworms taken from the roadside soils was 40.16 $mgg^{-1}$with a range of 21.14 $mgg^{-1}$and 67.03 mgg^{-1}. The average lead concentration of the earthworms from the control sites was 12.35 $mgg^{-1}$with a range of 10.22 $mgg^{-1}$and 14.03 mgg^{-1}.

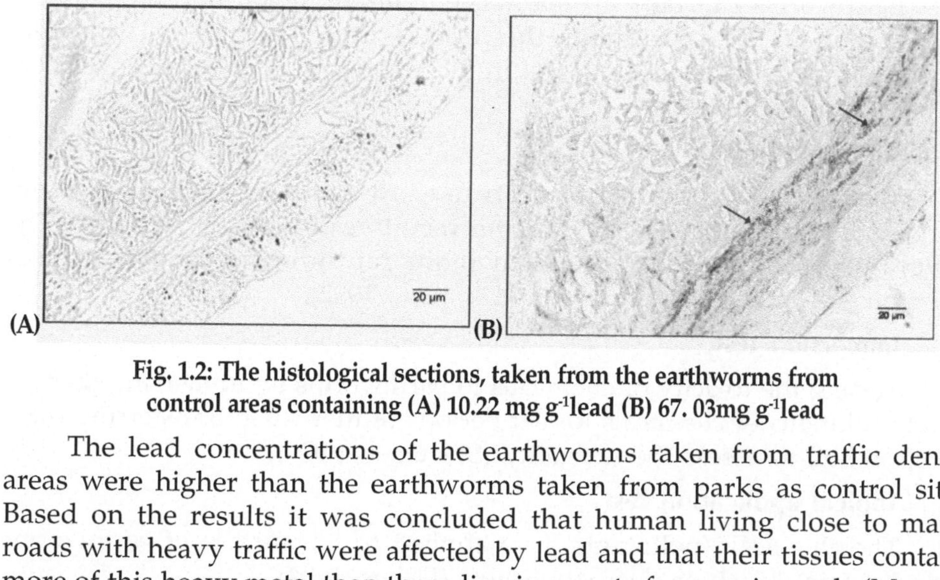

Fig. 1.2: The histological sections, taken from the earthworms from control areas containing (A) 10.22 mg g^{-1}lead (B) 67. 03mg g^{-1}lead

The lead concentrations of the earthworms taken from traffic dense areas were higher than the earthworms taken from parks as control site. Based on the results it was concluded that human living close to main roads with heavy traffic were affected by lead and that their tissues contain more of this heavy metal than those live in remote from main roads (Manay, 1999; Swaileh, 2001).

BIOASSAY METHODS

Field Methods

The design of field experiments to assess the toxicity of pollutants to earthworms in the field considers the following components.

Assessment Criteria

The most important criteria in assessing the overall effects of a pollutant on earthworms is the overall effect on populations of earthworms.

- Hand sorting a soil sample from a quadrat to a depth of 30-60 cm.
- Pouring 9 lit of dilute formalin onto the soil gradually and collecting the earthworms with forceps.
- Electrical method of sampling by passing a current from a 220v generator through soil.

Advantage of Field Tests

1. In laboratory tests only a single life stage or size of earthworm, natural mortality is minimized and the test worms are in optimal environmental conditions.
2. In field tests, a range of species of earthworms are exposed to chemicals simultaneously.
3. Laboratory tests can assess only the acute or direct toxicity of a chemical. But in field tests the chronic and indirect effects of chemicals are evaluated.
4. Earthworms can take up many chemicals from soil into their tissues and in field experiments this occurs under a range of different environmental conditions. But in the laboratory is only under selected constant conditions.

Laboratory Methods

Testing the toxicity of chemicals to earthworms in the field provides a realistic exposure pattern, but the results can be very variable. The laboratory experiments are much more reproducible and relatively inexpensive and quick (Edward and Bohlen, 1992).

❖ **Immersion test**

Testing the toxicity of chemicals to earthworms by immersing them in dilute solutions of chemicals for set periods of time, then transferring them to clean soil to assess the mortality (Stenersen, 1979).

❖ **Topical application test**

The chemicals/pollutants have applied to the surface of earthworms using a paint brush or microapplicator (Fisher, 1984).

❖ **Injection tests**

The chemicals are injected in an ethanolic solution into the coelomic cavity of earthworms that are then kept in soil and subsequently assessed for mortality (Fisher, 1984).

❖ **Forced feeding tests**

The test chemical was suspended in 1.5% agar-agar gel and injected into the oesophagus of an earthworm. The earthworm had been anaesthetized previously in a 10% aqueous ethanol solution. A motor driven

Hamilton syringe, fitted with a blunt glass needle was used to make the injection after which earthworms were placed on moistened paper in a plastic box and observed subsequently for an unspecified period (Stringer and Wright, 1976).

❖ **Feeding on treated food**

Leaf tissues treated with chemicals were offered to earthworms as food (Stringer and Wright, 1973). The earthworms were observed for any toxic or antifeedant effect of the test chemicals for 2 days.

❖ **Laboratory soil test**

Chemicals were applied to soil and exposed earthworms to them in containers in the lab. These tests have usually been in boxes or in plots (Stringer and Wright, 1973).

❖ **Contact filter paper test**

The contact filter paper test is to treat standard filter papers with chemicals, by dipping them in solutions of known concentrations or by spraying the chemical in solution on to them with a fine chromatograph spray and then exposing earthworms to the chemical residues. The test was standardized carefully for the EEC and OECD (Edwards, 1983).

EEC- European Economic Community

OECD- Organization for Economic Co-operation and Development guidelines

❖ **Artificial soil test**

To minimize the variability in natural soils, a standardized "artificial soil" was developed with an adsorptive capacity similar to that of a typical loam soil. The artificial soil was prepared from a mixture of 10% finely ground sphagnum peat (pH 5.5-6.0), 20% kaolinite clay (containing > 50% kaolinite), 69% industrial quartz sand, 1% calcium carbonate.

This was thoroughly mixed and brought to 45% dry weight water content. Then worms were exposed to the chemical, which was dissolved in water or an organic solvent, applied to artificial soil and then placed in a glass test container. The worms were then hand sorted from the soil and their mortality assessed (Edwards, 1983).

RESEARCH NEEDS

- Evaluating the genotoxic effects of pollutants o earthworms
- To establish a broader bio-monitoring method using earthworms to assess soil pollution

REFERENCES

Callahan, C.A. 1988. Earthworms as Ecotoxicological Assessment. In: Edwards, C.A., Neuhanser, E.F. (eds) Earthworms in Waste and Environmental Management. SPB Academic Publ. The Hague, The Netherlands,: 295-301.

Cambek, M., B. Iskli, M. Uyanoglu, T.A. Demir and A. Berber. 2005. Determination of Lead Accumulation in the *L. terrestris* (earthworm) Living in the Road Side Soils of Eskisehir. J. Art. Sci., 4: 47-53.

Chio, H. and J.R. Samborn. 1976. The Metabolism of ^{14}C-chlordane by the Earthworm, *Lumbricusterrestris* L. Chemosphere, 3: 161-166.

Drewes.C.D.ling amneri, A.1992. Use of Earth Warms in Eco neurotoxicology Testing. Sub-lethal Effects of Carbofuran in *Lumbricusterrestris*. In: Ecotoxicology of Earthworms. (Eds). P.W. Grieg-smith, H. Becker, P.J. Edward and F.heibach, Intercept, hants, U.K. pp. 197-206.

Edwards, C.A. 1983. Development of a Standardized Laboratory method for Assessing the Toxicity of Chemical Substances to Earthworms Commission of the European Communities, Brussels, Luxembourg.

Edwards, C.A. and J. Bohlem. 1992. The Effect of Chemicals on Earthworm. Rev. Environ. Contam. Toxicol.,125 : 22-95.

Edwards, C.A., A.R. Thompson and J.R. Lofty. 1968. Changes in Soil Invertebrate Populations Caused by Some Organophosphorus Insecticides. Proc. 4th Brit. Insectic. Fungic. Cont.,: 48-55.

Edwards, C.A., J.R. Lotfy and C.J. Stafford. 1971. Pesticides and the Soil Fauna. Rept. Rothamsted Exp. Stan., Part I, 194

Fanelli, R., M.P. Bertoni, M. Bontanti, M.G. Castelli, C. Chibarando, G.P. Martelli, M.A. Noe, A. Noseda and C. Sbarra. 1980. Routine Analysis of 2, 3, 7, 8-tetrachloro-dibenzo-p-dioxin in Biological Samples from the Contaminated Area of Seveso, Italy, Bull. Environ. Contam. Toxicol., 24: 818-823.

Fisher, S.W. 1984. A Comparison of Standardized methods for Measuring the Biological Activity of Pesticide to the Earthworm *L. terrestris*. Ecotoxicol Environ, Saf., 8: 564-571.

Huggett, R.J., Kirmle, R.A., Mehrle, O.M and Bergman, H.l. 1992. Biomarkers: Biochemical, Physiological an Hitological Markers of Anthrophogeneic, Lewis, Bocaraton.

Kuhle, J.C. 1983. Ecotoxicological Model Studies to Test the Suitability of Earthworms as Bioindicators. Verh. Dtsch. Zool. Ges,: 147-151.

Langdon, C.J., T.G. Piearce, A.A. Meharg and K.T. Sample. 2001. Resistance to Copper – Toxicity in Populations of the Earthworms *Lumbricusrubellus* and *Dendrodrilusrubidus* in Contaminated Mine-wastes. Environ. Toxicol. Chem., 20: 2336-2341.

Living Stone, D.R. 1990. Cytochrome. P. 450 and Oxidative Metabolism in Invertebrates.

Manay, N., L. Pereina and Z. Cousillas. 1999. Lead Contamination in Uruguay. Rev. Environ. Contam. Toxicol., 159 : 25-39.

Marquenie, J.M. and J.W. Simmers. 1988. A method to Assess Potential Bioavaiability of Contaminants. In: Edwards, C.A. and E.F. Neuhauser (eds) Earthworms in Waste and Environmental Management, SPB Academic Publ. The Hague, The Netherlands.: 367-376.

Moriarty, F. 1983. Ecotoxicology. Academic Press, New York, USA.

Salagovic, J. Gills, J., Verschaeve, L and kalian, I. 1996. The Context Assay for Detection of Genotoxic Damage in Earthwarms; A Promising Roll for Assessing the Biological Hazards of Pollutes Sites. Folia Biol., 42: 17-21.

Spurgeon, D.J. and S.P. Hopkin. 1995. Extrapolation of the Laboratory – based OECD Earthworm Toxicity Test to Metal – Contaminated Field Sites. Ecotoxicology, 4 : 190-205.

Stenersen, J. 1979. Action of Pesticides on Earthworms, Part 1: The Toxicity of Cholinesterase Inhibiting Insecticides to Earthworms as Evaluated by Laboratory Tests. Pestic Sci., 10: 66-74.

Stenersen, J. 1979. Action of Pesticides on Earthworms. Part 2: Elimination of Parathion by the Earthworm. *Eiseniafoetida* (Savigny). Pestic. Sci., 10: 104-112.

Stenersen, J., Kobro, S., Bjerke, M. and Arend, U. 1987. Glutathione Transferase in Aquatic and Terrestrial Animals from Nine Phyla. Comp. Biochem. Physiol., 86: 73-82.

Stenersen, J., Gilman, A. and (Vardanis, A. 1973. Carofuran: Its Toxicity to and Metabolism by Earthwarms (*Lumbricusterrestris*). J.Agric. Food Chem., 21: 166-171.

Stringer, A. and M.A. Wright. 1973. The Effect of Benomyl and some Related Compounds on *Lumbricusterrestris* and other Earthworms. Pestic. Sci., 4 : 165-170.

Swaileh, K.M., N. Rabaya's R. Salim, A. Ezzughayyar and A.A. Rabbo. 2001. Concentrations of Heavy Metals in Road Side Soils, Plants and Land Snails from the West Bank, Palestine. Environ. Sci. Health Part ATox. Hazard, Subst. Environ. Eng., 36(5): 765-778.

Thompson, A.R. 1970. Effects of Mine Insecticides on the Number and Biomass of Earthworms in Pasture. Bull. Environ. Contam. Toxicol., 5: 577.

Vebables, B.J., L.C. Fitzpatrick and A.J. Gover. 1992. Earthwarms as Indicators of Ecotoxicity In: Ecotoxicology of Earthwarms. In: P.W. grieg-smith, H.Becker. P.J. Edwards and F.Heimbach. Intercepts. Hans, UK. pp. 197-206.

Weeks, J.M. and C. Svendsen. 1996. Neutral – Red – Retention by Lysosomes from Earthworm (*Lumbricusrubellus*) Coelomocytes : A Simple Biomarker for Exposure of Soil Invertebrates. Environ. Toxicol. Chem., 15: 1801-1805.

Pages: 16-24

Vermitechnology, Farm and Fertilizer
Edited by: **Dr. Ashok K. Rathoure; Dr. Pawan Kumar 'Bharti' and Dr. Jaswant Ray**
ISBN: 978-93-88854-38-2
Edition: **2020**
Published by: **Discovery Publishing House Pvt. Ltd., New Delhi (India)**

2

Vermicomposting – A Sustainable Technology

V.Manivannan, E.Parameswari, K.Sivasubramaian and C.Harisudhan

INTRODUCTION

Earthworms have been on the earth for over 120 million years. Their purpose is simple, but very important. They are nature's way of recycling organic nutrients from dead tissues back to living organisms. Referring to an earthworm, Darwin said, "It may doubted whether there are many other animals in the world. Which have played so important part in the history of the world, as have these lowly organized creatures". Earthworms play a key role in soil biology by serving as versatile natural bioreactor to soil pathogens, thus:

> "Converting organic wastes into valuable products such as biofertilizers, biopesticides, vitamins, enzymes, antibiotics and proteinaceous worm biomass. Earthworm often called "Ecosystem engineers" because they are actively re-design the physical structure of the soil environment".

In recent years efforts have been made to use the potential of earthworms in recycling of nutrients,waste management and development of vermicomposting systems at commercial scale. These are also called as "Ecosystem engineers" as they increase the numbers and types of microbes in the soil by creating conditions under which these creatures can thrive and multiply. The objective of this article is to present an overview of the vermicomposting technology.

Dept. of Agronomy, Tamil Nadu Agricultural University, Coimbatore, (India)
[1] **Dept. of Environmental Sciences, Tamil Nadu Agricultural University, Coimbatore, (India)**
[2] **Regional Research Station, Tamil Nadu Agricultural University, Vridhachalam, (India)**

In India, the integration of crops and livestock and use of manure as fertilizer were traditionally the basis of farming systems. But development of chemical fertilizer industry during the green revolution period created opportunities for low-cost supply ofplant nutrients in inorganic forms which lead to rapid displacement of organic manures derived from livestock excreta. The deterioration of soil fertility through loss of nutrients and organic matter, erosion and salinity, and pollution of environment are the negative consequences of modern agricultural practices. In India, millions of tons of livestock excreta are produced annually (Table 2.1). Odour and pollution problems are of concern.Currently the fertilizer values of animal dung are not being fully utilized resulting in loss of potential nutrients returning to agricultural systems. The potential benefits of vermi composting of livestock excreta include control of pollution and production of avalue added product. Vermicomposting of different livestock excreta including cattle dung; horse waste; pig waste; goat waste; sheep waste; turkey waste and poultry droppings has been reported. Organic wastes can be ingested by earthworms and egestedas a peat-like material termed "vermicompost". Recycling of wastes through vermicomposting reduces the problem of non-utilization of livestock excreta. During vermicomposting, the important plant nutrients such as N, P, K, and Ca, present in the organic waste are released and converted into forms that are more soluble and available to plants. Vermicompost also contains biologically active substances such as plant growth regulators. Moreover, the worms themselves provide a protein source for animal feed.

Table 2.1
Livestock population and quantity of waste generated in India

Animal species	Population (In millions)	Daily average excreta animal^{-1} Wet weight (kg)
Cow	185.18	11.6
Buffalo	97.92	12.2
Sheep	61.47	0.76
Goat	124.35	0.70

Source: Livestock Census Report, 2003, Directorate of Economics and Statistics,Ministry of Agriculture, GOI)

VERMICOMPOSTING TECHNOLOGY

Vermicomposting is the process of degradation of organic wastes by earthworms to achieve three objectives *viz.*, (i) to upgrade the value of organic waste material so that it can be reused, (ii) to produce upgraded materials in-situ and (iii) to obtain a final product free of chemical or biological pollutants.

EARTHWORMS

Earthworms are as segmented worms, bilaterally symmetrical, with an external gland producing an egg case (cocoon), a sensory lobe in front of the mouth (prostomium), with the anus at the posterior end of the animal body, no limbs but possessing a small number of bristles (chaetae) on each segment. They are hermaphrodites and reproduction normally occurs through copulation and cross fertilization, following which each of the mated individuals can produce cocoons (oothecae) containing between one and twenty fertilized ova. The resistant cocoons, which can survive many years, are tiny and roughly lemon-shaped. After an incubation period that varies according to species and climatic conditions, the cocoons hatch. The young earthworms, which are white and only a few millimeters in length after emerging from the cocoons, gain their specific adult pigmentation within a day. Assuming favourable conditions, many species can reach sexual maturity within weeks after emergence, although species that live in soil take longer. Mature individuals can be distinguished easily by the presence of the clitellum, which is a pale- or dark-coloured swollen band, located behind the genital pores. The clitellum secretes the fibrous cocoon, and the clitellar gland cells produce a nutritive albuminous fluid which fills the cocoon. Earthworms can continue to grow in size after completing their sexual development, but never add segments (Dominguez and Edwards, 2004).

Characters of earthworm suited for vermicomposting

- Capable of inhabiting in high percentage of organic material
- Adaptability with respect to environmental factors
- High fecundity rate with low incubation period
- Smallest period of interval from hatching to maturity
- High growth rate, consumption, digestion and assimilation rates
- Least vermistabilisation time (period of inactivity after initial inoculation of organic wastes)

TYPES OF EARTHWORM

Different types of earthworm live in different niches performing different functions. As a result earthworms do not have the same requirements and will not survive under the same environments and will not survive under the same environmental conditions. In compost heaps the most common earthworm is *Eisenia foetida* more commonly known as the tiger worm. It likes to eat lots of organic matter and as such survives very well in the compost heap where it has a rich, plentiful supply. In moist soils, however, there is not enough organic matter present for the tiger worm to survive. Instead there are other types of earthworms which are specially adopted to living in the soil. Different species of earthworm inhabit different parts of the soil and have distinct feeding strategies. They can be separated into three ecological groups based on their feeding and burrowing habits (Reynolds, 1994)

- Soil surface dwelling or compost preferring species.
- Top soil dwelling species.
- Sub soil dwelling species.

Soil surface dwelling or compost preferring species are called *Epigenic* species. They prefer to live at or near the soil surface or in compost heaps and like to eat material which is high in organic matter *e.g.,* decaying plant roots and shoots, dung and leaves. They typically are small and adopted to the highly variable moisture and temperature conditions at the soil surface. These surface dwellers tend to be pigmented (or) highly coloured and they mix organic matter into soil. Examples of such species include the dung worm, *Lumbricus rubellus* and tiger worm *Eisenia foetida.*

The top soil dwelling species are called *Engogenic* species. These species usually live in the top 20-30 cmdepth of soil and feed primarily on soil and associated organic matter (geophages). They burrow through the soil (temporary channels) ingesting it as they go and mix the top soil layer. As they burrow they produce stable earthworm casts which help to improve the soil structure and increase the soil. After soil has passed through the gut of an earthworm the nutrients in the soil can be changed to a form more accessible to plants. The most common earthworm species is grey worm *Aporrectodea caliginosa.*

Subsoil dwelling species (or) deep burrowing species are called *Anecic* species. These species tend to make permanent burrows in the soil which can be more than three meters deep. They tend to forage about in the soil surface for food and they drag food such as leaves down into their burrows for consumption. This type of worms are useful in situations where large amounts of organic matter are left on the soil surface. Examples of these species are, the night crawler *Lumbricus terrestris* and *Aporrectodea longa.*

Epigenic earthworm like *Eudrilus eugeniae, Eisenia foetide* and *Perionyx excavatus* are some of the popularly used worms for vermicomposting. *Eudrilus eugeniae,* a tropical earthworm commonly called African night crawler, is large in size, grows rapidly, breeds fast and is capable of decomposing large quantities of organic material in valuable vermicompost.

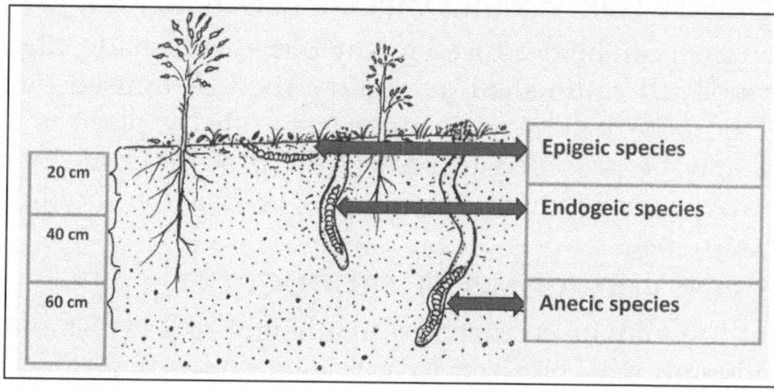

EARTHWORMS FOR VERMICOMPOSTING

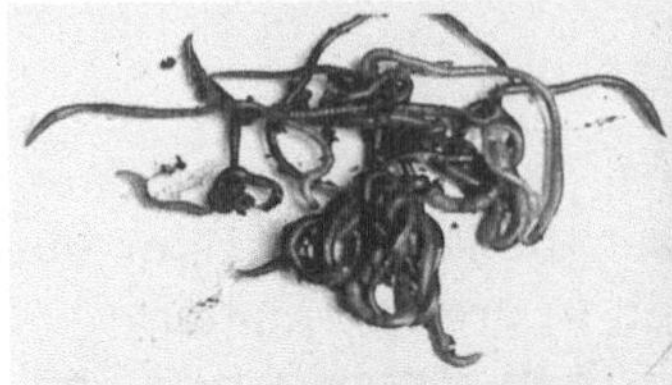

Eudrilus eugeniae

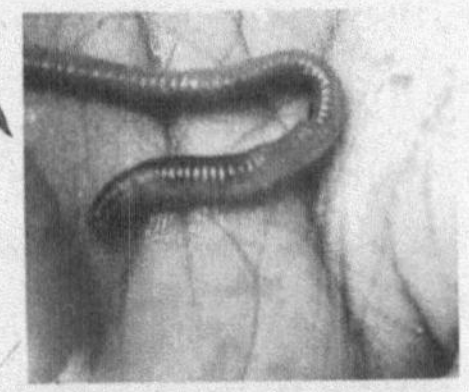

African earthworm (*Eudrillus euginiae*)

Eisenia foetida

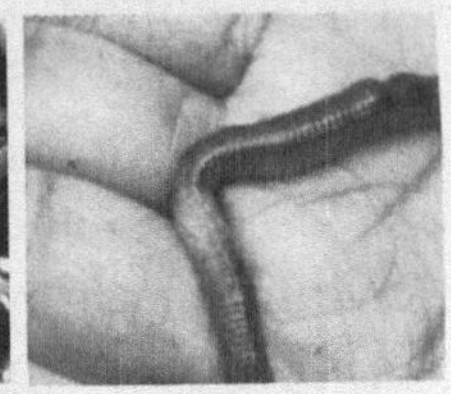

Tiger worm or Red wrinkle *Eisenia foetida*)

Perionyx excavatus

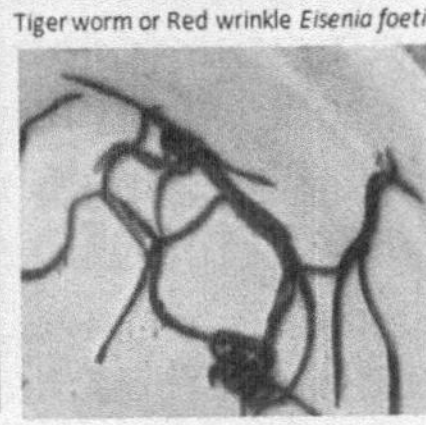

Asian worms (*Perinonyx excavatus*)

VERMICOMPOSTING PROCESS

It is an aerobic, bio-oxidation, non-thermophilic process of organic waste decomposition that depends upon earthworms to fragment, mix and promote microbial activity.

METHODS OF VERMICOMPOSTING

There are two methods having practical application:

(i) Solid waste materials are spread out over the soil surface, for incorporation directly into the soil by earhworms for burial and decomposition.

(ii) Wastes are stacked into heaps or placed in bins, where they are treated like compost heaps and earthworms are released.

SELECTION OF SITE FOR VERMICOMPOST PRODUCTION

Vermicompost can be produced in any place with shade, high humidity and cool. Abandoned cattle shed or poultry shed or unused buildings can be used. If if is to be produced in open area, shady place is selected. A thatched roof may be provided to protect the process from direct sunlight and rain. The waste heaped for vermicompost production should be covered with moist gunny bags.

STRUCTURES FOR VERMICOMPOST PRODUCTION

A cement tub may be constructed to a height of 2 ½ feet and a breadth of 3 feet. The length may be fixed to any level depending upon the size of the room. The bottom of the tub is made to slope like structure to drain the excess water form vermicompost unit. A small sump is necessary to collect the drain water.

In another option over the hand floor, hollow blocks/bricks may be arranged in compartment to a height of one feet, breadth of 3 feet and length to a desired level to have quick harvest. In this method, moisture assessment will be very easy. No excess water will be drained.

Vermicompost can also be prepared in wooden boxes, plastic buckets or in any containers with a drain hole at the bottom.

BEDDING

Bedding is any material that provides a relatively stable habitat to worms. For good vermicomposting, this habitat should satisfy the following criteria:

- High absorbency: As worms breathe through skin, the bedding must be able to absorb and retain adequate water.
- Good bulking potential: The bulking potential of the material should be such that worms get oxygen properly.
- Low nitrogen content (high Carbon: Nitrogen ratio): Although worms consume their bedding as it breaks down, it is very important that this be a slow process. High protein (or) nitrogen levels can result in rapid degradation and associated heating may be fatalto worms.

FOOD SOURCE

Regular input of feed materials for the earthworms is most essential step in the vermicomposting process. Earthworms can use a wide variety of organic materials as food but do exhibit food preferences. In adverse conditions, earthworms canextract sufficient nourishment from soil to survive. However earthworms feed mainly on dead and decaying organic waste and on free living soil microflora and fauna. Underideal conditions, worms can consume amount of food higher than their body weights, thegeneral rule-of-thumb is consumption of food weighing half of their body weight per day. Livestock excreta, *viz.*, goat manure, cattle dung or pig manure are the most commonly used worm feedstock as these materials have higher nitrogen content. When the material with higher carbon content is used with C: N ratio exceeding 40: 1, it is advisable to add nitrogen supplements to ensure effective decomposition. The food should be added onlyas a limited layer as an excess of the waste many generate heat. From the waste ingestedby the worms, 5-10% are being assimilated in their body and the rest are being excreted in the form of vermicast.

Pre-composting of organic waste: The death of *Eisenia foetida* after 2 weeks in the fresh cattle solids although all other growth parameters such as moisture content, pH, electrical conductivity, C: N ratio, NH_4 and NO_3^-

contents were suitable for the growth of the earthworms. They attributed the deaths of earthworms tothe anaerobic conditions which developed after 2 weeks in fresh cattle solids. It is established that pre-composting of organic waste is very essential to avoid the mortality of worms. For one-meter length, one-meter breadth and 0.5-meter height, 1 kg of worm (1000 numbers) is required. There is Earthworm will move inside on its own.

MOISTURE

Perhaps the most important requirement of earthworms is adequate moisture.They require moisture in the range of 60-70%. The feed stock should not be too wet otherwise it may create anaerobic conditions which may be fatal to earthworms.

AERATION

Factors such as high levels of fatty (or) oily substances in the feedstock or excessive moisture combined with poor aeration may render anaerobic conditions in vermicomposting system. Worms suffer severe mortality partly because they are deprived of oxygen and partly because of toxic substances (*e.g.* ammonia) produced under such conditions. This is one of the main reasons for not including meat or other fatty (or) oily wastes in worm feedstock unless they have been pre-composted to break down the oils and fats.

TEMPERATURE

The activity, metabolism, growth, respiration and reproduction of earthworms are greatly influenced by temperature. Most earthworm species used in vermicomposting require moderate temperatures from 10-35° C. While tolerances and preferences vary from species to species. Earthworms can tolerate cold and moist conditions far better than hot and dry conditions. For *Eisenia foetida* temperatures above 10° C (minimum) and preferably 15° C be maintained for maximizing vermicomposting efficiency and above15 °C (minimum) and preferably 20° C for vermiculture. Higher temperatures (> 35°C) may result in high mortality. Worms will redistribute themselves within piles, beds or wind rows such that they get favorable temperatures in the bed.

pH

Worms can survive in a pH range of 5 to 9, but a range of 7.5 to 8.0 is considered to bethe optimum. In general, the pH of worm beds tends to drop over time due to the 12 fragmentation of organic matter under series of chemical reactions. Thus, if the food sources are alkaline, the effect is a moderating one, tending to neutral or slightly acidic,and if acidic (*e.g.*, coffee grounds, peat moss); pH of the beds can drop well below 7. Insuch acidic conditions, pests like mites may become abundant. The pH can be adjusted upwards by adding calcium carbonate.

HARVESTING VERMICOMPOST

Tub method of composting, the casting formed on the top layer are collected periodically. The collection may be carried once in a week. Periodically the castings will be scooped out and put in a shady place as heap like structure. The harvestings of casting should be limited up to earthworm presence on top layer.This periodical harvesting is necessary for free flow of air and retain the compost quality. Otherwise the finished compost gets compacted when watering is done.

In small bed type of vermicomposting method, periodical harvesting is not required. Since the height of the waste material heaped is around 1 feet, the produced vermicompost will be harvested after the process is over.

HARVESTING EARTHWORM

After the vermicompost production, the earthworm present in the tub or small bed may be harvested be trapping method.In the vermibed, before harvesting the compost, small, fresh cow dung ball is made and inserted inside the bed in five or six places. After 24 hours, the cow dung ball is removed. All the worms will be adhered into the ball. Putting the cow dung ball in a bucket of water will separate this adhered worm. The collected worms will be used for next batch of composting.

STORING AND PACKING OF VERMICOMPOST

The harvested vermicompost should be stored in dark, cool place. It should have minimum 40% moisture. Sunlight should not fall over the composted material. It will lead to loss of moisture and nutrients it is advocated that the harvested composted material is openly stored rather than packed in over gunnies.Packing can be done at the time of selling. If it is stored in open place, periodical sprinkling of water may be done to maintain moisture level and also to maintain beneficial microbial population. If necessity comes to store the material, laminated gunnies are used for packing. This will minimize the moisture evaporation loss.Vermicompost can be stored for one year without loss of its quality, if the moisture is maintained at 40% level.

NUTRITIVE VALUE OF VERMICOMPOST

The nutrients content in vermicompost vary depending on the waste materials that are being used for compost preparation (Joshi *et al.*, 2015). If the waste materials are heterogeneous one, there will be wide range of nutrients available in the compost. If the waste materials are homogenous one, there will be only certain nutrients are available. The common available nutrients in vermicompost are as follows.

Organic carbon (%)	–	9.50-17.9
Nitrogen (%)	–	0.50-1.50
Phosphorus (%)	–	0.10-0.30

Potassium (%)	–	0.15-0.56
Sodium (%)	–	0.06-0.30
Calcium and Magnesium (meq/100g)	–	22.7-47.6
Copper (mg kg^{-1})	–	2.00-9.50
Iron (mg kg^{-1})	–	2.00-9.00
Zinc (mg kg^{-1})	–	5.70-11.5
Sulphur (mg kg^{-1})	–	128-548

CONCLUSION

As a processing system, the vermicomposting of organic waste is very simple. Worm singest the waste material, break it up in their rudimentary gizzards, consume the digestible portion, and then excrete a stable, humus like material that can be immediately marketed and has a variety of documented benefits to the consumer. Vermicompost technology can be a promising technique that has shown its potential in certain challenging areas like augmentation of food production, waste recycling, management of solid wastes *etc*. There is no doubt that in India, where on side pollution is increasing due to accumulation of organic wastes and on the other side there is shortage of organic manure, which could increase the fertility and productivity of the land and produce nutritive and safe food. So the scope for vermicomposting is enormous.

REFERENCES

Joshi, R., Singh, J. and Vig, A.P.2015. Vermicompost as an Effective Organic Fertilizer and Biocontrol Agent: Effect on Growth, yield and Quality of Plants. Rev Environ Sci Biotechnol.,:14: 137

Reynolds, J .1994. Earthwonns of the World. Global Diversity 4: 11-16.

Dominguez, J and Edwards, C.A. 2004. Vermicomposting Organic Wastes: A Review. In: Hanna SHS, Mikhail WZA (eds). Soil Zoology for Sustainable Development in the 21st Century. S.H. Shakir Hanna, Cairo, pp. 369-395.

Pages: 25-56

Vermitechnology, Farm and Fertilizer

Edited by: Dr. Ashok K. Rathoure; Dr. Pawan Kumar 'Bharti' and Dr. Jaswant Ray

ISBN: 978-93-88854-38-2

Edition: **2020**

Published by: **Discovery Publishing House Pvt. Ltd., New Delhi (India)**

3

Earthworms as Environmental Managers for Remediation of Contaminated Soil

Kalaiselvi, P., S.Mahimairaja, E. Parameswari, S. Paul Sebastian V. Davamani, K. Suganya and R. Poornima

INTRODUCTION

"Earth worms are the intestines of the soil" – Aristotle (about 330 B.C)

Earthworms are nature's clean-up crew, aiding in the production of lush, humus-rich top soil from spent plant and animal materials. They play a pivotal role in maintaining the productivity of our soils. Earthworms are key species within the ecosystem and often exposed to a wide range of anthropogenic compounds released to the terrestrial environment. As a consequence, they may suffer from the toxicity of these compounds. They also bioconcentrate these toxic compounds in their tissues. So earthworms may be a viable alternative to traditionally applied organisms as they are simple, well-studied creatures that can provide indications of bioavailability in a short time frame at relatively low costs. Development of reliable methods for testing the toxicity of chemicals to earthworms would allow experiments in which earthworms are used as "biomonitoring tools".

GENERAL FEATURES OF EARTHWORMS

Earthworms are classified within the phylum Annelida and the subclass Oligochaeta, which consists of as many as 36 families worldwide. About two-thirds of Oligochaete families comprise aquatic or semi-aquatic worms, and the remaining families comprise mostly terrestrial worms or earthworms. There are 7254 known earthworm species in Oligochaeta.

Department of Environmental Sciences, Tamil Nadu Agricultural University, Coimbatore, (India)

Distinct taxonomic groups have arisen on every continent except Antarctica, and some groups are now distributed throughout the world. Earthworms are the largest and most familiar soil invertebrates in soils. They are important members of the soil community because they can be the most abundant invertebrates by weight, reaching up to 1,000 lbs live weight.

Earthworms in Soil

Earthworm species can be grouped according to behavioral, morphological or physiological adaptations that enable them to partition available resources in the soil. The three main life history strategies are termed epi, anecic, and endogeic. Epigeic worms feed on plant litter, dwell on the soil surface or within the litter layer, heavily pigmented, and small- to medium sized. Anecic worms feed on plant litter and soil, live in nearly vertical permanent burrows, dorsally pigmented, and large. Endogeic species are soil-feeders, not heavily pigmented, form extensive horizontal burrow systems, size from small to large. Endogeic worms have been further divided into polyhumic, mesohumic, and oligohumic groups. Earthworm species do not always fall clearly into these three main categories and may even exhibit traits of different groups at different life stages or under different environmental conditions.The microbes associated with earthworm gut varies by ecological category, due to food choices and differences in gut morphology (Thakuria *et al.* 2010). Three major ecological categories based on their feeding and burrowing strategies (Bouche, 1977).

Epigeic species : (Litter dwellers) Live in crop or forest litter. They are not common in most agricultural soils

Endogeic species : (Topsoil dwellers) Live in the upper 2 to 3 inches of the soil

Anecic species : (Subsoil dwellers) Live in permanent vertical burrows that can be 5 or 6 feet deep.

EARTHWORMS AND ENVIRONMENTAL POLLUTANTS

Pollutant

A toxic chemical or pollutant is defined as a substance introduced to the environment by human activity that has a deleterious effect on biological organisms (Moriasty, 1983).

Pollutants are classified into two categories based on their chemical nature:

1. Inorganic pollutants (Heavy metals)
2. Organic pollutants (Pesticides)

Effect of Inorganic Pollutants

Among the different forms of pollutants the inorganic form of the pollutants includes heavy metals. Heavy metals are important contaminants in agricultural and non-agricultural soils. Bioaccumulation of heavy metals in earthworms has been studied in many different environments including.

1. Mine spoil tips
2. Land contaminated by the emissions from metal smelting or refining works
3. Land exposed to motor vehicle emissions
4. Municipal waste sites
5. Agricultural soils contaminated with metals applied to the soil as pesticides
6. Land exposed to contaminated sediments dredged from rivers
7. Sewage waste water
8. Sewage sludge

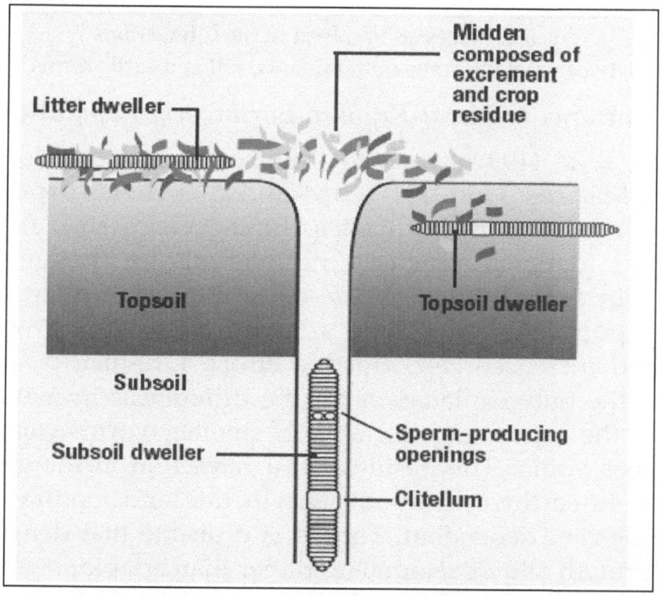

Fig. 3.1: Three major groups of earthworms are: Litter dwellers, topsoil dwellers, and subsoil dwellers

Residues of chemicals can bioaccumulate in earthworms and may be distributed by them to the tissues of animals in higher tropic levels within the food webs. A chemical accumulated in the tissues of the earthworms to be related more accurately to the concentration of the contaminant present in the soil. So they have been used to measure the level of contamination of soils due to heavy metals and long lived organic chemicals (Marquenie and Simmers, 1988).

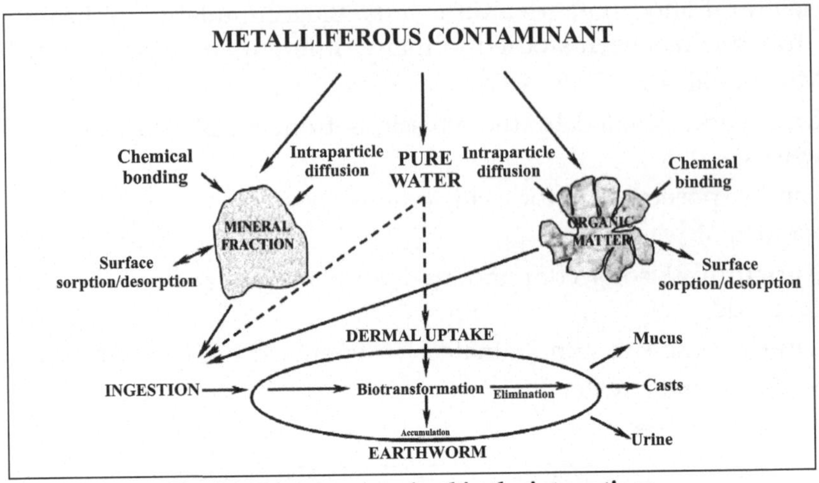

Fig. 3.2: Processes involved in the interactions between metalliferous contaminants, soil and earthworms

Life-History Patterns in Metal-Exposed Earthworm Populations

Spurgeon *et al.* (1999) assessed the growth and development of F1 *Lumbricusrubellus*bred from reference and one metal-exposed smelter populations in soils from both sites. In the clean soil, faster growth maturation was found at selected time intervals for the smelter worms. This result is in agreement with life-cycle models, which indicate that polluted-site populations will be adapted for faster growth, earlier maturation and increased reproductive effort. Life-history adaptation is not, however, the only explanation for the differences in maturation rates found. During the exposures, mortality of smelter worms was higher than for the reference strain. This resulted in a reduction in the density of the smelter strain. In earthworms, both growth rate and maturation time are known to be density dependent. Thus it is probable that density-mediated responses of growth and development, rather than adaptation, are primarily responsible for the observed life-history.

The effects of metal contaminants on the population density and species composition of earthworms were studied by spurgeon *et al.* (1996) at 22 sites around a primary smelting works situated at Avonmouth, southwest England. All worms were absent from six sites within 1 km of the factory and numbers were also reduced significantly at an additional four sites 2 km from the plant. Total earthworm density was found to be inversely related to concentrations of metals in soils. Some species of earthworms were found to be more 'sensitive' to metals and were absent from sites where more 'tolerant' species persisted. For example, *Lumbricusrubellus, Lurnbricuscastaneus*and *Lumbricusterrestris*were all present at sites close to the smelter where *Aporrectodearosea, Aporrectodeacaliginosa* and

Allolobophorachlorotica were absent. The first three 'tolerant' species have more active calcium secretion glands in their gut than the three 'sensitive' worms. Calcium is known to be involved in the sequestration and elimination of various metals through the chlorogogenous tissue.

Effect of Organic Pollutants

Effects of Toxic Chemicals on Earthworms

Earthworms are exposed to chemicals in a variety of ways. When land is treated with pesticides to control soil inhabiting pests, the chemicals are usually mixed thoroughly into the soil so that the pest comes into maximum contact with the pesticide. A wide range of non pest organisms such as earthworms are also exposed to the chemicals. Residues of chemicals can bioaccumulate in earthworm and may be distributed by them to the tissues of animals in higher trophic levels within the food web. The first compounds to be investigated for bioaccumulation into earthworms were the organochlorine insecticides (Fanelli *et al.*, 1980).

Responses of Earthworms to Toxic Chemicals

Acute Toxicity

Acute toxicity is usually the first criterion used in assessing the susceptibility of earthworms.

Chronic Toxicity

Many sublethal chronic toxicity symptoms of earthworms exposed to chemicals have been recorded some of which are serious and short term others of which are minor but involve long-term effects on the earthworms and their functions.

- Malformation
- Effects on activity
- Effects on nervous and physiological functions
- Effects on growth
- Effects on reproduction

Uptake and Metabolism of Chemicals by Earthworms

Uptake

❖ Organochlorine

One of the first reports on the uptake of chemicals into earthworms was by Barker (1985). He found large residues of DDT and its break down products in the tissues of earthworms taken from soil.

Loss toxic	:	HCH, DDT, Aldin, Dieldrin
Moderately toxic	:	Endosultan, Isobenzan
Extremely toxic	:	Chlordane

❖ Organophosphate insecticide

Most OP are not very toxic. Edwards *et al.* (1968) reported that earthworms from plots treated with the organophosphorus insecticide, chlorfenvinphos, did not contain appreciable quantities of this insecticide or its metabolites. But phorate was foundto be extremely toxic.

❖ Carbamate insecticide

The soluble insecticides such as aldicarb can be bioconcentrated very rapidly into earthworm tissues in large amounts when this is applied to flooded soils. It can be concentrated only as the parent compound, but not as metabolites. All carbamate insecticides are highly toxic.

❖ Pyrethroids

Pyrethroids synthetic and natural are found to be non toxic.

❖ Fungicides

Most of the fungicides are non toxic.

❖ Herbicides

Very few herbicides directly toxic to earthworms. They have indirect effects due to their influence on weeds as a source of supply of organic matter on which earthworms feed in soil.

Moderate effects : Atrazine, simazine, dinoseb

Metabolism

The microorganisms living in the earthworm gut can breakdown DDT to DDE (Edwards *et al.*, 1971). Aldrin to dieldrin, Heptachlor to Heptachlor epoxide (Chio and Sanborn, 1976). There is much less evidence of the role of earthworms in metabolizing organophosphate insecticides. Thompson (1970) reported that earthworms could metabolize fensultothion to its sulfone. Parathion was slowly converted to paraoxon which was then rapidly hydrolyzed to diethyl hydrogen phosphate (Steersen, 1979).

Table 3.1

Relative toxicities of some common pesticides to earthworms.

PESTICIDE	TOXICITY LEVEL
I. Vermicides	
Ammonium sulfate	Very toxic on acid soils only
Mowrah meal	Toxic with low environmental hazard
II. Fumigants	
Chloropicrin	Very toxic at normal rates
Methyl bromide	Very toxic at normal rates
Metham sodium	Very toxic at normal rates
Dichloropropane/Dichloropropene	Very toxic at normal rates

(Table Contd...)

PESTICIDE	TOXICITY LEVEL
III. Insecticides & Acaracides	
Organochlorines:	
Chlordane	Very toxic, used for earthworm control
Toxaphene	Very toxic, used for earthworm control
Heptachlor	Very toxic, used for earthworm control
Aldrin	Toxic at high rates only
Dieldrin	Toxic at high rates only
Endrin	Variable toxicity at does rate
Isobenzan	Variable toxicity
Organophosphates:	
Ethoprop	Very toxic at normal rates
Fensulfothion	Very toxic to some species
Phorate	Very toxic at normal rates
Fonofos	Moderately toxic at normal rates
Karathion	Moderately toxic
Methyl parathion	Moderately toxic
Thiomazin	Moderately toxic
Isofos	Slightly toxic at normal rates
Disulfoton	Slightly toxic at normal rates
Fenamiphos	Slightly toxic at normal rates
Chlorpyrifos	Relatively non-toxic at normal rates
Isofenphos	Relatively non-toxic
Malathion	Relatively non-toxic
Menazon	Relatively non-toxic
Phosalone	Relatively non-toxic
Terbufos	Relatively non-toxic
Trichlorfon	Relatively non-toxic
Carbamates:	
Aldicarb	Very toxic at normal rates
Bufencarb	Very toxic at normal rates
Carbaryl	Very toxic, used for earthworm control
Carbofuran	Very toxic
Dithiocarbamate	Highly toxic at normal dose rates
Methomyl	Highly toxic at normal dose rates
Oxamyl	Highly toxic at normal dose rates
Tirpate	Highly toxic at normal dose rates
IV. Fungicides	
Benomyl	Very toxic at normal rates
Carbenzadim	Very toxic at normal rates
Thiophanate methyl	Very toxic at normal rates
V. Herbicides	
All are relatively non-toxic at normal rates but some may be toxic at rates used to completely suppress plant growth.	

Earthworm as Biomarkers

Recently the use of biomarkers to estimate either exposure effects of chemicals have received considerable attention (Fassi *et al.*,1994).A biological response to, or toxic effect of, an environmental chemical and chemicals called biomarkers. The major reasons for the current interest in biomarkers are the limitations of the classical approach to environmental toxicology. In the classical approach the chemical concentration present in the ambient environment is related to adverse organism effects such as mortality, reproduction and growth. But under various environmental conditions the availability of the toxicant may differ, so it is difficult to extrapolate laboratory toxicity data to field conditions. The biomarkers quantifies only the bioactive fraction of the pollutants. They also integrate exposure or effects of complex pollution and can be applicable under both laboratory and field conditions (Weeks,1996).

DNA Alterations

DNA single strand breakage was also found in earthworms following exposure to chemicals. Chemicals may also cause DNA adducts. A dose – response relationship between pollutant and strand breakage frequency has been observed (Salago nic *et al.*, 1996).

Metallothionein and other Metal – Binding Proteins

Heavy metals entering earthworms may be bound in various fraction within the organism. One way of binding and detoxifying heavy metals in the tissues is by binding the metals to metallothionein (MT) and other metal – binding proteins (MBP).

Cholinesterase (ChE)

In earthworms, the inhibition of ChE by chemical compounds was observed.

Other Enzymatic Responses

Cytochrome p-450/MFO

This is one of the most important enzyme systems involved in the oxidation of endogenous and exogenous compounds in the Cytochrome p-450 dependent monooxygenase or mixed function oxidase system. This system was induced by a range of xenobiotic compounds (Livingstone,1990).

Glutathione S-transferase (GST)

This is a biotransformation enzyme that play an impotant role in binding or conjugating lipophilic molecules with an electrophonic atom. This is also induced by the chemical pollutants on exposure (Stenersen *et al.*, 1987).

Peroxidases

The exposure of chemicals reduces the activity of GP_X (glutathione peroxidase) activity.

Catalases

Catalases are hematin – containing enzymes that facilitate the removal of water. They are localized in the peroxisomes of the cells and are involved in fatty acid metabolism. The metal pollutants reduces the catalase activity.

Lysosomal Membrane Integrity

Lysosomes are a morphologically heterogenous group of membrane – bound subcellular organelles, which contain other substances acid hydrolases. The function of lysosomes in the cell is to catabolize organelles and macromolecules. Changes in Lysosomal membrane stability are thought to be a general measure of stress (Huggettet *et al.*, 1992). The membrane stability decreases in response to stress, and the membrane permeability increases.

Immunological Responses

In earthworm, the immune system is located in the coelom, consisting of coelomic fluid and coleomocytes. They are sensitive to foreign material. There are variety of different immunological responses have been measured in the nonspecific immune system, specific cell-mediated immune defence and humoral – mediated defence (Venables *et al.*, 1992).

Sperm Quality Responses

In earthworms, the number and the integrity of sperm have been studied. Earthworms exposed to the insecticides and metals the number of sperm cells in the testis and seminal vesicles decreased.

Neurological Responses

Measuring the velocity of nerve impulse,in addition to measuring ChE activity may assess neurotoxic effect. Changes in velocity of impulse medial (MGF) and lateral giant nerve fibers (LGF) have been measured (Drewes and lingamneni,1992) to assess the effect of pollutants. Changes in neural impulse velocity have mainly been studied in earthworms exposed to organic pollutants, observed a reduction of the velocity of MGF and LGF.

Behavioral Responses

Behavioral responses in connection with exposure to chemicals enable organisms to avoid intoxication. General behavioural responses observed are whole – body spasms and tight coiling, followed by partial relaxation, may be seen following exposure to various pesticide or some hazardous waste site soils (Stenersen *et al.*, 1973).

Earthworms for Environmental Biomonitoring

The impact of toxic and hazardous materials on the soil environment have multiplied in recent years and there has been an increased effort to find methods of evaluating these effects. Most current methods have assessed these impacts primarily in terms of human health (Callahan, 1988). There is an equally important need to assess the long term toxic impacts of chemicals on the terrestrial environment and its dynamic process.

Earthworms are excellent bioindicators of the relative health of soil ecosystems (Kuhle, 1983). Earthworm possess several qualities needed in animals used for biomonitoring of terrestrial systems. They are large, numerous, easy to sample and easily identified. They are widely distributed and relatively immobile, they are in full contact with the substrate and they consume large volumes of this substrate. Not only earthworms killed by toxic chemicals, and their growth rates, reproduction and behaviour affected, they also accumulate some chemicals into their tissues at levels higher than the medium in which they live. So that low levels of contamination of soil can be detected by monitoring number of earthworms and the residues they contain.

Langdon *et al.* (2001) reported that mature or immature *L. rubellus* collected from contaminated mine spoil at Devon Great consols showed yellowing in the posterior region of the body. This is the first report of yellow pigmentation of this kind in earthworms. The pigmentation may provide a useful indicator of exposure to soil contamination. The distinctive yellow coloration could provide a simple, non-destructive indicator of earthworms exposure to soil contamination that may be of value in assessment of soil health.

Determination of Lead Accumulation in the Earthworm

Canbek *et al.* (2005) conducted a study on *Lumbricusterrestris* in order to determine the level of vehicle derived lead contamination on living. *L. terrestris.* The average lead concentration of the earthworms taken from the roadside soils was 40.16 $mgg^{-1}$with a range of 21.14 mgg^{-1} and 67.03 mgg^{-1}. The average lead concentration of the earthworms from the control sites was 12.35 $mgg^{-1}$with a range of 10.22 $mgg^{-1}$and 14.03 mgg^{-1}.

The lead concentrations of the earthworms taken from traffic dense areas were higher than the earthworms taken from parks as control site. Based on the results it was concluded that human living close to main roads with heavy traffic were affected by lead and that their tissues contain more of this heavy metal than those live in remote from main roads (Manay, 1999; Swaileh, 2001).

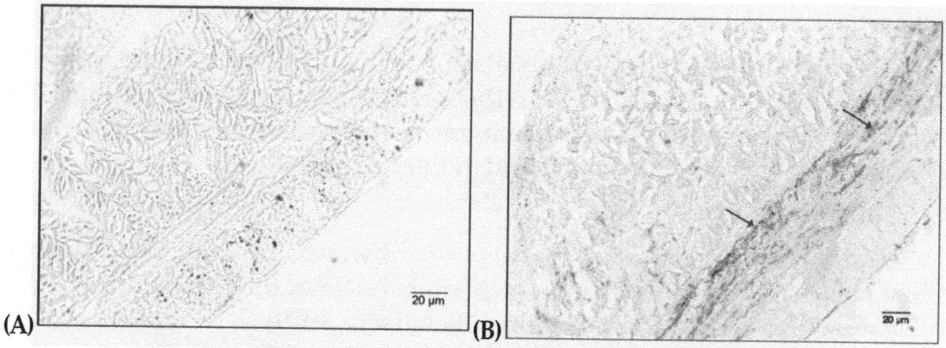

Fig. 3.3: The histological sections, taken from the earthworms from control areas containing (A) 10.22 mg g^{-1}lead (B) 67. 03mg g^{-1} lead

Bioassay Methods

Field Methods

The design of field experiments to assess the toxicity of pollutants to earthworms in the field considers the following components.

Assessment Criteria

The most important criteria in assessing the overall effects of a pollutant on earthworms is the overall effect on populations of earthworms.

- Hand sorting a soil sample from a quadrat to a depth of 30-60 cm.
- Pouring 9 lit of dilute formalin onto the soil gradually and collecting the earthworms with forceps.
- Electrical method of sampling by passing a current from a 220v generator through soil.

Advantage of Field Tests

1. In laboratory tests only a single life stage or size of earthworm, natural mortality is minimized and the test worms are in optimal environmental conditions.
2. In field tests, a range of species of earthworms are exposed to chemicals simultaneously.
3. Laboratory tests can assess only the acute or direct toxicity of a chemical. But in field tests the chronic and indirect effects of chemicals are evaluated.
4. Earthworms can take up many chemicals from soil into their tissues and in field experiments this occurs under a range of different environmental conditions. But in the laboratory is only under selected constant conditions.

Laboratory Methods

Testing the toxicity of chemicals to earthworms in the field provides a realistic exposure pattern, but the results can be very variable. The laboratory experiments are much more reproducible and relatively inexpensive and quick (Edward and Bohlen, 1992).

❖ **Immersion test**

Testing the toxicity of chemicals to earthworms by immersing them in dilute solutions of chemicals for set periods of time, then transferring them to clean soil to assess the mortality (Stenersen, 1979).

❖ **Topical application test**

The chemicals/pollutants have applied to the surface of earthworms using a paint brush or microapplicator (Fisher, 1984).

❖ **Injection tests**

The chemicals are injected in an ethanolic solution into the coelomic cavity of earthworms that are then kept in soil and subsequently assessed for mortality (Fisher, 1984).

❖ **Forced feeding tests**

The test chemical was suspended in 1.5% agar-agar gel and injected into the oesophagus of an earthworm. The earthworm had been anaesthetized previously in a 10% aqueous ethanol solution. A motor driven Hamilton syringe, fitted with a blunt glass needle was used to make the injection after which earthworms were placed on moistened paper in a plastic box and observed subsequently for an unspecified period (Stringer and Wright, 1976).

❖ **Feeding on treated food**

Leaf tissues treated with chemicals were offered to earthworms as food (Stringer and Wright, 1973). The earthworms were observed for any toxic or antifeedant effect of the test chemicals for 2 days.

❖ **Laboratory soil test**

Chemicals were applied to soil and exposed earthworms to them in containers in the lab. These tests have usually been in boxes or in plots (Stringer and Wright, 1973).

❖ **Contact filter paper test**

The contact filter paper test is to treat standard filter papers with chemicals, by dipping them in solutions of known concentrations or by spraying the chemical in solution on to them with a fine chromatograph spray and then exposing earthworms to the chemical residues. The test was standardized carefully for the EEC and OECD (Edwards, 1983).

EEC – European Economic Community
OECD – Organization for Economic Co-operation and Development guidelines

❖ **Artificial soil test**

To minimize the variability in natural soils, a standardized "artificial soil" was developed with an adsorptive capacity similar to that of a typical loam soil. The artificial soil was prepared from a mixture of 10% finely ground sphagnum peat (pH 5.5-6.0),20% kaolinite clay (containing > 50% kaolinite), 69% industrial quartz sand, 1% calcium carbonate.

This was thoroughly mixed and brought to 45% dry weight water content. Then worms were exposed to the chemical, which was dissolved in water or an organic solvent, applied to artificial soil and then placed in a glass test container. The worms were then hand sorted from the soil and their mortality assessed (Edwards, 1983).

REMEDIATION OF CONTAMINATED SOIL BY EARTHWORMS

Remediation of Metal Contaminated Soil

Bioavailability Monitoring of Heavy Metals

A study conducted by Savannah River Ecology Lab (SREL) of University of Georgia in soils contaminated with a variety of metals, including Ni and U as a result of nuclear materials production of the Savannah river site. Soil toxicity tests, using *Lumbricusterrestris* and *Eiseniafetida* to assess the bioavailability of metals and radionuclides showed that (Fig. 3.4 & 3.5) worms exposed to the 100% TB soil accumulated less U than worms in the 50% TB soil. This is due to the presence of calcium carbonate in the soil, which forms highly soluble uranyl carbonate complexes (Mason, 1997; Zabinski*et al.*, 1997).The digestive system of earthworms is capable of detaching heavy metal ions from the complex aggregates between ions and humic substances (Dominguez *et al.*, 2005). Various enzyme- driven processes seem to lead assimilation of the metal ions by the worms so they are locked up in organisms 'tissues rather than released back to soil (Yadav, 2016).

The metal concentrations in the TB hot spot used in the study are (mg/kg)

Ni – 264.9, U – 804.9, Cr – 37.9, Cu – 17.0, Pb – 27.1, Zn – 50.6

E. foetida and *L. terrestris* respond differently to contaminated substrates Ni, U and Zn are taken up in the highest concentrations relative to the other metals *E. foetida* accumulated more U at the 50% level than *L. terrestris*.

Bioavailability and Speciation of Arsenic (As) in Soil

The effect of earthworms on the bioavailability of As in the contaminated soil was examined by an incubation experiment conducted for 180days with earthworms (Mahimairaja, 2005).

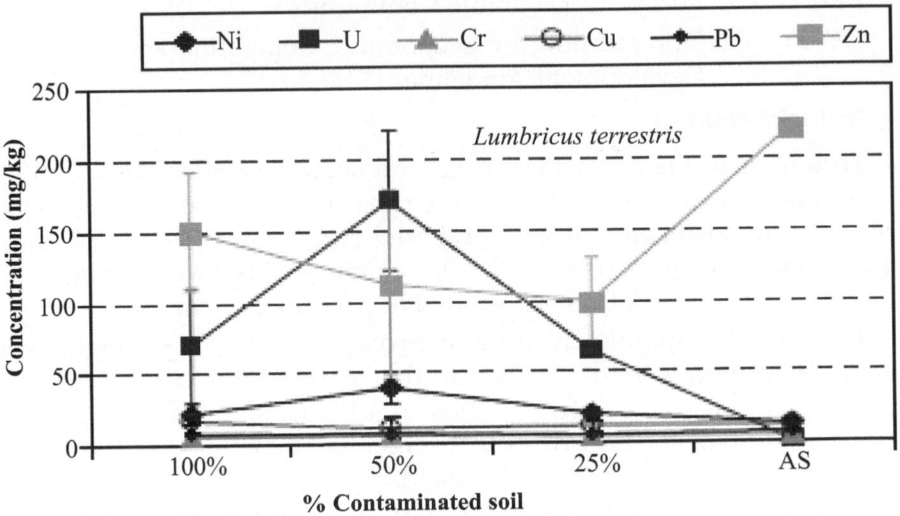

Fig. 3.4: Metal concentration in *Lumbricusterrestris*

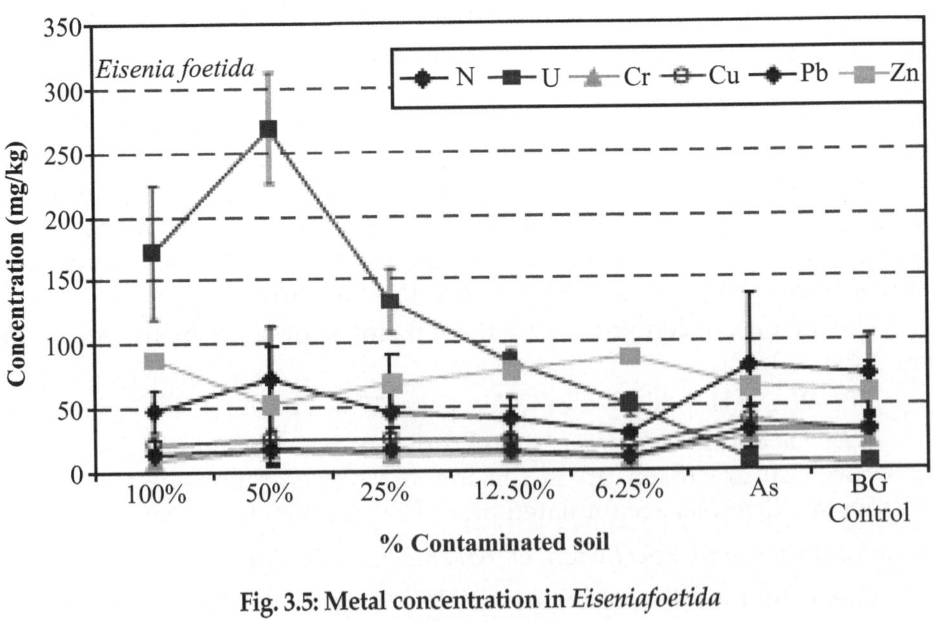

Fig. 3.5: Metal concentration in *Eiseniafoetida*

Table 3.2

Bioavailability and speciation of as in contaminated soil with and without crop

Treatment	pH (H_2O: 2.5)	$(NH_4)_2SO_4As$ (µgkg^{-1})	(NH_4) H_2P0_4-As (µgkg^{-1})	NH_4oxalate-As (µgkg^{-1})
1. Soil (initial)	5.20	171 ± 14	316 ± 28	13410 ± 385
2. Soil + crop	5.06	8 ± 0.6	629 ± 15	13640 ± 242
3. Soil + P + crop	5:77	741 ± 23	320 ± 22	13010 ± 96
4. Soil (no crop)	5.06	438 ± 79	511 ± 12	14225 ± 318
5. Soil (no crop) + P	5.12	833 ± 104	215 ± 21	15530 ± 472
6. Soil + Earthworms*	4.92	1484 ± 236	4114 ± 112	19210 ± 378

± Standard deviation* incubated for six months

The result showed that the bioavailability of As in the contaminated soil was tremendously increased due to the introduction of earthworms. Earthworms also appeared to have enhanced the adsorption of As in soil as the data have shown high values for sorbed – As (as extracted in 0.05 M (NH_4) H_2PO_4). Large amounts of As (25 mg kg^{-1}) was also found accumulated in the earthworm tissues.

Mehang *et al.* (1998) reported that bioconcentration of As in earthworms is due to the sequestration of As in tissues in forms that are not readily eliminated. An immunohistochemical study of arsenate – resistant *Lumbricusrubellus* from an As mine site has revealed the presence of metallothionein (Sturzenbaum *et al.,* 1998) around blood vessels in the chloragogenous tissue [a liver like tissue, separates the intestine from the coelomic cavity (Morgan *et al.,* 1994)]. The sulphur rich metallothionein may play a role in the detoxification and expulsion of As from contaminated earthworms.

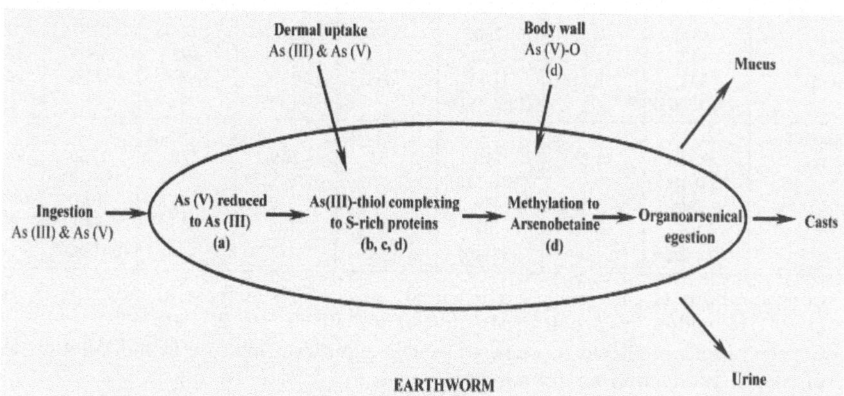

Fig. 3.6: Proposed metabolic pathway for arsenic through an earthworm

Toxicity in earthworms can be measured in two ways:

1. Sublethal effects
2. Mortality

In these environments, resistance to arsenic toxicity may influence survival, growth, reproduction (cocoon production), behaviour, metabolism, pigmentation and composition of the earthworm communities.

Effect of Metal Contamination on Earthworm (Eiseniafetida)

The effects of Cd, Cu, and Zn on survival growth, cocoon production and cocoon viability of the earthworm *Eiseniafetida* (Savigny) were determined (Spurgeon *et al.*, 1994). The results showed that the population densities and species diversities of earthworms declined with proximity to the smelting works. No earthworms were found within 1 km of the smelting factory. Comparison of toxicity values for the metalsshowed that Zn is most likely to be limiting earthworm populations in the vicinity of the works. Zn was atleast ten times more toxic to *E. fetida* in artificial soil than in contaminated soils collected from the field. This difference was due to the greater bioavailability of zinc in the artificial soil.

Table 3.3

EC_{50}[a] and estimated NOEC[b] determined in three toxicity experiments with the earthworm *E. fetida*

	Cadmium		Copper		Lead		Zinc	
	EC_{50}	Estimated NOEC	EC_{50}	Estimated NOEC	EC_{50}	Estimated NOEC	EC_{50}	Estimated NOEC
Experiment 1 Mortality	>300	>300	836 (721-939)	293	>10000	4793	1078 (789-1449)	442
Cocoons % Growth	-295 215 (167-292)	152 207	-716 601 (383-5823)	29 725	1629 2249	608 1966	-357 >400	237 >400
Experiment 2 Mortality Cocoons % growth	>312 -40 211 (172-264)	>312 18 83	>2609 -296 1763 (1392-2303)	>2609 119 481	>15996 -2131 10830 (8839-13521)	>15996 492 4064	>32871 3605 22371	>32871 1879 5444
Experiment 3 Mortality Cocoons % Growth	>16.0 (13.0-18.5) -5.6 1.7 (1.4-2.2)	4.3 2.1 1.7	110 (101-118) -59 38 (37-40)	51 40 39	759 (688-825) -391 258 (234-273)	375 275 265	1730 (1599-1830) -1001 740 (641-827)	1047 833 777

(a) Concentrations of each metal predicted to cause a 50% increase in mortality in 14 days or 50% reduction in cocoon production or growth rate in 21 days.

(b) Concentrations predicted to cause an exactly significant increase in mortality or decrease in cocoon production or growth rate.

The results from the population survey indicate that some species of earthworms are more sensitive to metal pollution than others.

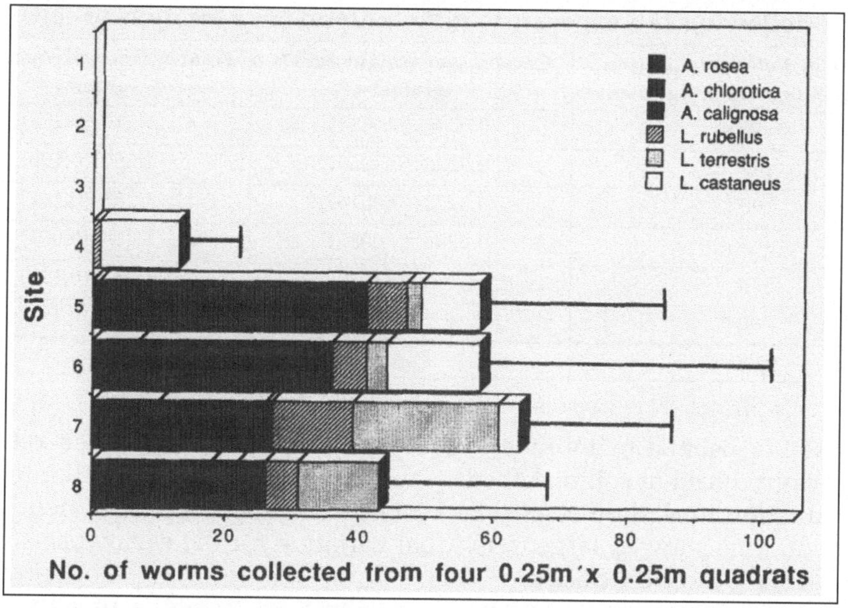

Fig. 3.7: Number of species of earthworms collected from the sampling sites

Aporrectodearosea (Savigny) and *Allolobophorachlorotica* (Savigny) appear to be more sensitive to metal contamination than *L. rubellus* and *L. castaneus* (Savigny). The former species are absent from soils containing ~ 2800 µg g^{-1} Zn, whereas, the later species survive in such soils. Species – specific responses to metal pollutants have been found in many groups of soil invertebrates including earthworms (Morgan and Morgan, 1991).

Toxicity of Nickel to the Earthworm

The toxic effects of Nickel (Ni) on survival, growth and reproduction of *Eiseniaveneta* were studied by Scott – Fordsmand and weeks (1998) following 4 weeks of exposure to a nickel-chloride spiked loamy sand soil. The ability of a simple earthworm biomarker, the lysosomal membrane stability of coelomocytes, to reflect Ni exposure was also studied. Ni caused a significant toxic effect on *E. veneta* at soil concentrations above 85 mg Ni kg^{-1}. Reproduction (cocoon production) was the most sensitive parameter being reduced at soil concentrations above 85 mg Ni kg^{-1}. Survival of adults was only reduced at concentrations above 245 mg Ni kg^{-1}, adult and cocoon wet weight were not affected by soil nickel concentrations upto 700 mg Ni kg^{-1}.

Table 3.4

Mean (±SD) cocoon and earthworm (*Eiseniaveneta*) wet weight following 28 d exposure to nickel chloride in a loamy sand soil

Soil nickel concentration (mg Ni/kg dry weight soil	Cocoon wet weight (±SD) (grams)	Final worm weight (±SD) (grams)
Control	0.0246 (0.0024)	1.247 (0.138)
50	0.0233 (0.0069)	1.350 (0.106)
100	0.0236 (0.0018)	1.255 (0.162)
300	0.0246 (0.0052)	1.434 (0.051)
500	0.0227	1.341 (0.129)
700	–[a]	1.151 (0.192)
1000	–[a]	–[b]

[a]No cocoons present· [b]No survivors

The lysosomal membrane stability, measured as neutral-red retention time was reduced at soil nickel concentrations. Similar to those that reduced reproduction and showed a dose-response relationship. The neutral-red retention time showed large individual variation for the earthworms within each exposure concentration.

The time required to obtain a ratio of 1 between the cells with leaked and non-leaked lysosomes was termed the neutral-red retention time (NRR-time).To measure the lysosomal membrane stability of any surviving worms, coelomic fluid was extracted and stained (Weeks and Svendsen, 1996). The viability of the extracted cells was checked with Eosin Y. For each earthworm, the lysosomal membrane stability was determined as the number of cells with fully stained – cytosols. Compared to the number of cells with unstained cytosols the ratio was determined. For each worm this ratio was assessed during 2 min. of counting every 4 min., until > 50% of the cytosols were stained red.

The neutral - red retention time for earthworms exposed to a range of soil nickel concentrations showed a general decrease with increasing nickel concentrations, a large individual variation was observed. Earthworms exposed to 700 mg Ni/kg had NRR-times of less than 2 min. The control and 50 mg Ni/kg exhibited NRR-times around 50 min. or more.

Physiological Fates of Metals

Kinetic studies can be used to predict the physiological fates of pollutants in exposed organisms. Excretion patterns gives useful information on probable detoxification mechanisms. Three potential pathways exist for the removal of chemicals from sensitive tissues.

1. Elements can be regulated by excretion from the body.
2. Bound within the matrix of inorganic granules
3. Attached to proteins or other ligands

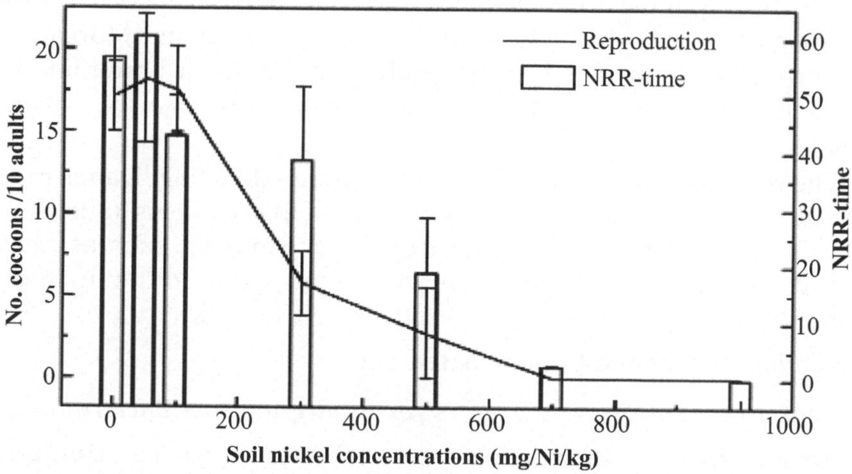

Fig. 3.8: Mean (± SEM) neutral-red retention time of coelomocyte lysosomes (NRR-time) and mean (± SEM) number of cocoons per 10 adult worms (reproduction), following 28 days of exposure to soil contaminated with nickel chloride

If metals are detoxified primarily by excretion, body concentrations should decrease when previously exposed individuals are transferred to a clean environment. If an element is bound in an inorganic matrix or to organic ligands, metal levels may remain constant, even after exposure has ceased (Tessier*et al.*, 1994)..

The difference found in the excretion kinetics of essential and xenobiotic elements in *E. fetida* suggest contrasting physiological fates for these metals. The high excretion rates found for copper and zinc indicate that these metals are detoxified primarily by excretion.

The ability of earthworms to eliminate excess copper and zinc is probably dependent on the essential nature of the element (Hopkin, 1995). Thus physiological pathways, possibly based on carrier systems, already exist for the physiological control of these elements (Morgan and Morgan, 1991).

For the xenobiotic metals, cadmium and lead, excretion was slow or absent. For these metals, the main detoxification pathways are sequestration within inorganic matrices or binding to organic ligands. The presence of storage detoxification systems for cadmium and lead have been demonstrated in a number of earthworm sps (Morgan *et al.*, 1989; Cancio *et al.*, 1995).

The main site of storage of metals is the chlorogogenous tissue, which is a sheath of modified peritoneal cells that line the outer wall of the gut (Fischer and Molner, 1993). X-ray micro analytical studies of this tissue have revealed that the cells contain two types of granules (chloragosomes).

The first granule form is represented by phosphate rich complexes containing calcium and to a lesser extent zinc (Morgan and Morgan, 1988). These granules are involved in the binding of type A or borderline metals such as lead by a process involving exchange with the matrix – associated calcium.

The second granule – type contains sulphur – donating ligands probably in the form of residues of metallothionein – like proteins (Suzuki *et al.*, 1980). Evidence that these proteins, bind type B metals, such as cadmium occur at increased levels in worms collected from contaminated soils (Sturzen-baum *et al.*, 1996).

Remediation of Organic Contaminated Soil

Earthworm Egg Capsules as Vectors for Biodegradative Bacteria of 2,4-D

Earthworms are saprotrophic invertebrates which contribute to the overall structure, drainage, and aeration of soil ecosystems. In addition, earthworms directly and indirectly influence soil microbial communities, mainly through the processes of feeding, burrowing, and fecal (cast) deposition. Earthworms can transport bacteria into the environment Recently, earthworms have been implicated as vectors and contributors for bacterial gene transfer. The majority of toxicity studies have focused only on adult earthworms and assessed only sublethal effects (juvenile growth, cocoon production or hatching, and immune system effects). None have examined the toxicity of chemicals to developing earthworms in cocoons directly. This study focused how developing cocoons or juvenile earthworms affect microbial communities (Daane and Haggblom, 1999).

The microorganisms are associated with earthworm egg capsules (cocoons). Morgan and Burrows (1982) reported that the internal fluid of *Eiseniafetida* cocoons contained bacteria of the genera *Nocardia, Pseudomonas,* and *Alcaligenes.* Zachmann and Molina (1993) were the first to quantify the bacteria present in egg capsules of *E. fetida,* with up to 10^8 CFU g^{-1} of cocoon. The cocoons may acquire bacteria from the environment from which they are formed. On examination of cocoon using scanning electron microscopy, determined the location of bacteria within the developing earthworm cocoon fragments containing well-developed juvenile earthworms revealed the presence of numerous rod-shaped microorganisms within the developingtissues. The microorganisms present did not appear to be detrimental to the developing earthworm tissue, which suggests a mutualistic association. So earthworm egg capsules could be used as biovectors for the introduction of beneficial bacteria, such as biological control, biodegradative, or plant-growth-promoting strains, into the environment.

The present study used the 2,4- dichlorophenoxyacetic acid (2,4-D)-degrading bacterium, *R. eutropha*JMP222N (pJP4), and the compost earthworm, *E. fetida*as a model system to determine whether bacterial strains acquired by earthworm egg capsules can be released from the cocoons into the soil for degradation of 2,4-D. In addition the ability of a degradative strain within the cocoon to influence the level of tolerance of the developing earthworm to 2,4-dichlorophenol (2,4-DCP) also been assessed.

The loss of 2,4-D was observed in soil containing cocoons with the degradative strain, *R. eutropha*JMP222N(pJP4). The concentration of 2,4-D fell to below the level of detection within 4 days in the *R. eutropha*JMP222N(pJP4) treatments. 2,4-D was utilized within 24 h after the remaining experimental microcosms were respiked at day 10 and day 11.The viability of the cocoon also assessed with different concentration of 2,4-DCP. The adult earthworms also exposed to 2,4-DCP in the same manner as cocoons to determine whether adults and developing worms have similar tolerance levels. Adult earthworms died within 48 h of exposure to 25 and 30 ppm of 2,4-DCP and survived up to 7 days in 20 ppm of 2,4-DCP. All of the adult earthworms survived long-term exposure (2 weeks) in 10 and 15 ppm of 2,4-DCP.

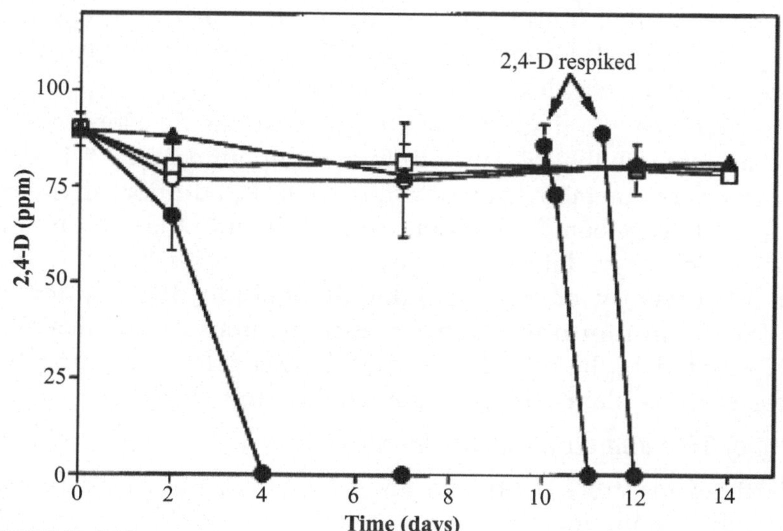

●, JMP222N(pJP4) cocoons

○, JMP222N cocoons

▲, No cocoons

Fig. 3.9: Degradation of 2,4-D in nonsterile soil with or without added earthworm cocoons

Table 3.5

Viability of cocoons exposed to various concentrations of 2,4-DCP with or without *R. eutropha* JMP 222N (pJP4)

Conc. (ppm)	Viability (%) after 23 days in cocoons	
	Without *R. eutropha* (pJP4)	Containing *R. eutropha* (pJP4)
0	100	100
5	100	100
10	100	100
15	60	100
20	0	100
25	0	83
30	0	67
40	0	0

Several studies have shown that 2,4-D is not toxic to adult earthworms even at high concentrations. The first intermediate of its degradation, 2,4-DCP, has been found to be highly toxic. The presence of the 2,4-D-degrading bacterium, *R. eutropha*(pJP4), within the developing cocoon greatly increases the tolerance to this highly toxic compound. Indeed, the exposure level allowing the successful hatching of juvenile earthworms was twice that of cocoons devoid of the degrading bacterium.

The presence of a degradative strain within the developing earthworm cocoon can increase the tolerance to toxic compounds, which indicates that the bacteria were metabolically active in vivo. In addition, that earthworm cocoons can release beneficial strains of bacteria into the soil upon hatching and initiate biodegradation. The present work with 2,4-D as the model system is currently being expanded to include degradation of more recalcitrant compounds such as polyaromatic hydrocarbons and polychlorinated biphenyls. It can also be used for including beneficial microbes such as plant pathogen antagonists and rhizobia.

Toxicity of Turf and Ornamental Insecticides and Miticides on Earthworms

Earthworms are essential to lawn health as macrodecomposers that help recycle organic matter and naturally aerate soil. Older insecticides in the chlorinated hydrocarbon group such as chlordane devasted earthworms creating unhealthy lawn environments. Currently used pesticides have lesser effects on lawn decomposers. Even among the current products some have potentially great impact on earthworms.

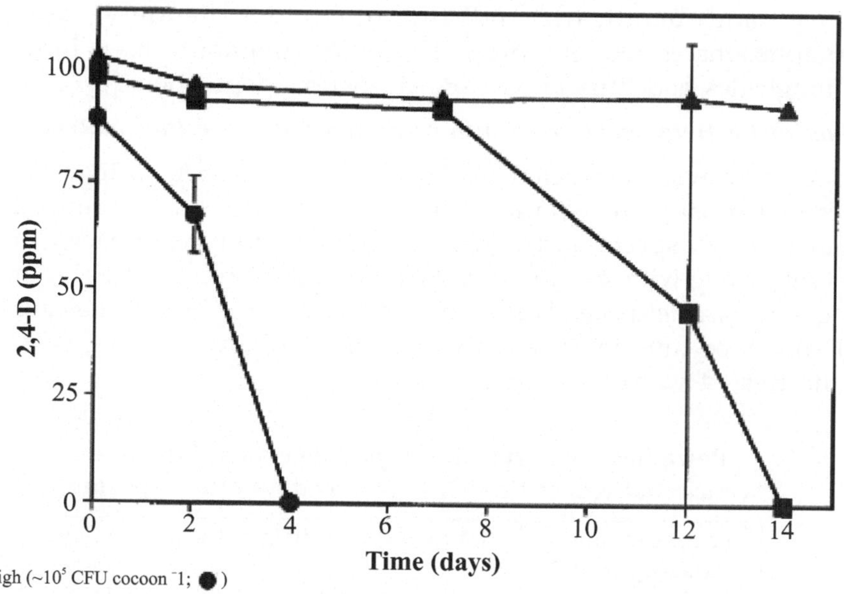

high (~10^5 CFU cocoon^{-1}; ●)

low (~10^2 CFU cocoon^{-1}; ■)

Fig. 3.10: Comparison of degradation of 2,4-D in nonsterile soil with cocoons containing high (10^5 CFU cocoon^{-1}) & low (10^2 CFU cocoon^{-1})

Recently Danpotter (1990) at the University of Kentucky studied the lawn care pesticide impact on earthworms.

Table 3.6
Effect of lawn pesticide on earthworm populations

Chemical	(% Population reduction)
Dursban 4E	(- 32.3)
Diazinon 14G	(- 58.4)
Triumph 4E	(- 59.4)
Benomyl	(- 60.0)*
Sevin SL	(- 89.8)*
Mocap 10G	(- 96.8)*
Turcam 2.5G	(- 99.0)*
Fonofos	(- 96)**
Thiophanate - methyl	(-88)**

*-these values indicate hazard under laboratory conditions.

Only a few of the tested products significantly impacted population two weeks after treatment. These includescarbamate insecticides such as carbaryl and bendicarb and the fungicides benomyl along the organophosphates like ethoprop. The other commonly used insecticides and fungicides had little impact on earthworm populations.

Impact of Pesticide on Earthworm Male Reproductive Parameters

A study was conducted by Bustos-obreget *al.* (2002) to explore the effect of exposure to commercial parathion (Pc) on the reproductive parameters like sperm and cocoon production and genotoxicity on male germ cells along with the survival, the body weight and the gross anatomical changes in *Eiseniafoetida*. Three dose of PC (1478, 739 and 444 mg/kg of soil) and three time intervals of exposure (5, 15 and 30 days) were used. All the treated warms were affected.

Table 3.7

Percentage of survival of *E. foetida* exposed to three concentrations of Pc at 5, 15 and 30 days after exposure

Pc concentration (mg/kg soil)	Survival (%) at different exposure days		
	5 days	15 days	30 days
0	95.0	97.5	76.3
444	97.5	90.0	32.5
739	90.0	91.3	13.8
1478	91.3	7.5	0

At the low Pc dose, survival is compromised only at long time after exposure (30 days). At the high dose marked effect is found at 15 days and no survivors by 30 days.

Table 3.8

Total number of *E. foetida* spermatozoa per mg of body weight exposed to three concentrations of Pc at 5, 15 and 30 days after exposure, *n* = number of worms

Pc concentration (mg/kg soil)	No. of sperm per mg of body (10^4) at different exposure days		
	5 days	15 days	30 days
0	11.26 (*n*=10)	7.57 (*n*=8)	7.76 (*n*=6)
444	14.01 (*n*=10)	16.59 (*n*=8)	15.29 (*n*=6)
739	12.71 (*n*=10)	13.15 (*n*=8)	15.02 (*n*=5)
1478	14.92 (*n*=10)	12.93 (*n*=4)	

Weight loss is a valuable indicator of physiological stress, related to the degree of intoxication and time of exposure. A similar trend has been reported for organochlorine pesticides intoxication and for the effects of fungicides and herbicides in *Lumbricusterrestris* and *E. foetida* (Helling *et al.*, 2000).

Alterations in reproductive parameters were obvious in regard to the number of sperm, cocoons and worms born. Neuromuscular function was also affected.

Table 3.9

Total number of capsules and worms born in *E. foetida* exposed to three concentrations compared with controls

Pc concentration (mg/kg soil)	Capsules (N_1)	Worms born (N_2)	N_2/N_1
0	220	315	1.4
444	77	126	1.6
739	84	110	1.3
1478	54	86	1.6

Coiling, another symptom seen in 100% of the Pc treated worms, because of this difficulties in locomotion of the treated worm and they are unable to feed themselves.

The number of capsules produced by Pc treated worms was clearly decreased, the viability of worms hatched from them was not much affected. This may imply that the quality of the ova is not damaged by Pc. Also the sexual characteristics of the worms were not affected. It clearly shows that Pc is genotoxic for male germ cells of *E. toetida* Reproductive parameters of earthworms exposed to agropesticide seem to be useful bioindicators of soil pollution and promising tools to predict genotoxic damage of the germ cell elements.

Effect of Organophosphate on Biomarkers of Earthworm

Two potential biomarkers of pesticide contamination were investigated in a common earthworm species following exposure to two widely used insecticide by Booth *et al.* (1998). *Apporectodeacaliginosa* was chosen as an indicator sps Juvenile earthworms were exposed to sub-lethal concentrations of the organophosphates chlorpyrifos and diazinon to assess their effect on cholinesterase and glutathione S-transforase activities.

Organophosphate and carbamate pesticides act by inhibiting chlinesteroses (ChE) which are a group of enzymes in the central nervous system. This enzyme may be a sensitive biomarker with which to assess environmental contamination by such pesticides. The activity of ChE in earthworms was severely inhibited by 72% by diazinon and 87% by chlorpyrifos within 24 hrs of exposure to sublethal level of pesticides and this activity showed no return to pre-exposure levels even after 14 days.

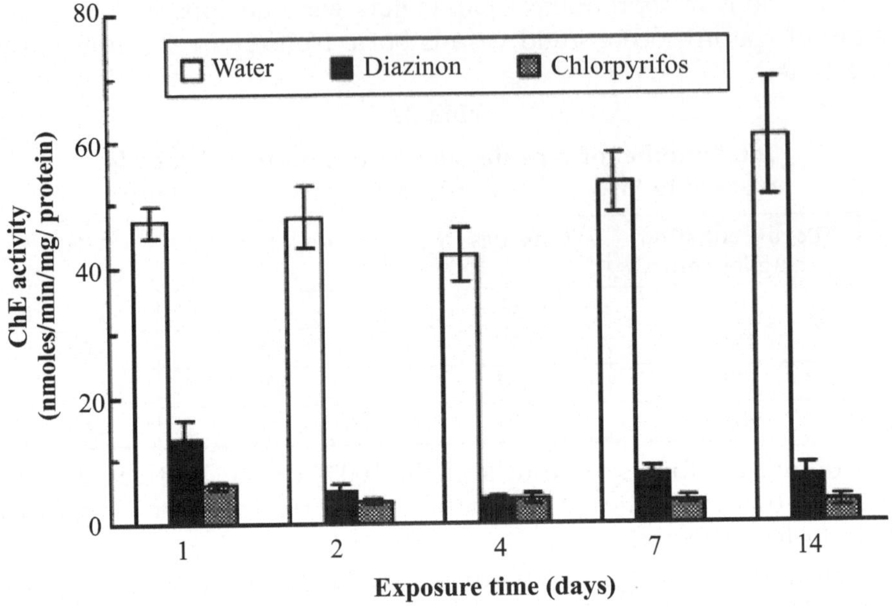

Fig. 3.11: ChE activity in *A. caliginosa* exposed to sublethal doses of diazinon. Values are mean activity standard error (n=5).

Glutathion S-transferase (GST) is involved in the detoxification of various xenobiotic chemicals. In Insects, GST plays an important role in the biotransformation of various insecticides (Lamoureux and Rusness, 1987) including the degradation of some organophosphorus compounds (Yang, 1976). So this enzyme could be useful as an indicator of pesticide exposure.

GST activity was induced by both chlorpyrifos and diazinon GST is induced by diazinom by 56% after 14 days and chlorpyrifos induced GST by 148% after 14 days exposure. But the maximum induction by other pesticdes likeEndosulphan by 250% (Hans *et al.*, 1993).

GST may be a useful biomarker for long-term exposure whereas ChE may be more indicative of acute exposures.

Kale and Krishnamoorthy (1982) reported up to 80% inhibition of ChE by carbaryl in the earthworm *Pontoscolexcorethrurus*. Sterersen (1979) exposred earthworms to a number of organophosphates and carbamates by dipping them in an aqueous solution and demonstrated upto 85% inhibition of Ache levels, compared to controls.

Effect of Agrochemicals on Growth and Development of Earthworm

The effects of insecticides, fungicides and herbicides against the earthworm *Pentoscolexcorethrurus* were tested by Awarknavar*et al.* (2005) under laboratory and cage house condition at Dharwad. From the acute toxicity study, it is revealed that the pattern of lethality based on LC_{50} was cypermethrin> carbazyl> alphamethrin> endosulfan> monocrotophos> atrazine > 2, 4-D <carbofuran > chlorpyrifos> triazophos> glyphosate >Gramaxane> Indofil> Captan> Ridomil whereas chronic study indicated that fungicides were less toxic followed by herbicides and insecticides. Among insecticides, chlorpyrifos was found to be the safest one as it recorded maximum weight (1463 mg), survivality (80.1%) and cocoons per worm (68) compared to other insecticides. But carbaryl, carbofuran and endosulfan were highly toxic insecticides to *P. corethrurns*.

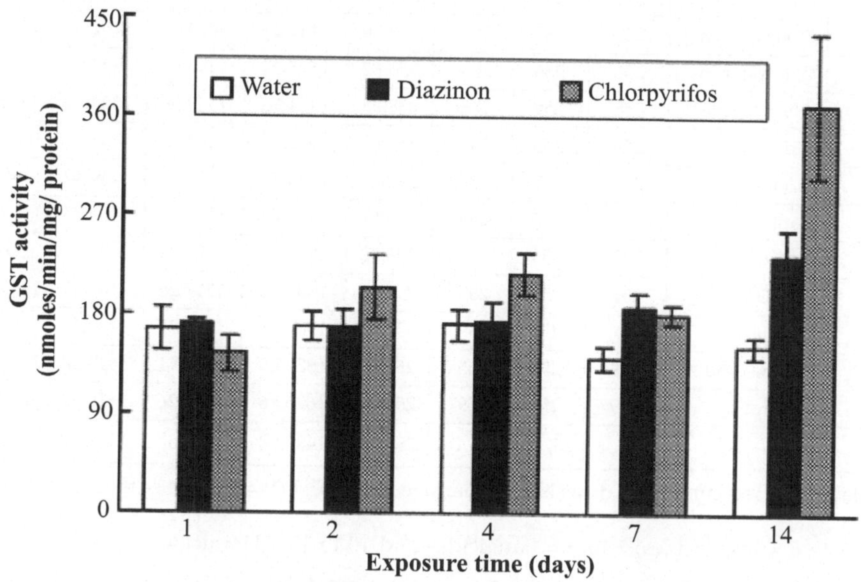

Fig. 3.12: GST activity in *A. caliginosa* exposed to sublethal doses of diazinon. Values are mean activity standard error (n=5)

Kring (1969) noticed drastically decreased *Lumbricusterrestris* population in carbofuran treated tobacco field. Reddy and Reddy (1992) found that application of Endosulfan @ 3 ml/ft^2 reduced 100% population of *Dravidawillsi* and *Lampitomauritii* chlorprophampropham, dinoseb and triazine herbicides such as simazine have moderate effects on earthworm population (Endwards and Thompson, 1973). Chio and Sanbporn (1978) reported that *L. terrest* couldmetabolise atrazine.

Earthworms for Radio Nuclei Contaminated Sites

Earthworms have also been used as bioindicators of radioactive soil pollution and radioactive materials including strontium 90 and cesium 137. Earthworms proved to be sensitive to a radiation background of ^{226}Ra. The levels of radiation affected the reproduction of earthworms and caused changes in the structure of the epithelium of the mid-gut and increase in mucus cells in the epithelium of the outer integument (Krivolutsky *et al.*, 1982).

Table 3.10

Effect of pesticides on weight (mg) of *Pentoscolexcorethrurus* at 0 day before release (DBR) and 90 days after release (DAR)

Sl. No.	ODBR					90 DAR			
	Pesticides	SN	N	DN	Mean	SN	N	DN	Mean
1.	Carbofuran	259	258	157	258.00	1376.03	1346.29′	1303.69	1342.0
2.	Carbaryl	256	259	255	256.67	1381.04	1352.73	1320.90	1351.4
3.	Endosulfan	257	257	259	257.67	1363.23	1338.26	1310.45	1337.3
4.	Monocrotophos	258	259	257	258.00	1459.38	1430.90	1402.43	1430.9
5.	Chlorphyrifos	256	256	255	255.67	1507.24	1460.89	1420.90	1463.01
6.	Alphamethrin	258	259	258	258.33	1374.36	1358.59	1328.31	1353.7
7.	Ridomil	256	258	259	257.67	1506.71	1464.95	1433.25	1468.30
8.	Indofil	257	257	258	257.33	1543.74	1503.12	1449.42	1498.59
9.	Captan	258	257	255	256.67	1561.25	1524.49	1460.85	1515.53
10.	Atrazine	257	259	259	258.33	1554.52	1503.82	1453.68	1504.0
11.	2-4. D	256	255	255	255,33	1532.42	1507.26	1459.42	1499.70
12.	Glyphosate	257	255	259	257.00	1508.16	1467.37	1426.34	1467.29
13.	Gramaxone	259	256	255	256.67	1537.08	1487.41	1447.48	1490.65
14.	Control	259	257	259	258.33	1625.66	1614.26	1619.91	1619.94
	Mean	257.36	257.28	257.14	257.26	1487.88	1454.30	1416.90	1453.03

SN - Half of the recommended dose; N = Recommended dose; DN = Double of the recommended dose.

Sl.No. 1 to 6 = Insecticides; 7 to 9 = Fungicides and 10 to 13 – Herbicides

A study had been conducted in 1969-1992 in the territory of the former USSR (Russia, Ukraine and Kazakhstan) for assessing the long-term effects of radiological accidents (Krivolusky, 1995). The ecological effects of the increased radiation caused by the radionuclides super (226) Ra, Super (232) Th, Super (238) U in the soils have been studied. There was appreciable reduction of populations abundance, disturbance of a breeding process, loss of the biological diversity at the polluted soil plots have been observed.

The secondary sick effects have been registered for active immigrants among terrestrial animals : birds, mammals, insects : their population abundance increased in zone with low level of irradiation and after the radiation decrease. A plot with a high level of super (226) Ra and a radiation level of about 100 p/hr contained a 7-fold reduction of soil inhabiting earthworms over the control. The irradiated earthworms were smaller in size. But there was not registered any negative ecological effects for surface living animals and plants in the same territory. Because the earthworms constantly swallow a lot of mineral soil particles with their food containing radionuclides. In the polluted soils they are influenced both from inside and outside of their body.

Another study was also conducted to understand the ecological effects of the Chernobyl reactor accident. In the investigation radiocesium Super (137) C_s levels in Eurasian woodcock, earthworms, litter, humus and mineral soil samples from a heavily effected (20-60Bqkg^{-1}) area in Norway. The highest concentration measured in earthworms (142Bqkg^{-1}) and wood cocks (730 Bqkg^{-1}) were below levels that should effect animal health, during the year 1986. Radiocesium concentrations decreased in earthworms (40%) and woodcock (95%) from 1986 to 1990. The decrease in radiocesium in woodcock and earthworms during the study (1986-90) probably resulted from decreasing bioavailability of radiocesium during the first years (Kaalaas *et al.*, 1994).

RESEARCH NEEDS

- Screening of earthworm species for specific metals and nonmetal contaminants.
- Developing suitable bioassay technique for biomarkers study.
- Developing methods to identify mechanism of metal resistance.
- There is a need to develop well-designed and harmonized test protocols relevant to the exposure of earthworms to chemicals under field conditions.

There is a need for a data bank on field and lab toxicity of chemicals to earthworms and the development of a simulation models to predict the toxicity of potentially toxic chemicals based on physico – chemical properties and characteristics.

SUMMARY

Bioindicators of pollution from metals and other substances are essential components of a comprehensive assessment of ecological and human health risks. Metals present in a bioavailable form may be bioaccumulated and thereby detrimentally affect long-term organism health. Metal bioavailability is usually determined using either geochemical methods or bioaccumulation studies. Geochemical techniques provide indirect evidence regarding metal-bearing minerals and the availability of metals to organism. However the relationship between geological parameters, metal uptake, and biological effects is frequently not clear due to complicating interactions between variables. Direct analysis of tissues from organisms exposed to specific field or lab conditions can provide evidence of bioavailability.

REFERENCES

Awaknoevar, J.S. and S.S. Karabhantanal. 2005. Effects of Agro-chemicals on Growth and Development of Earthworm, *Pentoscolex conethrurus*. J. Ecotoxicol. Environ. Monit., 15(2): 179-187.

Booth, L.H., V. Heppelthwaite and C.T. Eason. 1998. Cholinesterase and Glutathione S-transferase in the Earthworm *Apporectodea caliginosa* as Biomass of Organophosphate Exposure. Proc. of the 51st N_2 Plant Protection Conference: 138-142.

Bouche, M.B. 1977. Strategies Lombicienners, Biol. Bull., 25: 122-132.

Bustos-obeng, E. and R.L. Goicochea. 2002. Pesticide Soil Contamination mainly Affects Earthworm Male Reproductive Parameters. Asian J. Androl., 4: 195-199.

Callahan, C.A. 1988. Earthworms as Ecotoxicological Assessment. In: Edwards, C.A., Neuhanser, E.F. (eds) Earthworms in Waste and Environmental Management. SPB Academic Publ. The Hague, The Netherlands,: 295-301.

Cambek, M., B. Iskli, M. Uyanoglu, T.A. Demir and A. Berber. 2005. Determination of Lead Accumulation in the *L. terrestris* (Earthworm) Living in the Road Side Soils of Eskisehir. J. Art. Sci., 4: 47-53.

Chio, H. and J.R. Samborn. 1976. The Metabolism of ^{14}C-chlordane by the Earthworm, *Lumbricus terrestris* L. Chemosphere, 3: 161-166.

Chio, H. and J.R. Sambporn. 1978. The Metabolism Attrazine, Chlonemben and Decamba in Earthworms (*L. terrestris*) from Treated and Untreated Plots. Weed Sci., 26: 331-335.

Daane, L.l. and M.M. Haggblom.1999. Earthwarm Egg Capsules as Vectors for the Environemntsl of Introduction Biodegradative Bacteri. Appl. Environ. Microbiol., 65(6): 2376-2381.

Drewes.C.D. ling amneri, A. 1992. Use of Earth Warms in Eco Neurotoxicology Testing. Sub-lethal Effects of Carbofuran in *Lumbricus terrestris*. In: Ecotoxicology of Earthworms.(Eds). P.W. Grieg-smith, H. Becker, P.J. Edward and F.heibach, intercept, Hants, U.K. pp. 197-206.

Edwards, C.A. 1983. Development of a Standardized Laboratory method for Assessing the Toxicity of Chemical Substances to Earthworms Commission of the European Communities, Brussels, Luxembourg.

Edwards, C.A. and A.R. Thomson. 1973. Pesticides and Soil Fauna. Res. Rev., 45 : 1-79.

Edwards, C.A. and J. Bohlem. 1992. The Effect of Chemicals on Earthworm. Rev. Environ. Contam. Toxicol.,125 : 22-95.

Edwards, C.A., A.R. Thompson and J.R. Lofty. 1968. Changes in Soil Invertebrate Populations caused by some Organophosphorus Insecticides. Proc. 4th Brit. Insectic. Fungic. Cont.,: 48-55.

Edwards, C.A., J.R. Lotfy and C.J. Stafford. 1971. Pesticides and the Soil Fauna. Rept. Rothamsted Exp. Stan., Part I, 194.

Fanelli, R., M.P. Bertoni, M. Bontanti, M.G. Castelli, C. Chibarando, G.P. Martelli, M.A. Noe, A. Noseda and C. Sbarra. 1980. Routine Analysis of 2, 3, 7, 8-tetrachloro-dibenzo-p-dioxin in Biological Samples from the Contaminated Area of Seveso, Italy, Bull. Environ. Contam. Toxicol., 24: 818-823.

Fisher, S.W. 1984. A Comparison of Standardized methods for measuring the Biological Activity of Pesticide to the Earthworm *L. terrestri*. Ecotoxicol Environ, Saf., 8 : 564-571.

Hans, R.K., M.A. Khan, M. Farooz and M.U. Beg. 1993. Glutathione-S-transferase Activity in an Earthworm (*Pheretima posthuma*) Exposed to Three Insecticides. Soil Biol. and Biochem., 25(4): 509-511.

Helling, B., S. Reinecke and A. Reinecke. 2000. Effects of the Fungicide Copper Oxychlorideon the Growth and Reproduction of *Eisenia foetida* (Oligocheata). Ectoxicol. Environ. Saf., 46 : 108-116.

Hopkin, S.P. 1995. Deficiency and Excess and Essential and Non Essential Metals in Terrestrial Insects, In : Harrington, R. and N.E. Stork (Eds.) Insects in a Changing Environment, Academic Press, London.: 251-270.

Huggett, R.j., Kirmle, R.A., Mehrle, O.M and Bergman, H.l. 1992. Biomarkers : Biochemical, Physiological an Hitological Markers of Anthrophogeneic, Lewis, Boca raton.

Kaalaas, J.A., S. Bretten, I. Byrkjedal and O. Njaastad. 1994. Radiocesium (super (137) (S) from the Chernobyl Reactor in Eurasian Wood Lock and Earthworms in Norway. J. Wildl. Manage, 58(1) : 141-147.

Kring, J.B. 1969. Mortality of Earthworm *L. terrestins* Following Soil Application of Insecticides in a Tobacco Field. J. Econ. Ent., 62 : 963.

Kriralutsky, D., A. Turcaninova and Z. Mikhaltsova. 1982. Earthworms as Bioindicators of Radioactive Soil Pollution. Pedobiologia, 23 : 263-265.

Krivolutsky, D.A. 1995. Chernobyl Nuclear Disaster and Long-term Changes in Biodiversity induced by the Radiation Pollution. Ecol. Ind. Regions, 1(2) : 37-43.

Kuhle, J.C. 1983. Ecotoxicological Model Studies to Test the Suitability of Earthworms as Bioindicators. Verh. Dtsch. Zool. Ges,:147-151.

Lamoureux, G.L. and D.G. Rusness. 1987. Synergism of Diazinon Toxicity and Inhibition of Diazinon Metabolism in the Housefly by Tridiphane : Inhibition of Glutathione – s – transferase Activity. Pest. Biochem. Phys., 27 : 318-329.

Langdon, C.J., T.G. Piearce, A.A. Meharg and K.T. Sample. 2001. Resistance to Copper – Toxicity in Populations of the Earthworms *Lumbricus rubellus* and *Dendrodrilus rubidus* in Contaminated Mine-wastes. Environ. Toxicol. Chem., 20: 2336-2341.

Living Stone, D.R. 1990. Cytochrome. P.450 and Oxidative Metabolism in Invertebrates.

Mahimairaja, S. 2005. Phytoremeiation of Metals (As) Contaminated Soil. Postdoctoral Research Report. Institute of Natural Resource. Massy University, Palmerstone. North New Zealand.,: 41-46.

Manay, N., L. Pereina and Z. Cousillas. 1999. Lead Contamination in Uruguay. Rev. Environ. Contam. Toxicol., 159 : 25-39.

Marquenie, J.M. and J.W. Simmers. 1988. A method to Assess Potential Bioavaiability of Contaminants. In : Edwards, C.A. and E.F. Neuhauser (eds) Earthworms in Waste and Environmental Management, SPB Academic Publ. The Hague, The Netherlands.: 367-376.

Mason, C.F.V., R.J.R. Turner, B.M. Thomson, N. Lu, P.A. Longmire and C.J. Branse. 1997. Environ. Sci. Tech., 31 : 2707-2711.

Meharg, A.A., R.F. Share and K. Broadgate. 1998. Edaphic Factors Affecting the Toxicit and Accumulation of Arsenate in the Earthworms *Lumbricus terrestris*. Environ. Toxicol. Chem., 17 : 1124-1131.

Morgan, A.J., C. Winters and A. Yarwood. 1994. Speed-mapping of Arsenic Distribution in the Tissues of Earthworms Inhabiting Arsenious Soil. Cell Biology International, 18 : 911-914.

Morgan, J.E. and A.J. Morgan. 1991. Differences in the Accumulated Metal Concentration in Two Epigeic Earthworm species (*L. rubellus* and *D. rubidus*) living in Contaminated Soils. Bull. Environ. Contam. Toxicol., 47 : 289-301.

Morgan, J.E. and A.J. Morgan. 1991. Differences in the Accumulated Metal Concentration in Two Epigeic Earthworm species (*L. rubellus* and *D. rubidus*) living in Contaminated Soils. Bull. Environ. Contam. Toxicol., 47 : 289-301.

Moriarty, F. 1983. Ecotoxicology. Academic Press, New York, USA.

Reddy, M.V. and V.R. Reddy. 1992. Effect of Organochlorine, Organophosphorus and Carbamate Insecticides on the Population Structure and Biomass of Earthworms in a Semi Arid Tropical Grass Land. Soil Biol. Biochem., 24 : 1733-1738.

Salagovic, J. Gills, J., Verschaeve, L and kalian, I.1996. The Context Assay for Detection of Genotoxic Damage in Earthwarms; A Promising Roll for Assessing the Biological Hazards of Pollutes Sites. Folia Biol., 42: 17-21.

Spurgeon, D.J. and S.P. Hopkin. 1995. Extrapolation of the Laboratory – based OECD Earthworm Toxicity Test to Metal – Contaminated Field Sites. Ecotoxicology, 4 : 190-205.

Spurgeon, D.J. and S.P. Hopkin. 1995. Extrapolation of the Laboratory – based OECD Earthworm Toxicity Test to Metal – Contaminated Field Sites. Ecotoxicology, 4 : 190-205.

Stenersen, J. 1979. Action of Pesticides on Earthworms. Part 2: Elimination of Parathion by the Earthworm. *Eisenia foetida* (Savigny). Pestic. Sci., 10 : 104-112.

Stenersen, J. 1979. Action of Pesticides on Earthworms. Part 3 : Inhibition and Reactivation of Cholinesterases in *E. foetida* after Treatment with Cholinesterase – Inhibiting Insecticides. Pest. Sci., 10 : 113-122.

Stenersen, J., Kobro,S., Bjerke, M. and Arend, U. 1987. Glutathione Transferase in Aquatic and Terrestrial Animals from Nine Phyla. Comp. Biochem. Physiol.,86: 73-82.

Stenersen, J., Gilman, A. and (Vardanis, A. 1973. Carofuran: its Toxicity to and Metabolism by Earthwarms (*Lumbricus terrestris*). J.Agric.Food Chem., 21: 166-171.

Stringer, A. and M.A. Wright. 1973. The Effect of Benomyl and some related Compounds on *Lumbricus terrestris* and other Earthworms. Pestic. Sci., 4 : 165-170.

Stringer, A. and M.A. Wright. 1976. The Toxicity of benomyl and some related 2-subtituted Benzimidazoles to the Earthworm *Lumbricus terrestris*. Pestic. Sci., 7 : 459-464.

Sturzenbaum, S.R., P. Kille and A.J. Morgan. 1996. Heavy Metal Pollution: The Earthworm Response, In : Curry, J.P., T. Bolger, B. Kaye and B. Purvis, (Eds) Abstracts of the XII Int. Coloq. Soil Zoology, University College Dublin, Dublin, Ireland.

Sturzenbaun, S.R., P. Kille and A.J. Morgan. 198. The Identification, Characterization and Cloning of Earthworms Metallothionein. FEBS letters, 431 : 437-442.

Suzuki, K.T., M. Yamamura and T. Mori. 1980. Cadmium – binding Proteins Induced in the Earthworm. Arch. Environ. Contam. Toxicol., 9 : 415-424.

Swaileh, K.M., N. Rabaya's R. Salim, A. Ezzughayyar and A.A. Rabbo. 2001. Concentrations of Heavy Metals in Road Side Soils, Plants and Land Snails from the West Bank, Palestine. Environ. Sci. Health Part A Tox. Hazard, Subst. Environ. Eng., 36(5) : 765-778.

Tessier, L., G. Vaillancourt and L. Pazdernik. 1994. Temperature Effects on Cadmium and Mercury Kinetics in Fresh Water Mollusks under Laboratory Conditions. Arch. Environ. Contam. Toxicol., 26 : 179-184.

Thakuria, D. 2010. Gut Wall Bacteria of Earthworms: A Natural Selection Process. The ISME journal, 4(3), pp. 357-66.

Thompson, A.R. 1970. Effects of mine insecticides on the Number and Biomass of Earthworms in Pasture. Bull. Environ. Contam. Toxicol., 5 : 577.

Vebables, B.J., L.C. Fitzpatrick and A.J. Gover. 1992. Earthwarms as Indicators of Ecotoxicity In: Ecotoxicology of Earthwarms. In: P.W. grieg-smith, H.Becker. P.J. Edwards and F.Heimbach. Intercepts. Hans,UK. pp. 197-206.

Weeks, J.M. 1996. The Value of Biomarkers of Recological Risk Assessment: Academic Toy Orlegislative Toals?. Appl. Soil Ecol., 2: 215-216.

Yang, R.S.H. 1976. Enzyme Conjugation and Insecticide Metabolism. In: Biochemistry and Physiology of Insecticides. C.F. Wilkinson (Ed.): Plenum Press, New York : 177-187.

Zabinski, C.,P.M. Bertsch, T. Punshan and G.O. Quinn. 1997. Savannah Rive Ecology Laboratory. University of Georgia.

Zachmann, J.E. and J.A.E. Molina. 1893. Presence of Culturable Bacteria in Cocoons of the Earthwarm Eisenia Fetida. Appl. Environ. Microbiol., 59: 1904-1910.

Section II:
Farm and Farming

Pages: 59-70

Vermitechnology, Farm and Fertilizer

Edited by: Dr. Ashok K. Rathoure; Dr. Pawan Kumar 'Bharti' and Dr. Jaswant Ray

ISBN: 978-93-88854-38-2

Edition: **2020**

Published by: **Discovery Publishing House Pvt. Ltd., New Delhi (India)**

4

Farming System and Farming Approach

Prasann Kumar[1,2*], Shipa Rani Dey[1]

GRAPHICAL ABSTRACT

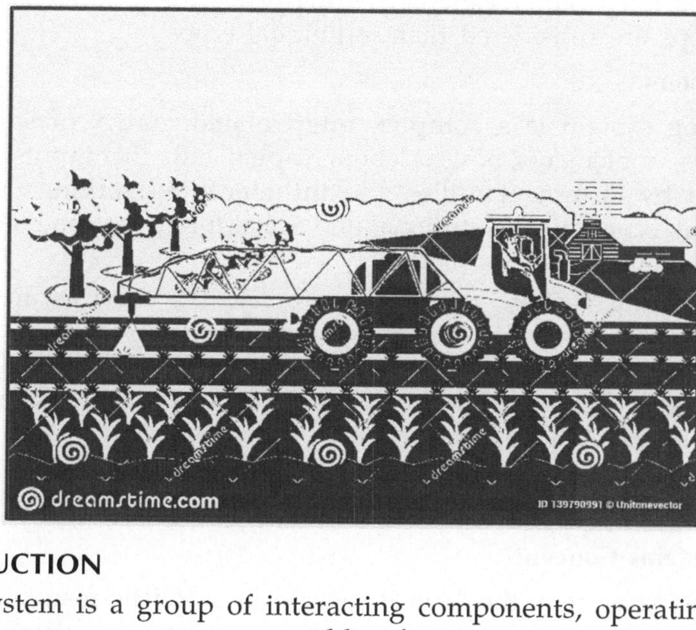

INTRODUCTION

- A system is a group of interacting components, operating together for a common purpose, capable of reacting as a whole to external stimuli.

[1] **Department of Agronomy, School of Agriculture Lovely Professional University, Jalandhar - 144 411 (Punjab) (India)**

[2] **Divison of Research and Development,, Lovely Professional University, Jalandhar - 144 411 (Punjab) (India)**

- A system is defined as a set of elements or components that are inter related and interacting among themselves.
- In system approach all the components and activities are linked, they affect each other. It is not sensible to look at one component by itself without recognizing that what it does and what happens to it, it will alsoaffect other parts of the system.
- In agriculture, management practices were usually formulated for individual corp.
- However, farmers are cultivating different crops in different seasons based on their adaptability to a particular season, domestic needs and profitability.
- Therefore, production technology or management practices should be developed in view all the crops grown in a year or more than one than one year if any sequence or rotation extends beyond one year.
- Such a package of management practices for all crops leads to efficient use of costly inputs, besides reduction in production cost.
- For instance, residual effect of manures and fertilizers applied and nitrogen fixed can considerably bring down the production cost if all the crops are considered than individual crops.

Farming System

- Farming system is a complex inter-related matrix of soil, plants, animals, implements, power, labour, capital and other inputs controlled in part by farming families and influenced to varying degrees by political, economic, institutional and social forces that operate at many levels.
- The farming system, therefore, refers to the farm as an entity of interdependent farming enterprises carried out on the farm. The farm is viewed in a holistic manner. The farmers are subjected to many socio-economic, biophysical, institutional, administrative and technological constraints.
- Farming system conceptually is a set of elements or components that are interrelated which interact among themselves.

Farming Systems Concept

- In farming system, the farm is viewed in a holistic manner.
- Farming enterprises include crops, dairying, poultry, fishery, sericulture, piggery, apiary tree crops etc. a combination of one or more enterprises with cropping when carefully chosen, planned and executed, gives greater dividends than a single enterprise, especially for small and marginal farmers.

- Farm as a unit is to be considered and planned for effective integration of the enterprises to be combined with crop production activity, such that the end-products and wastes of one enterprise are utilized effectively as inputs in other enterprise.

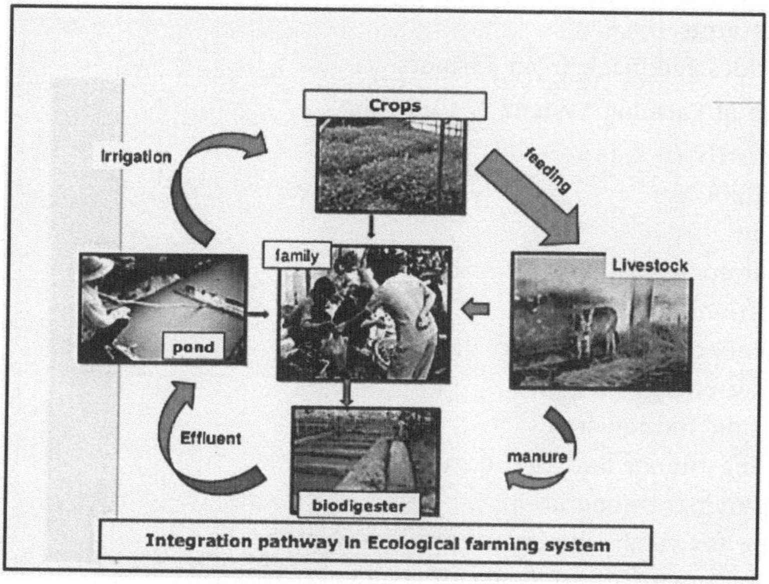

Fig. 4.1: Integrated pathway in Ecological Farming System

Source: Based on review of literature

Principles of Farming System

Minimization of Risk

- Recycling of wastes and residues
- Integration of two or more enterprises
- Optimum utilization of all resources
- Maximum productivity and profitability
- Ecological balance
- Generation of employment potential
- Increased input use efficiency
- Use of end products from one enterprise as input in other.

Characteristics of Farming System

1. Farmer oriented & holistic approach
2. Effective farmer's participation
3. Unique problem solving system
4. Dynamic system
5. Gender sensitive

6. Responsible to society
7. Environmental sustainability
8. Location specificity of technology
9. Diversified farming enterprises to avoid risks due to environmental constraints.
10. Provides feedback from farmers

Objectives of Farming System

- Productivity
- Profitability
- Potentiality
- Balanced food
- Environmental safety
- Income/cash flow round the year
- Saving energy
- Meeting fodder crises
- Solving timber and fuel crises
- Employment generation
- Scope for establishment of agro- industries
- Enhancement in input use efficiency

Determinants of Farming System

- **Factor A** represent the physical and biological elements which set limits to the type of agricultural produce to be produced in the given region. The physical elements include land, soil quality, topography, climate, water, location, distance etc.
- The biological elements include crops and livestock physiology, diseases etc., which determine the potential farm enterprises.
- **Factor B** represent endogenous human elements, which greatly influence the type of farming system adopted in a particular region. The system revolves around the farmer whose family and means of livelihood are interact linked.
- **Factor C** represents the exogenous human variables, which govern the allocation of available resources by the farmers.

Cropping System Related Terminology

- **Cropping system:** A cropping system refers to the principles and practices of cropping and their interaction with farm resources and edaphic environment to suit the region. It is an important component of farming system.
- **Cropping pattern:** The yearly sequence and spatial arrangement of crops and fallow on a given area.

Multiple Cropping

- Multiple cropping refers to intensification of cropping both in time and space. It includes sequential cropping, inter-cropping and mixed cropping.
- **Sequential cropping:** Growing two or more crops in a sequence on the same field in a farming year.
- **Intercropping:** It refers to growing of two or more dissimilar crops simultaneously on the same piece of land, base crop necessarily in distinct row arrangement.
- **Mixed inter-cropping:** Growing component crops simultaneously with no distinct row arrangement.
- **Strip inter-cropping:** Growing component crops in different strips wide enough to permit independent cultivation but narrow enough to the crop to interact agronomically.
- **Relay inter-cropping:** Growing component crops in relay, so that growth cycles overlap.
- **Mixed cropping:** Mixed cropping is growing of two or more crops simultaneously on the same piece of land.
- **Ratoon cropping:** The cultivation of crops're-growth coming out of roots or stalks of the preceding crop after harvest, although not necessarily for grain is termed as ratoon cropping/ratooning.

CONCEPT FARMING SYSTEMS APPROACH

Simmonds (1984) clarified the FSA as follows:

- It is an academic activity comprising of theory, concepts, principles and approaches
- It creates an opportunity for developing diversified models for different types and categories of farmers
- New farming system models can be developed by means of on-farm research and extension.

Objectives of FSA

- To develop farm - household systems of rural communities on a sustainable basis
- To improve efficiency in farm production
- To raise farm and family income
- To increase welfare of farm families and satisfy basic needs

DIFFERENT FARMING SYSTEMS

The following farm enterprises could be promoted

- Agri+ Livestock
- Agri + Livestock + Poultry

- Agri + Horticulture
- Agri + Horticulture + Sericulture
- Agri + Fisheries + Duckery + Poultry etc.,

METHODOLOGY

I. Analysis of existing farming system

- Identification of major socio-economic situations
- Understanding dominant enterprises and most common farming systems
- Analysis of economic viability of existing farming systems
- Understanding relationship between different enterprises within the system
- Analysis of linkages between different farming systems

II. Understanding the modifications made in existing farming system by innovative farmers

- Understanding the changing scenario in rural areas and its impact on existing farming system
- Identification of new market opportunities and its impact and relevance to socio-economic situation
- Suitable modification made by innovative farm families in existing farming system
- Type of modification made (diversification or intensification of the enterprises)

III. New options recommended by the researchers

- Identification of new suggested options by researchers around each dominant enterprise
- Understanding thetechnological details about new options.

IV. Economic analysis of recommended options:

- Analysis of relative profitability of recommended options as compared to existing farming system
- Understanding of implications of each options with regard to reallocation of resource

V. Testing of recommended options

- Selecting representative village/farm families
- Training about technical skills
- Testing the effectiveness of recommended options

VI. Feedback evaluation

- Analysis of farming system profit loss ratio.

- Understanding the pros and cons
- Further requirement/modification protocols

INTEGRATED FARMING SYSTEM FOR WET LAND

Crop based IFS: Here, crop production is the major activity, utilizing a greater share of available resources and often contributing more of total income. Other activities complement the crop production activity by way of recycling of organic waste and supplementing the income. The crop by products can be utilized for the allied enterprises.

For example,

Crop + Dairy

Crop + Poultry

Crop + Fish

Livestock based IFS: Here, rearing of livestock is the major activity, which contributes the major share of income. Cropping is to plan in such a way to meet the fodder and feed requirement of the livestock.

For example,

Poultry Farm

Goat/sheep Farm

Fish + Piggery + Crop.

Crops in Wetland

rice–rice–rice

rice–rice–rice

fallow–rice–rice

rice–rice–upland crop (ground nut)

upland crop–rice–rice

rice–rice–cotton

Components/enterprises proposed for IFS under wetland conditions

- Multiple cropping including sequential cropping, inter and relay cropping.
- Integrating livestock, cow, goat, piggery etc., along with cropping enterprises.
- Combining fish (Aquaculture) cum poultry in the existing system.
- Agro-forestry on tree components in the existing system.
- Inclusion of mulberry cultivation and sericulture or lac culture with crops.
- Mushroom cultivation with cropping.
- Inclusion of apiary and horticultural crops etc.

Integrated Farming System for Irrigated Upland

Crops

Crops that can tolerate mild winter

Legumes – green gram, black gram, soybean, and groundnut.

Cereals – maize, sorghum, pearl millet and ragi.

Other crops – cotton, sunflower and vegetables.

Crops that can tolerate cool winter are wheat, barely, mustard and potato.

Integrated farming system model for irrigated upland system at Jalandhar, India

(Crop + Dairy + Poultry)

Integrated Farming System for Dry Land

Crop production depends entirely on the quantity of rainfall received or with conserved moisture. Hence, there is every likelihood of crop being facing with mild to severe stress during its growth period. The major constraint is the wind and water erosion.

Cereal + Pigeon Pea

Cereal + Cotton

Single crop area - Sorghum, Chickpea, Sunflower, Coriander

Double crop area - Sorghum/Pearl millet/Pulse during rainy period. Sunflower/Safflower/Chickpea during post rainy period.

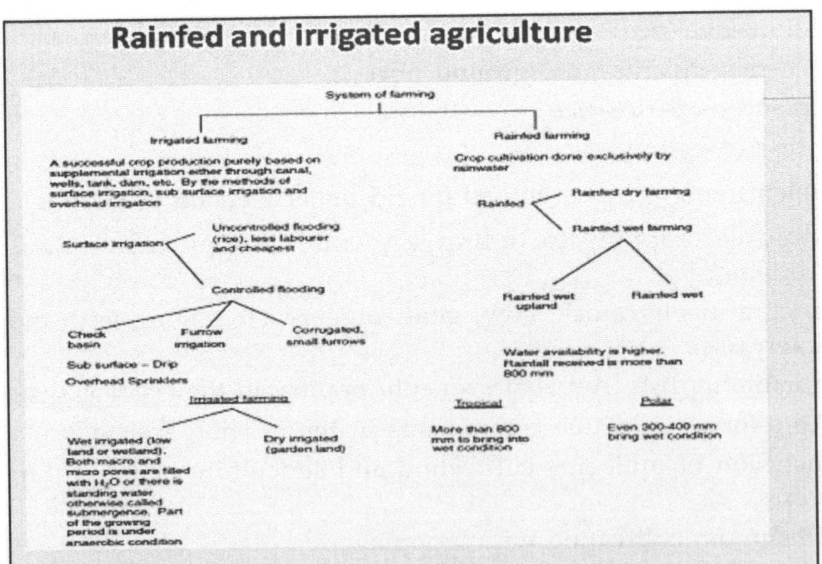

Fig. 4.2: Rainfed and Irrigated agriculture

Source: Based on review of literature

Irrigation Methods

The irrigation methods are broadly classified as:

1. Surface method or gravity method of irrigation
2. Sub surface or sub irrigation
3. Pressurized or micro irrigation - Drip irrigation, sprinkler irrigation and rain gun irrigation.

Surface Irrigation

Border strip method - The field is divided into number of long parallel strips by providing small parallel earthen bunds along both sides of the strips. The end along the strip may or may not be closed, which is based on the length of the strips. If the length of the strip is very long, the end will be closed to have a uniform distribution and to avoid run off loss. Each strip is irrigated independently from upper end (turned on) and water flow as thin sheet and uniformly spread along the strips. The water is turned off when the required volume is delivered to the strip. The application efficiency of this system is 75–85%.

Dryland Agriculture

- Dry farming
- Dry land farming
- Rainfed farming

Dry Farming

- *Dry farming* is cultivation of crops in regions with annual rainfall of less than 750 mm. Crop failure is most common due to prolonged dry spells during the crop period.

  Arid regions

  Crop growing period - <75 days

  Moisture conservation practices - necessray

  Dryland Farming

- *Dry land farming* is cultivation of crops in regions with annual rainfall of 750 - 1150mm. In spite of prolonged dry spells, crop failure is relatively less frequent.

  Semi -arid regions

  Crop growing period – 75-120 days

  Moisture conservation practices –necessray

  Adequate drainage - required

RAINFED FARMING

- *Rainfed farming* is cultivation of crops in regions with annual rainfall of more than 1150 mm. Crops are not subjected to soil moisture stress during crop period.

    Humid regions

    Crop growing period - >120 days

    Adequate drainage facility

Fig. 4.3: Rainfed farming

Source: Based on review of literature

The important improved Dry land technologies are:

1. Selection of efficient crops and their varieties
2. Crop planning as per length of cropping season
3. Developing suitable varieties for dry lands
4. Seeding time for Dry land crops
5. Timely seeding for pest avoidance
6. Intercropping
7. Fertilizer use in Dry land
8. Weed Management
9. Crop planning as per land use capability
10. Crop planning for aberrant weather situation in dry lands
11. Mid - season correction practices (eg. Foliar nutrient spray)
12. Soil and water conservation practices

Drought

- The condition under which crops fail to mature because of insufficient supply of water through rains.
- The situation in which the amount of water required for transpiration and evaporation by crop plants in a defined area exceeds the amount of available moisture in the soil.
- A situation of no precipitation in a rainy season for more than 15 days.

Classification of Drought

- Meteorological drought: If annual rainfall is significantly short of certain level (75 per cent) of the climatologically expected normal rainfall over a wide area, then the situation is called by this term.
- Hydrological drought: This is a situation in which the hydrological resources like streams, rivers, reservoirs, lakes, wells etc., dry up because of marked depletion of surface water. The ground water table also depletes.
- Agricultural drought: This is a situation which is a result of inadequate rainfall. Because of this, the soil moisture falls short to meet the demands of the crop during its growth. Since the soil moisture available to a crop is insufficient, it affects growth and finally results in the reduction of yield.

CONCLUSION

- Modification of microclimate by use of shelter-belts and artificial barriers to reduce evapotranspiration and wind movement.
- Maintaining optimum plant population.
- Best possible seed-bed preparation to hold and absorb maximum moisture and better weed management.
- Tillage practices to minimise runoff and evapotranspiration.
- Crops that evade or endure periods of drought shall be sown.
- Drought tolerant crops for which row spacing can be increased without affecting the final yield can be identified and practiced.
- The dates of sowing shall be adjusted such that the reproductive stage of the crop shall not pass through the drought, in addition to other stages for critical crop growth.
- Effective control of pests and diseases and use of recommended doses of fertilizers.
- Correcting nutrient deficiencies and use of recommended doses of fertilizers.
- Application of anti-transparent and use of mulches will reduce evapotranspiration.
- Application of irrigation at appropriate stages of crop growth.
- Weed control by keeping the land fallow has an added effect in conserving the moisture.
- Ploughing of range lands with heavy disks or similar equipment to make a more rapid and complete infiltration.
- Shaping of land so that the water stays where it falls or runoff from a slope to irrigate a level bench below the slope.

REFERENCES

www.fao.org/farmingsystems/description_en.htm
www.hillagric.ac.in/.../Lecture%201%20Farming%20system%20scope%20...
https://en.wikipedia.org/wiki/Farming_systems_in_India
https://www.slideshare.net/.../concept-definitions-types-of-farming-system
agritech.tnau.ac.in/agriculture/agri_majorareas_ifs.html
https://www.nap.edu/read/2132/chapter/8
https://www.manage.gov.in/studymaterial/FSA-E.pdf
www.iloencyclopaedia.org/part-x-96841/agriculture.../farming-systems
www.economicsdiscussion.net/.../farming-types-4...systems...farming/2141...

Pages: 71-85

Vermitechnology, Farm and Fertilizer

Edited by: Dr. Ashok K. Rathoure; Dr. Pawan Kumar 'Bharti' and Dr. Jaswant Ray

ISBN: 978-93-88854-38-2

***Edition:* 2020**

***Published by:* Discovery Publishing House Pvt. Ltd., New Delhi (India)**

5

Mechanization and Profitability of Small Farms through Improved Animal Drawn Implements

Amit Namdeo, M. Din and R.K. Tiwari

ABSTRACT

Despite rapid increase in tractors and power-operated machinery, the use of mechanical power in agriculture has increased but draught animal power (DAP) continues to be used on Indian farms due to small holdings and hill agriculture. In India, more than 35% of net or gross sown area is still being managed by using draught animals. Study reveals that the command area with per animal pair per season ranges from 1.5 -2.0 ha to ensure timeliness in field operations. Under the project, AICRP on UAE, improved animal drawn implements have been developed by the centres and studies showed that the improved implement system gave 32% more field capacity, 25% saving in labour and 60% cost of operations over conventional implement system. Bullock drawn air mist canopy sprayer saves 82.2 per cent cost and 88.4 per cent time for spraying of cotton and pigeon pea over the manual knapsack sprayer. The cost of operation with improved animal drawn implement was found to be Rs 714 per ha as compared to Rs 893 per ha in case of conventional method of manual broadcasting. The average grain yield and B:C ratio for mechanized rice with improved animal drawn implement were found to be 4.8 t/ha and 1.42 as compared to 4.2 t/ha and 1.24, respectively for conventional method.For small farmers having farm area of 1.5-2.0 ha, the animal based cultivation system has been found to be cost-effective and energy efficient. Animal based farming system get best fit to the size of the farms for practicing conservation farming, integrated farming and organic farming with management of appropriate technology practices on-farm.

Keywords: *Small Farm mechanization, animal based farming system and efficient implements.*

ICAR-Central Institute of Agricultural Engineering, NabiBagh, Berasia Road, Bhopal - 462 038 (M.P.) (India)

INTRODUCTION

Draught animal power has traditionally been the main source of power in Indian Agriculture. These animals are mainly used for tillage, sowing, interculture, sprayinghaulage, water lifting and other purposes. India possesses finest draught breeds of cattle in the world. There are 24 cattle breed along with a large number of non-descript breeds. Nagori, Helicar, Amritmahal, Kangeyam, Malvi, Haryana, Deoni, Dangi, Red Khandhari, Khillar, Gaolao, Krishna Valley, Gir, Ongole, Tharparkar and Sahiwal are popular draught breed in India.

Bullocks and he-buffaloes over two years of age are main source of draught power for field operations. Camels (both male and female) are also used fortractivepower in few states such as Rajasthan, Gujarat, Haryana, Punjab and Uttar Pradesh.They are also used for transport cart and as pack animal.

Draught animal power (DAP) is the predominant power source for 117.1 million for marginal and small farmers of the country who constitute 84.97% of total number of land holdings (2011-12). The country has a draught animal population of 49.69 million among which bullocks constitute 44.48 million, buffalo 4.09 million and 1.12 million other important draught animals namely camel, equines, donkey, horse, pony, mule, yak and mithun. It is used for tillage, sowing, weeding, spraying, water lifting, haulage, and other purposes. India is endowed with the best bovine fauna in the world. The DAP has potential to generate annually 21924 million kWh energy (at 1800 working hours per year).

The average size of an operational land holding has declined from 2.7 hectares in 1960-61 to 1.16 hectares in 2011-12. Marginal and small groups of farmers cover 70.5 million ha which is 49.6% of the total cultivated area of the country. The average size of farms is less than 2.0 ha, too small for economic operation with large size machines. Further, farm holdings are getting fragmented year after year. This area is within the command area of one pair of bullocks. In fields (hilly terrain, terraced cultivation, coastal, wet fields and desert lands) where tractor or self-propelled machinery cannot reach, animals are used for field preparation, puddling, sowing and transportation. In hilly areas, animals can assist with contour ploughing and terracing also. Animal power still has relevance for the mechanization of small farms. There is a great deal of stress now days on sustainable agriculture, sustainable development, environment protection, prevention of pollution, and methods of low energy use, etc. In these situations, use of animal power for small farms will not decline significantly for many years.

Animal energy is environmental friendly which saves about Rs. 60,000 crores worth of fossil fuel annually. They are fed by crop-residue and also produce manure. Draught animals produce about 40 billion tonnes of dung which is used to make farm yard manure. Thus, draught animal system is more oriented towards organic farming. Organic farming is coming up in a big way in the country. At present about 90% of the registered farmers adopting organic farming has been from small and marginal farmers having up to 2 ha holdings.

For small farms, the animal human system is the best fit for practicing resource conservation, organic and integrated farming system. It gives higher economic value to the farmers by means of quality green/organic produce without damaging the soil and environment. Similarly, non-motorized transport using animal carts and pack load transport still constitute a significant portion of total transport sector. There are at present more than 12 million animal carts. Population of carts is on increase.

It is expected that draught animals would continue to play an important role in Indian agriculture for the next two decades, especially in the backward and remote parts of the country, where fuel availability and tractorization are likely to by behind. Therefore, it is imperative to utilize the draught animals properly economically and enhance their productivity.

Improved Animal drawn Implements for Tillage, Seedbed Preparation, Farm-yard Manure Application, Sowing and Planting, inter-culture and harvesting.

Equipment package have been developed for tillage, sowing, weeding, spraying and harvesting which gave higher area coverage and lower cost of operation in comparison to existing size of implements. The increase in output ranged from 30-70%.

IRON PLOUGH

A steel shovel is fixed at the lower end of plough and can be replaced when worn out. The power required to operate *tendua* plough is 0.38 kW, which is significantly less than the power requirement of 0.60 kW in case of traditional plough. An iron plough is suitable for deep tillage in irrigated fields. Pant hill plough has a width of 150 mm and weighs 5 kg. Due to its light weight, farmers in the hills can easily carry it. Cost of unit is Rs. 500/-. This implement has also become popular with the farmers. The draught requirement is 400 N. It has a field capacity of 0.022 ha/h. It is lighter than the traditional plough and the field capacity is 53% higher.

MOULDBOARD PLOUGH

Animal drawn mould board plough is used extensively for primary tillage in many parts of the country. It inverts soil and tills weed unlike traditional plough and also contribute to increase yield. MB plough size 100 mm is found suitable for small bullocks. Field capacity is 0.016 ha/h and draught requirement is 430 N. Cost of operation was found Rs. 1200-1500/ha.

Iron Plough

Mouldboard Plough

BLADE HARROW

Animal drawn blade harrow is a commonly used tillage implement for primary and secondary tillage. The developed improved blade harrow with V shaped blades using 600 mm blade is suitable for primary tillage and 900 mm blade, V shaped blades for secondary tillage. The blade harrow gave 25% saving in cost of operation per hectare over the traditional method. The field capacity of the 600 mm and 900 mm blade harrow is 0.073 and 0.10 ha/h, respectively.

S. No.	Variables		Values
1.	Dimensions (lxwxh), mm	:	1120×850×650
2.	Weight of implement, kg	:	45
3.	Size of blade, mm a. Primary tillage b. Secondary tillage	:	 600 900
4.	Depth of operation, mm	:	60-100
5.	Draught, N	:	600
6.	Cost of operation, Rs/ha	:	410

DISC HARROW

The disc harrow consists of a frame, two gangs having, 6 discs and an operator's seat and its weight is 35 kg. The field capacity of disc harrow was 0.15-0.3 ha/h, 5-10 times of traditional plough and gave 75% saving in cost of operation per hectare.

S. No.	Variables		Values
1.	Working width, mm	:	540
2.	Draught, N	:	400
3.	Weight of implement, kg	:	35

Blade harrow

Disc harrow

CULTIVATOR

The width of three tyne cultivator is 420 mm. The field capacity of the modified cultivator is 0.052 ha/h, 3-5 times of that traditional plough and inter-culture tool. It saves 50-75% in cost of operation per hectare. The draught required is 350 N, which corresponds to 8.4% of body weight and is within the draught capacity of local bullocks.

PATELA HARROW

Patela harrow is used for breaking clods and trash collection. It consists of sal wood plank, trash collection hooks, cogwheel and lever for lifting device. The width of the harrow is 2 m for large bullocks and 1.5 m for small and medium size bullocks. The field capacity ranges from 0.30 to 0.40 ha/h with cost of operation of Rs. 200-250/ha. It saves 60% cost of operation per hectare as compared to planking and manual picking of trash.

S. No.	Variables		Values
1.	Dimensions (lxwxh), mm	:	1500×230×100
2.	Weight, kg	:	65
3.	Draught, N	:	450-500
4.	Depth of operation, mm	:	60-70

Cultivator

Patela harrow

ANIMAL OPERATED CLOD CRUSHER CUM PUDDLER

A developed bullock operated clod crusher cum puddler can be used for clod breaking and puddling. Field capacity was 0.26 ha/h. It can also be used for puddling operations in wet soil.

S. No.	Variables		Values
1.	Overall dimensions (lxwxh), mm	:	1300×665×810
2.	Weight of implement, kg	:	35
3.	Depth of operation, mm	:	50
4.	Width, mm	:	1200
5.	Type of soil working element	:	Zig zag blades consisting of 40×5 mm MS flat fitted on the periphery of ring at 72° angle, total of 5 rings
6.	Handle	:	25 mm dia pipe; length 330 mm; height 140 mm

BULLOCK DRAWN STUBBLE COLLECTOR

The developed animal operated stubble collector is used for collection of stubbles of cotton in the field. It takes 2.5 h per ha for stubble collection. The cleaning efficiency and output power was 87.93% and 0.80 kW, respectively. It has become popular in Maharashtra region.

Clod crusher cum puddler

Stubble collector

IMPLEMENTS FOR PUDDLING

A lug wheel puddler having two passes of the puddler is adequate to prepare the puddle bed. The field capacity of the implement is 0.10 ha/h. It saves 50% time and 60% cost of puddling per hectare as compared to traditional spike tooth harrow.

S. No.	Variables		Values
1.	Dimensions (lxwxh), mm	:	1360×1200×1200
2.	Working width, mm	:	1200
3.	Weight, kg	:	80
4.	Draught, N	:	700
5.	Cost of operation, Rs/ha	:	450-500

FARMYARD MANURE SPREADER

The farmyard manure spreader can be used both for transport of manure as well as spreading. The average draft requirement during spreading operation varies between 520-640 N. Manure application rate varies from 4.62 t/ha to 18.53 t/ha. Field capacity of the spreader for manure spreading was 0.18 ha/h.

Lug wheel puddler

Farm yard manure spreader

IMPLEMENTS FOR SOWING AND PLANTING

Three Row Seed cum Fertilizer Drill

Three row seed cum fertilizer drill for line sowing of paddy has been developed by IGKV, Raipur. The draught requirement of the implement is 554 N with field capacity of 0.10 ha/h. Line sowing of paddy results in 10-15% increase in yield.

S. No.	Variables		Values
1.	Dimensions (lxwxh), mm	:	1070×640×940
2.	Working width, mm	:	600
3.	Size of seed and fertilizer box (lxwxh), mm	:	382×333×244
4.	Capacity of seed box, kg	:	5-7
5.	Type of furrow opener	:	Reversible shovel
6.	Metering mechanism	:	Fluted roller
7.	Weight, kg	:	32
8.	Number of rows	:	3
9.	Power transmission	:	From ground wheel through chain and sprocket
10.	Cost of operation, Rs/ha	:	400-500

ZERO TILL SEED DRILL

An animal drawn zero till seed drill with one, two and three rows is suitable for sowing of wheat after rice. One row unit is ideal for narrow terraces of hills. This opens a narrow slit with minimum soil disturbance. The weight of unit varies from 4.5 to 25 kg depending on the size. Draught requirements vary from 400-600 N. The field capacity of the implement varies from 0.02 to 0.06 ha/h.

Three row seed drill

Zero till seed drill

MULTI-CROP SEED CUM FERTILIZER DRILL

Animal drawn multi-crop seed cum fertilizer drill has been developed for sowing of seed spices. Two pneumatic wheels are provided for transportation on either side of main frame. A clutch is provided to engage or disengage the power transmission to seed metering device. Five nos. shoe type furrow openers are provided. The draught was 250 N and field capacity was 0.23 ha/h.

BULLOCK DRAWN 8-ROW DRUM SEEDER

It has been developed by OUAT, Bhubaneswar for sowing of pre-germinated paddy. The seed rate was observed to be 30.0 kg/ha. Field capacity of drum seeder was 0.18 ha/h with field efficiency of 68.25%. The cost of seeding with this drum seeder was found to be Rs. 118 per hectare.

Multi crop seed cum fertilizer drill

8 row drum seeder

IMPLEMENTS FOR WEEDING AND INTER-CULTURE OPERATIONS

The developed improved animal drawn blade hoe is suitable of weeding in two rows, having working width of 200 mm. Its field capacity is 0.10 ha/h and weeding efficiency, 62-79% and draught requirement 550 N.

ANIMAL DRAWN 3 TYNE FERTI-HOE

Three tyne cultivator type hoe with fertilizer application attachment has been developed by MAU, Parbhani. Draft requirement for the ferti-hoe is 510 N at operating speed of 2.2 km/h. The time required to cover 1 hectare was 5 hour and observed weeding efficiency was 84%. It saves 50-60% cost of operation over traditional method.

BULLOCK DRAWN EARTHING-UP CUM INTER-CULTURING

An earthing-up cum inter-culturing implement has been developed by MAU, Parbhani to remove weed as well as placement of fertilizer at a time in the crop. Field capacity of for inter-culturing, light earthing-up and final earthing-up operation were 0.151, 0.146, 0.117 ha/h, respectively for sugarcane and 0.196 ha/hr, 0.177 ha/h and 0.128 ha/h, respectively for turmeric.

S. No.	Variables		Values
1.	Weeding Efficiency,%	:	90
2.	Field efficiency,%	:	62
3.	Draft, N	:	525

Bullock Drawn Earthing-up cum Inter-culturing

PLANT PROTECTION EQUIPMENTS

Bullock Drawn Pre-emergence Herbicide Applicator

CIAE Bhopal centre developed an attachment of pre-emergence herbicide applicator using battery operated knapsack sprayer in existing animal drawn seed-cum-ferti drill. It has three flat fan type nozzles which areoperated at pressure of 1.8 kg/cm^2 to meet the desired application rate of herbicide. The actual field capacity was found 0.13 ha/h and draft varied from 470 to 560 N. There is a saving of 36% in labour requirement.

Bullock drawn pre-emergence herbicide applicator

Bullock drawn traction sprayer

BULLOCK DRAWN TRACTION SPRAYER

MAU, Parbhani Centre developed an animal operated traction sprayer suitable for medium and heavy pair of bullock. The maximum height of sprayer's nozzles from ground is 1.2 m. The sprayer uses stub axles and can therefore also be used as a high clearance sprayer for cotton and pigeon pea crops. Fourteen hollow cone nozzles of discharge 720 ml/min are used to produce fine droplets. Average discharge of nozzles varies from 712.0 to 715.0 ml/min with average boom discharge varies from 9.96 to 9.97 l/min at nozzle height of 450 mm from plant canopy. The field capacity of the sprayer is 1.33 ha/h with field efficiency of 84% whereas the draught requirement varies from 654 to 709 N. The cost of operation is reduced by 50-60% as compared to manual knapsack spraying.

BULLOCK DRAWN SOLAR POWERED HIGH CLEARANCE SPRAYER

In order to utilize available solar energy and labour saving, a solar powered bullock drawn high clearance sprayer has been devepoed for spraying in cotton and pigeon pea crop. The area covered by the solar powered sprayer was about 0.95 to 1.0 ha/h. The cost of operation of bullock drawn solar powered high clearance sprayer was Rs. 128.10/ha for cotton and Rs. 119.60/ha for red gram crop. The percentage of financial saving over the manual knapsack sprayer was 56 per cent for cotton and 67.1 per cent for red gram crop. The percentage of labour saving over the manual knapsack sprayer was 56.6 per cent for cotton and 59.48 per cent for red gram crop.

BULLOCK DRAWN AIR MIST CANOPY SPRAYER

UAS, Raichur Centre developed a bullock drawn air mist canopy for control of pests and diseases on top and underneath side of leaves, plant stem and other canopy surface of crop. It comprised of bullock cart, spray boom, air blower, HTP pump, diesel engine, spray tank, control valves, power transmission system, battery (12-volt), self-starter and pressure gauge. A pair of bullock is used for pulling the cart which acts as a traction device and the diesel engine has been selected as power source for operating canopy sprayer. The average field capacity of canopy sprayer was worked out as 0.70 ha/h for cotton crop and 0.60 ha/h for red gram crop, respectively. The financial saving for spraying operation on cotton and pigeon pea were 82.24 and 82.01 per cent. The time saving for spraying operation on cotton and pigeon pea over the manual knapsack sprayer was 88.43 per cent and 88.46 per cent, respectively. The energy requirement for spraying operation on cotton and pigeon pea crops was 65 and 85 MJ/ha, respectively.

Bullock drawn solar powered high clearance sprayer

Bullock drawn air mist canopy sprayer

CIAE MULTIPURPOSE TOOL CARRIER

It has been attachment of tools for tillage, seeding and interculture. The unit consists of main frame, tool bar and wheel (Pneumatic/Iron wheels) with provisions for attachment of tools and lifting of tools on turns. The wheeled tools carrier showed advantage in terms higher command area (1.5-2.5 times) than the conventional implements. Its field capacity is 0.032 ha/h at the forward speed of 2.95 km/h during the ploughing operation. For harrowing operation, its field capacity is 0.23 ha/h at the forward speed of 3.47 km/h. The average draft and power output is found 600 N and 0.66 kW.

PNEUMATIC WHEELED TYPE MULTIPURPOSE TOOL CARRIER

Tool carrier consists of a rectangular frame made of MS pipe. Power to the seed and fertilizer metering mechanism is given through a pneumatic transport wheel by a set of bevel gear and telescopic shaft. The size of the plough in light soil is 225 mm and in heavy soil it is 150 mm. The average field capacity observed in light and heavy soil is 0.05 and 0.035 ha/h, respectively. The draught requirement for operating the plough is 518 N in light soil and 700 N in heavy soil. For secondary tillage with 3 tyne cultivator, using sweep or shovel, the average field capacity is 0.176 ha/h, which is nearly a 300% increase as compared for indigenous plough. Draught requirement was found 700 N. For raised bed formation and sowing with raised bed planter, the draught requirement and field capacity is 635 N and 0.18 ha/h, respectively.

MAU, Parbhani has adopted Multipurpose Tool Carrier and made provision for attachment of inclined plate planter, sprayer and three tyneferti-hoe. The average draft required for operating the planter-cum-sprayer with seed covering device was 620 N. The field capacity for the planter-cum-sprayer with seed covering device and three tyne hoe having two furrow opener was 0.19 and 0.30 ha/h, respectively. The average discharge from each nozzle was in the range of 195.9 and 197.6 ml/min. The uniformity coefficient of the sprayer was 74%. The weeding efficiency was found to be 84% in soybean

LIGHTWEIGHT NON-WHEELED TYPE TOOL FRAME

This tool frame is very light, weighing about 2 kg. Even with an attachment fitted, it weighs only about 4 kg. The tool frame was evaluated with different attachments, namely cultivator with shovel, ridger, MB plough and reversible plough. Farmer can easily lift the tool frame with implement. During operation, the tool frame remained very stable without giving any mechanical problems.

CIAE multipurpose tool carrier

Pneumatic wheeled type

GARLIC DIGGER

An animal drawn garlic digger with curved type blade having size 550 mm was developed at CIAE Bhopal. The average draft and power output were found to be 683.5 N and 0.55 kW, respectively at average 12% (db) moisture content and 550 kPa soil cone index. The field capacity of developed digger was found to be in the range of 0.08 to 0.1 ha/h with 86% digging efficiency. By using animal drawn garlic digger, and 175.70 MJ/ha energy as compared to manual digging. The newly developed animal drawn garlic digger saved 75% cost and 45% energy as compared to traditional method.

ANIMAL DRAWN SINGLE ROW IMPROVED POTATO DIGGER

It is used for digging of potato tubers grown on raised beds. It consists of mild steel plate, shank, L Shape clamps (02 no.), main frame, clevis, beam and handle. The light weight digger can work up to 100 mm depth. The working width of digger is 200 mm and its required draught of 350N.

Garlic digger

Potato digger

BULLOCK DRAWN TURMERIC AND GINGER DIGGER FOR RAISED BED PLANTING

The bullock drawn turmeric and ginger digger to be used for digging of turmeric and ginger plant on raised beds. The main components of bullock drawn turmeric and ginger digger are main frame, handle, beam, ground wheel, shank, sweep and extension bars. It was evaluated in the field having row spacing of 300 mm and bed width of 1500 mm between two ridges. The average depth of operation was found to be 18 mm for turmeric and 17 mm for ginger.The average draft requirement of the turmeric and ginger digger is 843 and 833 N, respectively. The average actual field capacity and field efficiency is 0.18 ha/h and 81% for turmeric and 0.17 ha/h and 84% for ginger, respectively. The digging efficiency for turmeric and ginger is 92 and 89 percent respectively. There is saving of 55.25 and 38.55% in cost of digging for turmeric and ginger crop over totraditional digging method.

Bullock Drawn Turmeric and Ginger Digger

REFERENCES

Anon, 2011, Annual Report of AICRP on UAE, IGKV, Raipur Centre. Faculty of Agricultural Engineering, Indira Krishi Vishwavidyalaya Raipur, Chhattisgarh.

Anon, 2015. Biennial Report of AICRP on UAE, IGKV, Raipur Centre. Faculty of Agricultural Engineering, Indira Krishi Vishwavidyalaya Raipur, Chhattisgarh.

Chandraker, A.K., Victor, V.M. and Khalkho, D. 2014. A Study on Status of Farm Power and Scope of Farm Mechanization in the Agro-climatic Zone of Chhattisgarh Plains. *Prabhandhan. Indian Journal of Management, Vol.: 7, issue -11, pp: 40-47.*

Deepak Chaudhuri, R.C. Singh, 2013. Improved Technology for Utilization of Draught Animals, All India Coordinated Research Project on Increased Utilization of Animal Energy With Enhanced System Efficiency, CIAE Bhopal. Technical Bulletin No. CIAE/ UAE/2013/160.

Dhruwe, N.K.; Victor, V.M., Namdeo, A. and Jogdand, S. 2017. Development of Five Row Animal Drawn Planter for Planting Various Seeds. Trends in Bioscience 10(2): 7-773.

M.Din, R.C.Singh, S.N. More, A.P.Magar, R.K. Tiwari, 2018. Three Decades of Silent Achievements AICRP on UAE, CIAE Bhopal, Technical Bulletin No. CIAE/UAE/ 2018/243.

M. Veerangouda, K.V. Prakash, Jag Jiwan Ram and M. Din, 2018. Bullock Drawn Solar Powered High Clearance Sprayer - A promising Renewable Energy Technology, Published in Akshayurja.

Namdeo A, Victor VM and Dhruwe NK.Status of Farm Mechanization under Animal Farming in Northern Hills Agro-Climatic Zone of Chhattisgarh, India. Int. J. Curr. Microbiol. App.Sci. 2018,7(2): 2162 2168. https://doi.org/10.20546/ijcmas. 2018.702.

Namdeo A, Victor VM and Dhruwe NK. A Case Study on Status of Farm Mechanization Under Animal Farming in Chhattisgarh. Trends in Biosciences 11(3), Print: ISSN 0974-8431, 2018, 239-243.

V.M.Victor, A.K. Chandrakar, S. Jogdand, Ajay K.Verma, A.K. Dave and N. Kerketta, 2018. Animal Drawn Machinery System for Mechanising Rice Cultivation in Small and Marginal Farms of Chhattisgarh, IGKV/Pub. Book/2018/02, pp. 255-264. National Seminar On Sustainable Rice Production Technology For Increasing The Farmers Income, Technology For Rice Production.

S.K. Swain, A.K. Mohapatra, A.K. Dash, B.R. Nayak, D.K. Mohanty and D. Sahoo. 2016. Performance Evaluation of Bullock Drawn Groundnut Digger in Farmers Field in Different Districts of Odisha. *Journal of Extension Education*, Vol. XXI(1): 99-102.

S.K. Swain, A.K. Mohapatra and A.K. Dash. 2016. Adoptive Trial of CIAE Three Row Seed Drill and CIAE Three Row Seed cum Fertilizer Drill for Line Sowing of Oilseed and Pulse Crops in Odisha. *Journal of Extension Education*, vol. XXI(2): 99-102.

Singh, G. Spatial Distribution and use of Draught Animal Power in India. Indian Journal of Animal Sciences. 2002, 72: 689-694.

Singh G. Characteristics and use of Draught Animal Power in India. Ind. J. Anim. Sci. 2007, 69(8): 621-627.

Singh, P.K., Availability and use of Draught Animal Power in Gujrat State, Indian Journal of Animal Production Management, 1993. 9 (4); 157-160.

Tiwari R.K., and Chauhan S.K., 2017. Farm Mechanization Strategy for Promotion of Improved Equipment under Animal Based Farming in Nagaland-India. *Agricultural Mechanization in Asia, Africa, and Latin America*.Vol. 48 No. 1, Page No. 71-75.

Tiwari RK, SN Yadav and Deepak Chaudhuri 2016. Status of Draught Animal Power Availability in Selected Villages of East and South Districts in Sikkim, India *Agric. International* 3(1) : 1-8.

Pages: 86-102

Vermitechnology, Farm and Fertilizer
Edited by: Dr. Ashok K. Rathoure; Dr. Pawan Kumar 'Bharti' and Dr. Jaswant Ray
ISBN: 978-93-88854-38-2
Edition: **2020**
Published by: **Discovery Publishing House Pvt. Ltd., New Delhi (India)**

6

Effect of Paper Mill Sludge on yield Potential of Green Gram Farming

Anitha G[1] and Esakkimuthu M[2*]

INTRODUCTION

In the present scenario of intensive agriculture, shrinkage of cultivable land area is inevitable due to urbanization and industrialization. The soil is over exploited due to intensive cultivation with high yielding crops and use of high analysis inorganic fertilizers leading the soil ecosystem to become unproductive. In addition, commercial farming system on net profit- loss planning without any fallow period also destroys the inherant nature of the soil. Hence, soil is unable to replenish its original condition of health. Under these circumstances, application and recycling of organic wastes, by-products of agro industries waste as well as wastes from paper, hotel, hostel, urban and rural area etc., as source of manure is the only way to boost the soil health.

The pulp of paper industry plays an integral role in the global economy. India is the 15th largest paper producer in the world. Today, there are 759 pulp and paper mills present in India with an installed capacity of 12.7 million tonnes producing 10.11 tonnes of paper and paperboards which is 2.52 per cent of the total world production of 402 million tonnes per annum (Kulkarni, 2013). In Tamil Nadu, there are about 31 paper units with an installed capacity of 0.64 million tonnes, producing fine duplex paper boards per annum. The pulp and paper industry is ranked third in the world after

[1] **Anitha G., Assistant Professor (Soil Science and Agricultural Chemistry), S. Thangapazham Agricultural College, Vasudevanallur, Tamil Nadu (India)**

[2] **Esakkimuthu M., Assistant Professor (Agricultural Extension), Regional Agricultural Research Station, Pilicode, Kerala (India)**

primary metals and chemical industries in terms of fresh water use, consuming around 250 to 300 m^3 fresh water per ton of paper produced. The corresponding wastewater generation is also much higher, ranging from 75 to 250 m^3 per ton of paper produced.

The disposal of industrial wastes is a problem of increasing importance throughout the world due to public health menace. Sludge from paper mills are produced in large quantities in most of the industrial countries of the world. Today due to the intensive usage of paper constitute one of our most serious environmental problems. Paper industries produce large amount of solids and its application increases theinput of OM, and the availability ofmacronutrients and micronutrients (Trepanier *et al.*, 1996). The effect of paper mill sludge application on chemicalproperties would be directly associatedwith the improving of biological properties, vital for the nutrient turnover and long-term productivity. Hence, the present study was undertaken to examine the effect of paper mill sludge as an amendment for alkali soil and its influence on the growth and yield of green gram.

Green gram *[Vignaradiata*(L.) Wilczek] is one of the important pulse crops of the world. It is a short duration grain legume having wider adaptability and low input requirements with minimum care. Green gram, commonly known as *'Mung*bean or *Moong'*, being a legume crop has high demand on sulphur to produce several proteins ·containing amino acids and fatty acids. It is a prehistoric crop and grown throughout Asia, Australia, West Indies, South America, Tropical and Subtropical Africa. India is the largest producer and consumer of greengram and it accounts for about 65 per cent of the world acreage and 54 per cent of the world production. Being rich in quality proteins, minerals and vitamins, green gram is an inseperable ingredient in the diets of majority of population in the Indian subcontinent.

Production of pulses in the country is 18.24 million tonnes in an area of 26.28 million hectare with an increase of 28.45 per cent over 2006-07 (Department of Agriculture and Co-operation, 2010-11). ref Inspite of increased production over the past years, the average productivity in India is yet to see major breakthrough to meet the per capita availability of 80g pulses/day (WHO) to alleviate protein energy malnutrition. Whereas real situation is different and the per capita availability of pulses has declined sharply from 41 g (1990-91) to 33 g (2009-10) due to the additional population of 350 million during this period. To make up this short fall in supply besides further demand from burgeoning population about 26.5 million tonnes of pulses are required by 2050 to meet the national self sufficiency in pulses. The additional production has to come through productivity enhancement and rest through horizontal expansion in other major pulses crops including green gram.

Sulphur (S) is an essential plant nutrient which plays a key role in sustaining higher production of pulse crop, and also in the formation of protein, vitamins and enzymes and its a constituent of amino acids, *viz.*, cysteine, cystine and methionine. Besides, it also involved in various metabolic and enzymatic process including photosynthesis, respiration and legume-rhizobium symbiotic nitrogen fixation. It is also required for the formation of chlorophyll, vitamin, glycosides and ferrodoxins. Sulphur is also associated with the metabolism of carbohydrates and oils.

Sulphur deficiency in Indian soils were wide spread (30-40%) in area of 57 m ha^{-1} and it is a major constraint in increasing crop productivity, product quality and farm income generation.

At present, nearly 70% of pulses are produced only through rainfed farming. The average yield of pulses in India is black gram 300 kg/ha, green gram 375 kg/ha and red gram 240 kg/ha. The nutrient availability and dynamics is purely decided by chemical behavior of soil. Under salted soil ecosystem, reclamation of alkali soil by application of gypsum or post methonated effluent ameliorate the soil to normal condition. Recently, it was reported that application of sulphur rich paper industry solid (sludge) waste acts as a best soil conditioner to alleviate the alkaline problem of soil to normal condition. Paper mill sludge is the major residue from paper industry and it contains water, fiber, organic compounds, inorganic salt, and mineral fillers etc., (Maschio *et al.*, 2009). Paper mill sludges have been evaluated and used to amend problem soils successfully, fostering revegetation and reducing erosion (Feagley *et al.*, 1994; Kost *et al.*, 1997; Fierro *et al.*, 1999 a).

Paper mill bio-soilds can provide multidimentional benefits to the soil ecosystem (Price and Voroney, 2007). Mixed paper mill sludges are an important source of N for crop production (Dayegamiye *et al.*, 2003). Over 70% of solid wastes (by products) generated in the manufacture of paper pulp are presently disposed of in landfills. Most of these by products are compostable and reusable in horticulture, landscaping and agriculture (Das *et al.*, 2001). Paper sludge is the biggest source of lignin. Lignin application to arable soils can not only improve the plant growth *in vitro*, but also reduce the accumulation of the heavy metals like Cu, Zn, Cd, Pb, Cr and Ni in plants (Zhang *et al.*, 2004). Application of fresh paper mill sludge and their compost, creates a sustainable conducive effect on soil aggregation (Bipfubusa *et al.*, 2005).

"Sometimes on rare occasions what everybody says happens to be true" writes Richards Bach in his Book "Running from safety" and always it is wise to know the people's opinion and expert's statement before starting our research. In this chapter, such contemporary reviews are presented under the following headings relevant to the objectives that were formulated at the start of research.

In the modern agriculture, the use and handling of agrochemicals has grown gigantically causing serious problems to the environment. Under this situation the use of paper mill sludge is a viable alternative to improve the soil fertility and profitability of crops, particularly for medium and small-sized farms under intensive production systems.

Paper mill sludge (PMS) is a waste in the paper processing industry. Total annual production in India is approximately 402 million tonnes. Until recently, most of the sludge has been discarded in landfill, high tipping fees, increasing environmental concerns and governmental regulations. The utilization of PMS as a soil conditioner or as a container media in the nursery may provide beneficial alternatives. The high cellulose content in PMS improves infiltration, water holding capacity, stabilizes soil structure, increases cation exchange capacity and nutrient content of barren soils. Consequently, plant growth and production could be increased. Since, 1950s, PMS has been used for land reclamation, and in forestry or agricultural management projects. Several plant species have been evaluated for their growth in PMS- amended media. e.g. grains, grasses, woody plants and horticultural crops. The objective of the study was to the effect of paper mill sludge as an amendment in alkali soil and its influence on the growth and yield of green gram.

Sulphur assumes greater significance in increasing growth and yield of pulses, as far as green gram is concerned no work have been done earlier with regard to sources and level of sulphur on growth and yield of rice fallow green gram. The low values recorded under the no sulphur treatments could be due to poor availability of S and other nutrients to meet the crop demand particularly during post flowering stage.

CHARACTERISTICS OF PAPER MILL SLUDGE FROM PAPER INDUSTRY

The TNPL lime sludge had higher concentration of Ca and Mg recording 8.60 and 11.0 per cent, respectively but essential nutrient status was very low (Hameed, 1994). Paper mills landfill their sludge for ecofriendly management (Edwards and Someshwar, 2000). The disposal of industrial wastes is a major problem and acquiring importance throught the world due to public health meanace. Sludge from paper mills are produced in large quantities in almost all nations throughout world today due to the intensive usage of paper, which constitute one of our most serious environmental threat (Suriynarayanan *et.al.,* 2010).

Paper mill biosolids are produced as a byproduct of the pulp and paper industry. The characteristics of biosolids are highly heterogeneous and directly related to the technology used to pulp the wood, manufacture of the paper and type of effluent treatment. The wastes generated from paper and pulp industry is utilized in several ways and further different techniques and practices are also available for the safe management of sludges (Mladenov and Pelovski, 2010).

Nutrient Content of Paper Mill Sludge

The TNPL lime sludge had higher concentration of Ca and Mg recording 8.60 and 11.0 per cent, respectively but essential nutrient status was very low (Hameed, 1997).The biocompost prepared from the combination of paperboard mill sludge, flyash, farm yard manure and coir pith with addition of microbial cultures had higher nutrient content and vigorous microbial activity than the amendments in the combinations tried alone (Prasanthrajan, 2010). Vermicompost is prepared by using tis mixture of paper mill sludge along with cow dung showed higher pH, N, P, K, Ca, Mg and micronutrients (Jayanthi, 2007).Compost made from organic wastes mixed with different quantities of recovered paper and wastes of the paper industry satisfy the requirements like maturity and of suitability for plant growth. Alina (2013) reported that the sludge from pulp and paper mills has significant total solids, volatile solids, N and COD values.

EFFECT OF PAPER MILL SLUDGE ON SOIL QUALITY

Physico-chemical Properties

The paper mill by-products can be used as soil amendments, although they contain high in organics, including microorganisms, cellulose, lignin and wood extracts, and is relatively low in trace metals and calcium carbonatereported byAlyson L. (1975). Zibilske *et al.* (1987) observed that the multiple applications of paper mill sludge as applied once, applied in alternate years, or applied annually. Increase or maintenance of soil carbon were observed when sludge was applied annually or biennially. Significant increases were observed in soil aggregation and water holding properties.Feagley *et al,* (1994) revealed that paper mill sludge will add nutrients such as Ca, K, Mg, N and P when applied to mine soil which is usually low in all these nutrients. Paper mill sludge when applied to the soil increased the cation exchange capacity and better soil nutrient retension capacity (Bellamy *et al,* 1995).

Incorporation of paper mill wastes in agricultural and mine soils has been found to be an environmentally sound practice to improve soil organic matter content (Fierro *et al.,* 1999.b), water storage capacity (Trépanier *et al.,* 1996) and nutrient availability (Cabral and Vasconcelos 1993). Zibilske *et al.* (2000) observed that the multiple applications of paper mill sludge as applied once, applied in alternate years, or applied annually. Increase or maintenance of soil C were observed when sludge was applied annually or biennially. Significant increases were observed in soil aggregation and water holding properties. A field experiment was conducted by Simard (2001) on cabbage –sweet corn sequence with primary/secondary paper mill sludge, reported that high N content in paper sludge.The marketable yields and N uptake increased with increasing amounts of PMS applied. PMS applications had a very significant residual effect on corn yield. Ou-Yang *et.al.* (2002)

observed that composted PMS mixed with peat at ratio of 80% PMS (volume basis) supported plant growth and relative leaf chlorophyll content of periwinkles comparable to commercial container medium.Application of biosludge @ 12.5 t ha^{-1} recorded significant increase in the soil organic carbon content and available nitrogen contents (Satishkumar, 2002).

According to Gagnon *et* al. (2003)observed thatreduction in pH, increased the inorganic N and nutrient by addition of paper mill sludge (17 Mg ha^{-1}) in blueberry fruit. Madejon *et al.* (2003) observed that the total organic carbon content significantly increased in soils treated with the paper mill sludge.Combining organic amendments like manures and paper mill sludge with mineral nitrogen fertilizer increased the yield of potato, nitrogen use efficiency and specific gravity. This shows that nitrogen fertilizer needs to be added with organic amendments to achieve potato yield and for nitrogen nutrition (Dayegamiye *et al.*,2003). Bipfubusa *et al.* (2005) reported that the application of fresh paper mill sludge and their compost, creates a sustainable conducive effect on soil aggregation.

Accordingly, Suguna Devakumari (2005) reported that selecting integration of bio-sludge and fly ash solid by products of paper industry enhanced the productivity of fodder grass at the same time reduced 25 per cent on cost of fertilizer input. Curnoe *et al.* (2006) identified the positive effects of factory lime sludge paper on maize crop yield. Land application of paper mill sludge is one of the best methods to manage solid waste and is more economically and ecologically sound than landfill practice (Zule *et al.*, 2007). Nunes *et al.* (2008) suggested that the soil amended with secondary paper mill sludge in wheat crop shown that, the pH significantly decreased as well as nutrient concentration increased, and also it reduced the heavy metal ions in soil.

According to Suriyanarayanan *et al.* (2010) observed that the soil amended with paper mill sludge application significantly increased the C: N ratio and also increased the Ca ion concentration. Amos *et al.* (2011) reported that the application of sludge and manure would increase plant growth and biomass production similar to that of commercial fertilizer relative to the control, and sludge and manure treatments would increase CEC, organic matter and the concentration of nutrients in the soil and plant foliage. Gallardo *et al.* (2012) reported that addition of paper mill sludge has improved the chemical properties of the soil, organic matter and P content in the soil with increasing amounts of sludge. Paper mill sludge used as mulch with higher rate (100 t ha^{-1}) and also the combined N and K mineral fertilizer treatments increased yield of rainfed winter wheat (Amini *et al.*, 2012).

Effect of Paper Mill Sludge on Biological Properties

The decomposition of organic matter by soil organisms has an immense influence on soil fertility, plant growth, soil structure, and carbon storage.

Effects of high salts and N deficiency have been minimized by controlling sludge application rates and by delaying planting for some period after treatment, and/or by applying fertilizer to soil or sludge (Simpson *et al.*, 1983). Pulp mill residuals increased the beneficial soil organisms and reduced plant pathogens and also increased water and water retention (Foley and Copperband, 2002). Pulp mill residuals improved the soil's ability to suppress crop diseases (Leon *et al.*, 2006).

Effect of gypsum on Soil Health

Application of lime, sulphur, and gypsum alone and in combination with manure and found that infiltration was the greatest with gypsum + manure treatment and the highest decrease in ESP occurred in case of gypsum treated plots. Decrease in pH was more in upper 12 inches soil (Bower *et al.* 1951). They observed that sulphuric acid was more effective in decreasing soil pH than gypsum and sulphur. Kausar and Muhammad (1972) reported that reclamation of sodic soil by gypsum application followed by leaching took shorter time as compared to biological methods. They also observed an increase in hydraulic conductivity, exchangeable and soluble Ca + Mg and decrease in exchangeable Na, K, ESP, free lime, pH, ECe and SAR with gypsum treatment.

Muhammad and Khaliq (1975) reported that decrease in ECe, lime, pH and increase in hydraulic conductivity, soluble and exchangeable Ca and Mg was more with sulphur than with gypsum alone or in combination with FYM.Gupta and Bajpai (1977) observed that addition of gypsum, H_2SO_4 or $CaCl_2$ improved the physical as well as chemical properties of saline-alkali soil under regular flushing. Abrol *et al.* (1978) reported thata major amount of gypsum added to the soil is utilized in neutralizing or precipitating the soluble carbonates and bicarbonates. Since carbonates and bicarbonates in the soil are in the solution phase, they freely react with added gypsum.

Sharma *et al.* (1982), observed the soil pH, ECe $CaCO_3$, exchangeable Na^+, Cl^- and dispersion ratio decreased considerably; whereas, exchangeable Ca^{2+} + Mg^{2+}, hydraulic conductivity, water infiltration and redistribution increased as a result of gypsum application.Hussain *et al.* (2000) reported that splitting of gypsum into two equal doses (25% GR.) was very useful to reclaim the saline sodic soil, although the reclamation time was increased. Hussain *et.al* (2001) observed that the sodicity parameter (SAR) of the soil decreased significantly when soil was treated with sulfuric acid, gypsum, FYM and their various combinations. Muhammad (2001) reported that the gypsum applied will replace the sodium (Na^+) with calcium (Ca^{++}) from the soil exchange complex and will be leached down below root zone with irrigation water resulting in better and productive soil and more crop yield per unit area. Efficiency of gypsum in the reclamation of saline-sodic and sodic soil varies considerably depending upon the type of the soil to be reclaimed, the methods of gypsum application, the fineness of the gypsum particles, combination of gypsum with other amendments and breaking of the soil hard pan, if exists.

Use of gypsum in combination with FYM, finer gypsum (80-100 mesh) and breaking of soil hard pan were significantly better in improving the physical and chemical properties of soil and crops yield. The influence of chlorophyll combined with higher photosynthetic rate, dry matter production and seed yield per plant has been reported by Gowsami *et al.* and Wagh *et al.* (2003). Sagheer *et al.* (2006) reported that the application of gypsum had significantly removed greater amounts of sodium (Na^+) from the root zone leaving behind minimum level of sodium adsorption ratio (SAR) and the greatest ECe: SAR ratio in post-amelioration soil. Mohamed (2012) reported that application of gypsum combined with Water Hyacinth or Rice Straw Compost enhanced reclamation and caused more decreases in salinity as well as sodicity. Ahmed *et al.* (2013) reported thatthe application of sulphur had significant influence on plant height, biological yield, economic yield, Na^+ and K^+ content in leaves.

Effect of Vermicompost on Crops

Sultan *et al.* (2003) observed that the combination of VC and VW, gave the best results as the soil pH reduced by 7.8 per cent while the soil organic carbon and available phosphates increased by 117 per cent. The yields of spinach (5.08 t ha^{-1}), onion (6.28 t ha^{-1}) and potato (11.67 t ha^{-1}) were also highest under this treatment. Vermitech pattern was more suitable for sodic soils than chemical treatment of the same through gypsum application. Reddy (2005) revealed that the application of vermicompost @ 10 t ha^{-1} increased plant height, number of leaves per plant, leaf area, bulb length, diameter, weight and yield of onion.Application of vermicompost @ 5 or 10 t ha^{-1} in strawberries increased the dehydrogenase activity and microbial biomass- N increased amounts of NH_4-N, NO_3-N and orthophosphates of soil (Arancon*et al.*, 2006).

Abdullah (2007) reported that the application of vermicompost has significantly decreased the pH in sodic soil. Abdullah (2008) reported that the application of vermicompost reclaimed the sodic soils and improved the productivity of potato (*Solanumtuberosum*), spinach (*Spinaciaoleracea*) and turnip (*Brassica campestris*) crops. It also improved the soil quality.Sodic soil is reclaimed by application of vermicompost and paddy, wheat crops yield has increased through vermitechnology. (Abdullah and Sultan, 2008). Reddy *et al.* (2011) reported that increased yield in case of onion and radish through integrated use of vermicompost and nitrogen fertilizers when compared to the application of either nitrogen fertilizer or vermicompost alone. This adds to the significance of vermicompost in increasing the nutrient availability through its decomposition in soil and also through higher soil enzyme activities.

Mahmoud and Ibrahim (2012) reported that the soil treated with mixtures of vermicompost and water treatment residuals, gave the highest reduction in salinity, sodicity and soluble Cl^- and Na^+. Consequently, the grain weight of barley has increased. It was indicated that the application of 10g kg^{-1} soil at 2:1 (Vermi: WTR) mixed ratio resulted in the best barley growth. Abduli*et al.* (2013)observed a significant rise in growth of tomato plants by increasing ratio of vermicompost combined with soil. The stem diameter, height, the number of leaves per plant, and yielding of tomato plants obtained the highest rate in four tested beds after 40 days in vermicompost to soil ratios of 1:3, 1:1, 1:3, and 1:2, respectively. Uz and Tavali (2014) reported that thevermicompost has a potential to be used as an alternative to farmyard manure to improve and maintain soil biological activity in alkaline calcareous soils as well as increase the bacterial activity in soil.

Effect of Vermicompost on Soil Physical, Chemical and Biological Properties

The uptake of N, phosphorus (P), potassium (K) and magnesium (Mg) by rice (*Oryzasativa*) plant was highest when fertilizer was applied in combination with vermicompost by Jadhav*et al.* (1997). The application of vermicompost along with fertilizer N gave higher dry matter (16.2 g $plant^{-1}$) and grain yield (3.6 t ha^{-1}) of wheat (*Triticumaestivum*) and higher dry matter yield (0.66 g $plant^{-1}$) of the following coriander (*Coriandrumsativum*) crop in sequential cropping system. Similarly, a positive response was obtained with the application of vermicompost to other field crops such as sorghum (*Sorghum bicolor*) (Patil and Sheelavantar 2000) and sunflower (*Helianthus annuus*) (Devi and Agarwal, 1998).The application of vermicompost gave higher germination (93%) of mung bean (*Vignaradiata*) compared to the control (84%).

Further, the growth and yield of mung bean was also significantly higher with vermicompost application. Likewise, in another pot experiment, the fresh and dry matter yields of cowpea (*Vignaunguiculata*) were higher when soil was amended with vermicompost than with biodigested slurry (Karmegam and Daniel, 2000). The application of organic matter including vermicompost favorably affected soil pH, microbial population and soil enzyme activities (Maheswarappa *et al.*, 1999). The fresh weight of flowers such as *Chrysanthemum chinensis* increased with the application of different levels of vermicompost. Also, the number of flowers per plant (26), flower diameter (6 cm) and yield (0.5 t ha^{-1}) were maximum with the application of 10 t ha^{-1} of vermicompost along with 50% of recommended dose of NPK fertilizer. However, the vase life of flowers (11 days) was high with the combined application of vermicompost at 15 t ha^{-1} and 50% of recommended dose of NPK fertilizer (Nethra *et al.*, 1999). Marinari *et al.* (2000) reported an increased macropore space ranging from 50 to 500 ìm, resulting in improved air-water relationship in the soil which favorably affected plant growth by addition of vermicompost. Sreenivas *et al.* (2000) reported that an integrated effect of application of fertilizer and vermicompost on soil available nitrogen (N) and uptake of ridge gourd (*Luffaacutangula*) increased significantly with increasing levels of vermicompost and highest N uptake was obtained at 50% of the recommended fertilizer rate plus 10 t ha^{-1}vermicompost.

Effect of Paper Mill Sludge on Soil Microbial Biomass Carbon

Thekraft mill sludge application increased theinput of OM, and the availability ofmacronutrients and micronutrients. Theeffect of sludge application on chemicalproperties were directly associatedwith the improvement in microbial biomass carbon, vital for the nutrient turnover and long-term productivity by Gallardo *et al.* (2007). The microbial biomass carbon was evaluated with the application of paper mill sludge @ 0, 10, 20, 30 and 50 t ha^{-1} in Andisol. The different soil-sludge mixtures were incubated at controlled temperature for 60 days and microbial respiration, microbial biomass carbon, fluorescein diacetate hydrolysis and acid phosphatase activity were evaluated throughout the incubation time. The maximum microbial biomass carbon were observed at 30 and 50 t ha^{-1} (Gallardo *et al.*, 2010).

The literature reviewed suggests that the PMS is extensively tested on edible crops like wheat, maize, cabbage, sweet corn, soybean, potato and strawberry. Considering all the valuable points, our study was planned to test the effect of paper mill sludge as an amendment in alkali soil and its influence on the growth and yield of green gram [VBN (Gg) 2].

CONCLUSION

The results revealed that the application of PMS @ 30, 45 and 60 t ha^{-1} significantly reduced the soil pH in high pH soil. In the case of EC and exchangeable Ca+Mg+K, PMS application showed higher contents than gypsum and vermicompost applied treatments. The application of PMS @ 30 t ha^{-1} (T_2) significantly increased the organic carbon and available sulphur contents in alkali soil. The different levels of PMS @ 30, 45 and 60 t ha^{-1}, treatments gave favourable results with the presence of Ca and S during incubation experiment. Among the different levels, application of PMS @ 30 t ha^{-1} was fixed for field experiment based on gypsum requirement (15 t ha^{-1}).

REFERENCES

Abduli, M.A., L Amiri, E. Madadian, S. Gitipour and S. Sedighian. 2103. Efficiency of Vermicompost on Quantitative and Qualitative Growth of Tomato Plants. *Int. J. Environ. Res., 7(2):467-47.*

Abdullah, A.A. 2007. Soil Profile Studies during Bioremediation of Sodic Soils through the Application of Organic Amendments (Vermiwash, Tillage, Green Manure, Mulch, Earthworms and Vermicompost). *World J. Agric. Sci.,* 4 (5): 550-553.

Abdullah, A.A. 2008. Effect of Vermicompost on the Productivity of Potato (*Solanumtuberosum*), Spinach (*Spinaciaoleracea*) and turnip (*Brassica campestris*). *World. J.Agrl. Sci.*, 4 (3): 333-336.

Abdullah, A.A and Sultan A.I. 2008. Reclamation of Sodic Soils through Vermitechnology. *Pakistan J. Agric. Res.*, 21:1-4.

Abrol, I.P., A.X. Soha and C.L. Achrya, 1978. Effect of Exchangeable Sodium on some Soil Physical Properties. *J. Ind. Soc. Soil Sci.*, 25: 98-105.

Ahmad K.M., A. Mohammad and J.M. Martin 2013. The Effect of Sulphur Application on yield and yield Components of Corn in Two Different Planting methods in Saline Condition.*Int. J. Agron. Plant. Prod.*, 4 (7): 1474-1478.

Alina, H.2013. Sludge from Pulp and Paper Mills for Biogas Production. *Karstad. Univers. Stud,* Karstad, Sweden, p. 1-58.

Alyson, L.1975. Soil Degradation and the use of Agricultural and Organic Industrial by Products as Soil Amendments. Soils of the Desert Southwest University of Arizona Press.

Amini, S., M.Naeini and K. Mashayekhi. 2012. Effects of Paper Mill Sludge as a Mulch Versus Topsoil Incorporation on Potassium uptake and the Grain yield of Rain-fed Wheat in a High Specific Surface Loess Soil with Illite Dominance in Clay Fraction. *Appl. Environ. Soil Sci.*, 4: 120-145.

Amos K.Q., A.V. Timothy, H. Sasha, J. L. Donald and S. Charles. 2011. Impacts of Paper Sludge and Manure on Soil and Biomass Production of Willow. *Biomass and Bioenergy.*, 35.

Association of Official Agricultural Chemists (AOAC). 1962. Official and Tentative methods of Analysis of Association of Official Agricultural Chemists, Washington, p. 354.

Arancon, N.Q., C.A. Edwards and P. Biermam. 2006. Influence of Vermicompost on Field Strawberries: Part 2. Effects on Soil Microbiological and Chemical Properties. *Biores. Technol.*, 97(6): 831-840.

Arnon, D.I., 1949. Copper Enzymes in Isolated Chloroplast Polyphenol Oxidases in *Beta vulgaris*. *Plant Physiol.*,pp: 24: 31.

Arul, P. 2002. Impact of Treated Paperboard Mill Effluent and Solid Wastes on yield and Quality of Marigold-soil Ecosystem. M.Sc. Thesis, Tamil Nadu Agric. Univ., Coimbatore.

Bellamy, K.L., C. Chong and R.A. Cline. 1995. Paper Sludge Utilization in Agriculture and Container Nursery Culture. *J. Environ. Qual.*, 24: 1074-1082.

Bipfubusa, M.A., N'Dayegamiye and H.Antoun. 2005. Effects of Fresh Paper Mill Sludge and their Composts on Soil Macro Aggregates. *Canadian J.Soil Sci.*, 85(1): 47-55.

Bower, C.A., L.R. Swarner, A.W. March, and F.M. Tileston, 1951. The Improvement of Alkali Soils by Treatments with Manure and Chemical Amendment. *Organs Agric. Expt. Stat. Tech. Bull.*, No.22: 37.

Burghardt, H. 1962. Uber die Bedeeutungdeschlorstur die pflanznernahrungbesenderer Beruck Sichtigung des chlond/sulfat problems. *Angewandle Botanik* XXXV: 5 (c.f. A. Surat and H. Boulay (ed.) 1985. Sulphate of Potash Fertilizers).

Cabral, F. and Vasconcelos, E. 1993. Agricultural use of Combined Primary/Secondary Pulpmill Sludge. *Agrochimica* 37: 409-417.

Curnoe, W.E., D.C. Irving, C.B. Dow, G. Velema and A. Unc. 2006. Effect of Spring Application of a Paper Mill Soil Conditioner on Corn yield. *Agron. J.*, 983(3): 423-429.

Dart, P.J.1997. Infection and Development of Leguminous Nodules. In: A Treatise on Dinitrogen Fixation Section III. (Biology) Hardy R.W.F. and Silver, W.S. (eds), John Wiley and Sons, New York, USA, pp. 367-372.

Das, K.C., E.W.Tollner and T.G. Tornabene. 2001. Composting by-products from a Bleached kraft Pulping Process: Effect of Type and Amount of Nitrogen Amendments. *Compost Sci. Util.*, 9(3): 256-265.

Dayegamiye, A.S., S. Huard and Y. Thibault.2003. Influence of Paper Mill Sludges on Corn yield and Nitrogen Recovery. *Canadian J. Soil Sci.*, 83(5): 497-505.

Department of Agriculture and Co-operation. 2010-11. In: Annual report, Production of pulses. Ministry of Agriculture, Government of India. pp. 15.

Devi, D and S.K. Agarwal. 1998. Performance of Sunflower Hybrids as Influenced by Organic Manure and Fertilizer. *J. Oilseeds Res.*, 15(2): 272-279.

Edwards, J.H and A.V. Someshwar. 2000. Chemical, Physical, and Biological Characteristics of Agricultural and Forest by-products. In: Land Application of Agricultural, Industrial, and Municipal Soil Science Society of America, Madison, Wisconsin, USA, pp. 17-54.

Feagley, S.E., M.S. Valdez and W.H. Hudnall. 1994. Paper Mill Sludge, Phosphorous, Potassium and Lime Effect on Clover Grown on Mine Soil. *J.Environ. Qual.*, 23: 759-765.

Fierro, A., Angers, D. A. and Beauchamp, C. J. 1999a. Restoration of Ecosystem Function in an Abandoned Sandpit: Plant and Soil Responses to De-inking Sludge. *J. Appl. Ecol.*,36: 244-253.

Fierro, A., D.A. Angers and C.J. Beauchamp. 1999b. Decomposition of Paper de-inking Sludge in a Sandpit Minesoil during its Revegetation. Soil. Biol. Biochem., (In Press).

Foley, B and L. Cooperband. 2002. Paper Mill Residuals and Compost Effects on Soil Carbon and Physical Properties. *J.Environ. Qual.*, 31(6): 2086-2095.

Gallardo, F., M.L Mora, M.C Diez. 2007. Kraft Mill Sludge to Improve Vegetable Production in Chilean Andisol. *Water Sci. Technol.*, 55, 31-37.

Gallardo F., C. Bravo, G. Briceño, M.C Di. 2010. Use of Sludge from Kraft Mill Wastewater Treatment as Improver of Volcanic Soils: Effect on Soil Biological Parameters. *R.C. SueloNutr. Veg. 10(1): 48-6.*

Gallardo, F., M. Cea, G.R. Tortella and M.C. Diez. 2012. Effect of Pulp Mill Sludge on Soil Characteristics, Microbial Community and Vegetable Production of *Loliumperenne*. *J. Environ. Manage.*,95: 193-198.

Gagnon, B., Simard, R. R., Lalande, R. etLafond, J. 2003. Improvement of Soil Properties and Fruit yield of Native Lowbush Blueberry by Papermill Sludge Addition. *Can. J. Soil Sci.*, 83: 1-9.

Gowsami, R.K., S.M. Hireman, M.B. Chetti, P.M .Salimth and R.V. Koti, 2003. Physiological basis for Higher Productivity in Green Gram. 2nd *Intl. Cong. Plant. Pathol.*, Jan 8: 12-20.

Gowtham, V. 2012. Impact of Treated Paperboard Mill Effluent Irrigation and Solid Waste on yield and Quality of China Aster (*Callistephuschinensis* (I.) Ness.) and Soil Health. M.Sc. Thesis, Tamil Nadu Agric. Univ., Coimbatore.

Gupta, R.P., and C. Dakshinamoorthy. 1980. Procedures for Physical Analysis of Soil and Collection of Agrometeorological Data. Indian Agricultural Research Institute, New Delhi.

Gupta, B.R. and P.D. Bajpai, 1977. Effect of some Inorganic Ameliorants on Reclamation and Phosphorous Availability in Salt-affected Soil. *IndianJ. Agric. Res.*, 11: 97-103.

Hameed, S.M and C. Udayasoorian. 1994. Use of Pulp and Paper Mill Sludge and Effluent to Increase Production of Tree Species. *Sustain. Environ.*, 321-328.

Hameed, S.M. 1997. Influence of Paper mill (TNPL) Solid Wastes as Amendments for Forest Nursery and their Impact on Soil Properties. M.Sc. Thesis, Tamil Nadu Agric. Univ., Coimbatore.

Hussain, N., B.H. Niazi, M. Salim, A. Ali and G. Hassan, 2000. Effect of Split Application of Gypsum on Wheat yield and Properties of Saline Sodic Soil Irrigated with Brackish Water. *Int. J. Agri. Biol.*, 3: 234-6.

Hussain N., G. Hassan, M. Arshadullah and F. Mujeeb. 2001. Evaluation of Amendments for the Improvement of Physical Properties of Sodic Soil. *Int. J. Agri. Biol.*,3(3): 319-322.

Jadhav A.D., S.C. Talashilkarand A.G Pawar. 1997. Influence of the Conjunctive use of FYM, Vermicompost and Urea on Growth and Nutrient Uptake in Rice. *J. Maharas. Agrl. Univ.*, 22(2): 249-250.

Jacson, M.L. 1967. Soil Chemical Analysis. Prentice Hall of India (Pvt.) Ltd., New Delhi, p. 105.

Jacson, M.L. 1973. Soil Chemical Analysis. Prentice Hall of India (Pvt.) Ltd., New Delhi, p. 109.

Jayanthi, T. 2007. Impact of Paperboard Mill Sludge Vermicompost and Effluent Irrigation on yield and Quality of Colesiacristata and Soil Health. M.sc. Thesis, Tamil Nadu Agric. Univ., Coimbatore.

Jenkinson, D.S and D.S Powlson. 1972. The Effects of Biocidal Treatments on Metabolism in Soil. V A Method for Measuring Soil Biomass. *Soil Biology & Biochemistry 8:* 209-213.

Karmegam N and T. Daniel. 2000. Effect of Biodigested Slurry and Vermicompost on the Growth and yield of Cowpea [*Vignaunguiculata*(L.)]. *Enviro. Ecol.*, 18(2): 367-370.

Karthika, V. 2013. Impact of Treated Paperboard Mill Effluent Irrigation and Solid Waste on yield and Quality of Bhendi (*Abelmoschusesculentus* L.) and Soil Health. M.sc. Thesis, Tamil Nadu Agric.Univ., Coimbatore.

Kausar, M.A. and S. Muhammad, 1972. Comparison of Biological and Chemical Methods for Reclaiming Sodic Soils. *Pakistan J. Sci. Res.*, 24: 252-61.

Kost, D.A., D.A. Bouutelle, M.M. Larson, W.D. Smith and J.P. Vimmerstedt. 1997. Papermill Sludge Amendments, Tree Protection, and Tree Establishment on an Abandoned Mine Soil. *J. Environ. Qual.*, 26: 1409-1416.

Kothule, V.G., R.K. Bhalearo and B.V. Sathe. 2003. Effect of Exogenous Application of Growth Regulators on Growth, Biomass Partitioning and yield in Soybean. *Annual Review of Plant Physiol*, 17: 95-9.

Kulkarni, H.D. 2013. Pulp and Paper Industry Raw Material Scenario-ITC Plantation a Case Study. Ippta., 82(2): 157-165.

Kumar, S. and T.B. Singh. 2009. Effect of varying Levels of Sulphur with and without Rhizobium on yield, Quality and Nutrient uptake of Black Gram. *Asian J. of Soil Sci.*, 4: 154-155.

Leon, M.C.C., A. Stone and R.P Dick. 2006. Oraganic Soil Amendment: Impact on Snap Bean Common Root Rot (Aphanomyceseuteiches) and Soil Quality. *Appl. Soil Ecol.*, 31(3): 199-210.

Lindsay, W.L. and W.A. NorvelL, 1978, Development of DTPA Soil Test for Zinc, Iron, manganese and Copper. *Soil Sci. Soc. of Am. J.*, 42: 421-428.

Madejon, E., P. Burgos, R. Lopez and F. Cabrera, 2003. Agricultural use of Three Organic Residues: Effect of Orange Production and on Properties of a Soil of the 'Comarca costa de huelva' (swspain). *Nutri. Cyc. Agro-Eco.*, 65(3): 281-288.

Mahmoud, E.K and M.M. Ibrahim. 2012. Effect of Vermicompost and its Mixtures with Water Treatment Residuals on Soil Chemical Properties and Barleygrowth. *J. Pla. Nut. Soil Sci.*,12 (3): 431-440.

Maheswarappa., H.P, H. Nanjappaand M.R Hegde.1999. Influence of Organic Manures on yield of Arrowroot, Soil Physico-chemical and Biological Properties when Grown as Intercrop in Coconut Garden. *Annals of Agric. Res.*, 20(3): 318-323.

Mahimairaja, S., N.S. Bolan, M.J. Hedley and A.N. Macgregor. 1995. Dissolution of Phosphate Rock during the Composting of Poultry manure. An Incubation Expriment. *FertilizerRes.*, 40: 93-104.

Marinari S., G Masciandaro, B. Ceccantiand S. Grego. 2000. Influence of Organic and Mineral Fertilisers on Soil Biological and Physical Properties. *Bioresource Tech.*, 72(1): 9-17.

Maschio, S., E. Furlani, G. Tonello, N. Faraone, E. Aneggi, D. Minichelli, L. Fedrizzi, A. Bachiorrini and S. Bruckner.2009. Fast Firing of Tiles Containing Paper Mill Sludg, Glass Cullet and Clay. *Waste. Manage.*,29: 2880-2885.

Mladenov, M and Y. Pelovski. 2010. Utilization of Wastes from Pulp and Paper Industry. *J. Uni. Chem. Techol. Metallurgy*, 45(1): 33-38.

Mohamed K. Abdel-Fattah. 2012. Role of Gypsum and Compost in Reclaiming Saline-sodic Soils. *J.Agric .Veterinary. Sci.*, 1(3): 30-38.

Muhammad, S. and A. Khaliq, 1975. Comparison of Various Chemical and Organic Amendments for Reclaiming Saline-sodic Soils. *Bull. Irrig. Drain. Flood Cont. Res. Council.*, 5: 50-54.

Muhammad Ramzan Chaudhry. (2001). Gypsum Efficiency in the Amelioration of Saline Sodic/Sodic Soils. *Int. J. of Agric & Biol.*, 3(3): 276-280.

Nethra N.N., K.V. Jayaprasad and R.D. Kale.1999. China aster [*Callistephuschinensis*(L)] Cultivation using Vermicompost as Organic Amendment. *Crop Res, Hisar.*,17(2): 209-215.

Nunes, J.R., F. Cabral and A.L. Pineiro. 2008. Short-term Effects on Soil Properties and Wheat Production from Secondary Paper Mill Sludge Application on Two Mediterranean Agricultural Soils. *Biores. Technol.*, 99(11): 4935-4942.

Olsen, S.R., L.L. Cole, F.S. Watanable and D.A. Dean. 1954. Estimation of Available Phosphorus in Soils by Extraction with Sodium Bicarbonate. U.S.D.A. Cric., p. 939.

Ou-Yang and W.S. Wu, 2002. Investigations of Paper Mill Sludge as a Component of Container Medium. Plant Pathol. Bull. 11: 19-24.

Panse, V and P.V. Sukhatme. 1976. *Statistical methods for Agricultural Workers*. ICAR, New Delhi.

Patil, S.L and M.N. Sheelavantar. 2000. Effect of Moisture Conservation Practices, Organic Sources and Nitrogen Levels on yield, Water use and Root Development of Rabi sorghum [*Sorghum bicolor*(L.)] in the Vertisols of Semiarid Tropics. *Annals of Agric. Res.*, 21(21): 32-36.

Pearce, R.B., R.H. Brown and R.E. Blaster.1968. Photosynthesis of Alfalfa Leaves as Influenced by Age and Environment. *Crop Sci.* 8: 677-680.

Phukan, S and K.G. Bhattacharyya. 2003. Modification of Soil Quality Near a Pulp and Paper Mill. *Water Air Soil Pollu.*, 146 (1-4): 319-333.

Piper, C.S. 1966.Soil and Plant Analysis, Inter Science Publications, New York, pp. 368.

Ponmani, S.2008. Impact of Treated Paperboard Mill Effluent and Solid Wastes on Vegetable Crop and Soil Ecosystem. M.Sc. Thesis, Tamil Nadu Agric. Univ., Coimbatore.

Prasanthrajan, M. 2010. Biocompost from Paperboard Mill Solid Wastes. M.Sc. Thesis, Tamil Nadu Agric. Univ., Coimbatore.

Prasanthrajan, M., C. Udayasoorian and P. Singaram. 2004. Impact of Paperboard Mill Solid Sludge Biocompost and Treated Effluent Irrigation on Growth and yield Attributes of Vegetable Cowpea. *Madras Agric. J.*, 91(7-12): 483-488.

Prathiba, S. 2005. Impact of Treated Paperboard Mill Effluent and Solid Wastes on yield and Quality of Vegetable Crops and Soil. M.Sc. Thesis, Tamil Nadu Agric. Univ., Coimbatore.

Preethi, A. 2012. Impact of Treated Paperboard Mill Effluent and Solid Wastes on yield and Quality of Tomato and Soil Ecosystem. M.Sc. Thesis, Tamil Nadu Agric. Univ., Coimbatore.

Price, G.W. and R.P. Voroney, 2007. Paper Mill Bio-solids Effect on Soil Physical and Chemical Properties. *J. Environ. Qua.*, 36 (6): 1704-1714.

Reddy, K. 2005. Different Levels of Vermicompost and Nitrogen on Growth and yield in Onion (*Allium cepa*) – Radish (Raphanussativus) Cropping System. *J. Res.Angrau.*, 33(1): 11-17.

Reddy, T.P., G. Padmaja and P. C. Rao. 2011. Integrated Effect of Vermicompost and Nitrogen Fertilizers on Soil Nutrient Status and yield of Onion-radish Cropping System. *Crop Res.*, 41(1-3): 148-155.

Rios, D., C. Perez and M. Sandoval. 2012. Phytotoxic Effect of Paper Pulp Sludge on Alkali Soil. *J. Pla. Nut. Soil Sci.*, 12(2): 315-327.

Sagheer A., G. Abdul, Q. Manzoor and M.A. Abbas (2006). Amelioration of a Calcareous Saline-Sodic Soil by Gypsum Application and Different Crop Rotations. *Int. J. Agric & Biol.*, 8(2): 142-146.

Satishkumar, B. 2002. Ecofriendly Agrocycling of Solid and Liquid Wastes of Paper Mill. Ph.D. Thesis.Tamil Nadu Agric. Univ., Coimbatore.

Sebastian, P.S., C. Udayasoorian, R.M. Jayabalakrishnan and E. Parameswari. 2009. Improving Soil Microbial Biomass and Enzyme Activities by Amendments under Poor Quality Irrigation Water. *World Appl. Sci. J.*, 7(7): 885-890.

Shamsuddoha, A.T.M., M. Anisuzzaman, G.N.C. Sutradha, M.A. Hakim and M.S. Bhuiyan. 2011. Effect of Sulphur and Boron on Nutrients in Mungbean (*Vigna radiate* L.) and Soil Health. *Plant Res. Manage.*, 2: 224-229.

Sharma, M.L. 1971. Physical and Physic-chemical Changes in the Profile of a Sodic Soil Treated with Gypsum. *Australian J. Soil Res.*, 9: 73-82.

Sharma, D.P., K.K. Mehta and J.S.P. Yadav. 1982. Effect of Reclamation Practices on Soil Properties and Crop Growth on Farmers Field. *J. Ind.Soc. Soil Sci.*, 29: 356-60.

Sharma, R., S.S. S.M. Mohinder, R.K. Malik and D. Singh. 2008. Effect of Sulphur and Phosphorusinteration on Growth and Nutrient Content in Green Gram (*Phaseolusaureus* L.). *Har. Agric. Univ. J. Res.*, 38: 41-47.

Simard, R.R., Coulombe, J., Lalande, R., Gagnon, B. and Yelle, S. 1998. Use of Fresh and Composted de-inking Sludge Incabbage Production. Pages 349-361 *in* S. Brown *et al*., eds. Beneficial co-utilization of Agricultural, Municipal and Industrialby-products. Kluwer Academic Publishers, Dordrecht, The Netherlands.

Simard, R.R. 2001. Combined Primary/Secondary Papermill Sludge as a Nitrogen Source in a Cabbage-sweet Corn Cropping Sequence. *Canadian J. Soil Sci.,* 81(1): 1-10.

Simpson, G.G., L.D. King, B.L. Carlile and P.S. Blickensderfer. 1983. Paper Mill Sludges, Coal Fly Ash, and Surplus Lime Mud as Soil Amendments in Crop Production. *Tappi Journal* 66: 71-74.

Singh, A.B. 2001. Influence of Phenolic Compounds on yield and Protein Quality of Green Gram (Vigna radiate L. Wilczek). *Indian J of Plant Physiol,* 24: 366-70.

Sinha, R.K., Sunita Agarwal, Krunal Chauhan, Dalsukh Valani. 2010. The Wonders of Earthworms & its Vermicompost in Farm Production: Charles Darwin's 'Friends of Farmers', with Potential to Replace Destructive Chemical Fertilizers from Agriculture. *J.Agrl.Sci.,*1 (2): 76-94.

Sreenivas C., S. Muralidhar and M.S. Rao. 2000. Vermicompost, a Viable Component of IPNSS in Nitrogen Nutrition of Ridge Gourd. *Annals of Agric. Res.,* 21(1): 108-113.

Stanford, S. and L. English. 1949. Use of Flame Photometer in Rapid Soil Tests of K and Ca. *Agron. J.,* 41: 446-447.

Subbiah, B.V and G.L. Asija. 1956. A Rapid Procedure for Estimation of Available Nitrogen in Soils. *Curr. Sci.,* 25(8): 259-260.

Suguna Devakumari, S. 2005. Integrated Management of Treated Paper Mill Effluent and Solid Wastes on Soil, Groundwater and Productivity of Fodder Grass (CO_3) and Sugarcane (CO86032) and Biobleaching of Kraft Pulps by Elite Fungal Species. Ph.D. Thesis, Tamil Nadu Agric. Univ., Coimbatore.

*Sultan A.T.S, S. Sundaravadivel, J.M. Reddy, K.S. Geetha and Abdullah A.A.2003. Bioremediation of Sodic Soil through Vermitech.

Suriyanarayanan. S., A.S. Mailappa, D. Jayakumar, K. Nanthakumar, K. Karthikeyan and S. Balasubramanian. 2010. Studies on the Characterization and Possibilities of Reutilization of Solid Wastes from a Wastes from a Waste Paper based Paper Industry. *Global J. Environ. Res.,* 4(1): 18-22.

Trepanier, L., J. Caron, S.Yelle, G.Theriault, J. Gallichand, C.J. Beauchamp. 1996. Impact of Deinking Sludge Amendment on Agricultural Soil Quality. In: Proceeedings of TAPPI Environment Conference, MAY, 1-9.

Uz and I.E. Tavali. 2014. Short-Term Effect of Vermicompost Application on Biological Properties of an Alkaline Soil with High Lime Content from Mediterranean Region of Turkey. *J. Sci. World.*

Wagh, R.S., R.S. Patil, R.W. Bharud and M.N. Bhalekar. 2003. Physiological and Nutritional Assessment of Somatic Hybrid Derivatives of Tomato (*Lycopersiconesculentum* Mill.). 2nd *Intl. Cong. Plant. Pathol.,* Jan 8-12, New Delhi, 28.

Walkley, A and I.A. Black. 1934. An Examination for the Outline of method for Determining Soil Organic Matter and a Proposed Modification of the Chromic Acid Titration method. *Soil. Sci.,* 3(1): 29-30.

Williams, R.F. 1946. The Physiology of Plant Growth with Special References to the Concept of Net Assimilation Rate. *Ann. Bot.,* 10: 41-72.

Xiao, C., L.Q. Ma and M.W. Brooder. 1993. Microbial Progression in the Decomposition of Corn Stalk Residue in Soil. *Soil Sci.,* 155: 48-42.

Yadav, K.S. and K.R. Dadarwal. 1997. In: Biotechnological Approaches in Soil Microorganisms for Sustainable Crop Production (Ed. Dadarwal, K.R.). Scientific Publishers, Jodhpur. pp. 293-308.

Zang, X and E.H. Ervin. 2004. Cytokinin-containing Seaweed and Humic Acid Extracts Associated with Creeping Bentgrass Leaf Cytokinins and Drought Resistance. *Crop Sci.,* 44:1-10.

Zhang, S., S. Wang, X.Q. Shan and H.Mu. 2004. Influences of Ligni from Paper Mill Sludge on Soil Properties and Metal Accumulation in Wheat. *Bio. Fert. Soils.,* 40(4): 237-242.

Zibilske, L.M. 1975. Dynamics of Nitrogen and Carbon in Soil during Paper Mill Sludge Decomposition. *Soil Sci.,*143: 26-33.

Zibilske, L.M., W.M. Clapham and R.V. Rourke. 2000. Multiple Applications of Paper Mill Sludge in an Agricultural System: Soil Effects. *J. Environ. Qual.,* 29(6): 1975-1981.

Zule, J., F. Cernec and M. Likon. 2007. Chemical Properties and Biodegradability of Waste Paper Millsludges to be used for Landfill Covering. *Waste Manage, Res.,* 25(6): 538-546.

*Originals not seen.

Pages: 103-111

Vermitechnology, Farm and Fertilizer

Edited by: Dr. Ashok K. Rathoure; Dr. Pawan Kumar 'Bharti' and Dr. Jaswant Ray

ISBN: 978-93-88854-38-2

Edition: **2020**

Published by: **Discovery Publishing House Pvt. Ltd., New Delhi (India)**

7

Organic Farming and its Need, Importance, Ministries and Constraints for its Adoption

Yaman[1*] and Prasann Kumar[1,2*]

ABSTRACT

Now a days maximum of the farmers are only bothered about yield of the crops and how they increase their crop productivity. For this they use huge amount of inorganic fertilizers in their crops and overuse of the agrochemicals for management of different diseases, insect-pest and weeds. All these practices has very harmful effect on the soil health, environment and cause serious diseases problem in human beings. All these problems can be solved by the organic farming which totally exclude the use of the inorganic inputs for the crop production which maintain the ecological balance and provide sustainability in agriculture, more importantly does not cause any harmful effect to the peoples. So there are many Government departments and ministries for encouragement of the organic farming and provide certification of the organic production to farmers. But there is lack of awareness to farmers for adopting organic farming which can be solved by some awareness programmes both at farmers and consumer level. Hence organic farming has the potential to maintain long term fertility of soil and avoid all types of pollution from agricultural techniques.

Keywords: *Abiotic, Biotic, Crop, Density, Economy, Forage.*

INTRODUCTION

Agriculture is the backbone of the Indian economy which provide employment to 70% of the population and 50% of the workforce depends upon agriculture. There is contribution of 17.42% of India's gross domestic

[1] **Department of Agronomy, School of Agriculture, Lovely Professional University, Jalandhar - 144 411 (Punjab) (India)**

[1, 2] **Division of Research and Development, Lovely Professional University, Jalandhar - 144411 (Punjab) (India)**

product (GDP) by the agriculture sector. So increase or decrease in Indian economy highly depends upon agriculture sector. India is a developing country. To make it developed country agriculture is very crucial sector. So it is very important to maintaining the soil health for sustainability in agriculture. But now a day there is decrease in soil fertility due to excessive use of the agrochemicals results in loss of natural habitat balance.Earlier than 1960's in India there was only use of organic source of nutrients in the soil which has no negative effect on the soil fertility. But at that time there is increase in population and total agricultural production is insufficient to feed the nation. So this was very serious problem for the Indian Government. To increase the agricultural production there was the need of improved technologies. All these happenings give birth to the era of green revolution. To enhanced the agricultural production and productivity improved seeds, machinery, huge amount of fertilizers, pesticides and others agrochemicals are used and also gives the positive results. India came in position to feed the nation and also able to export the agricultural produce. But with time due to excessive use of fertilizers and pesticides there is deterioration in soil health which cause gradual decrease in the agricultural production and also responsible for environmental degradation. All these facts receive the consideration of the world when International Panel on Climate Change (IPCC) found that agriculture cause one fifth of the anthropogenic greenhouse effect produce about 50% and 70% of total anthropogenic methane and nitrogen oxides emissions respectively (Reddy, 2010).In modern agricultural practices there is overuse of the fertilizers, pesticides and other agrochemicals which disbalance the natural resources and also cause soil erosion, decrease in water table, environmental pollution and reduce the food quality. Because of these excessive use agrochemicals are now enter to our food chain which is not good indication for the human health.To overcome all these problems there is need of alternative farm strategies and techniques which is organic farming. Term indicates that only the use of organic products in the farm for the crop production and totally exclude the inorganic substances like fertilizers, agrochemicals and genetically modified organisms for maintaining the soil health and sustainability in agriculture.

ORGANIC FARMING

Definition according to USDA (United States Department of Agriculture), "organic farming is a system which avoids or largely excludes the use of synthetic inputs such as fertilizers, pesticides, hormones, feed additives etc and to the maximum extent feasible rely upon crop rotations, crop residues, animal manures, off farm organic waste, mineral grade rock additives and biological system of nutrient mobilization and plant protection".According to IFOAM(The International Federation of Organic Agriculture Movements), "Organic agriculture is a production system that sustains the health of soils, ecosystems and people". In modern day farmers only concerned for the measures by which he can increase the crop yield and give more importance to the quantity of the food grains rather than the quality. That's why he uses inorganic fertilizers and pesticides in larger amount for increase the production with out much more concerned about the soil health, environment and also human health. This overuse of chemicals reduces the quality of food results in various diseases to human beings like cancer as well as affect immunity of body. Application of fertilizers in the field has very short-term effect on the crop productivity but has more negative effect on the environment and their leaching down into the soil contaminate the ground water and water bodies. Due to heavy rain there is runoff water carried lot of nutrients to the waterbodies from the soil and there is excessive growth of the algae which reduces the available oxygen in water called as "eutrophication" as a result of this process fishes and many water organisms are killed. Due to the excessive use of hybrid seeds season after season for increasing yield pose threat to local and indigenous varieties. So, organic farming has the potential to solve all these problems by using the organic and natural sources for crop production and provide ecologically and economically pure food. Organic farming has the potential to maintaining the sustainability in agriculture and make farmers self sufficient for the agricultural inputs.

PRINCIPLES OF ORGANIC FARMING

Organic farming includes four principles which are following:

1. **Principle of health:** Organic agriculture plays very important role for the survival of microbes present in the soil otherwise they are deteriorated by the excessive use of the fertilizers. Soil microbes plays very crucial role for maintaining the soil health. Soil health is very important for producing the healthy crops that enhance the health of people and animals. Hence organic farming plays major role in sustaining the health of ecosystem and all the living organisms.
2. **Principle of ecology:** Organic farming is depends upon the living ecological systems and also helps to sustain the ecological systems. There is a specific production environment for each living things on this earth. For example, for the production of the crops there is need of healthy soil and for the marine organisms like fish there is need of aquatic environment. Organic agriculture is able to maintain the ecological balance in nature and save the environment, climate, biodiversity, water and air.
3. **Principle of fairness:** Organic farming ensure the fairness towards the life, environment and all those which are involved in the farming viz. farmers, labour and consumers. Because in conventional agriculture there is overuse of agrochemicals which are dangerous for the health

of user and also reduce the food quality. So organic agriculture has the main aim to feed the nation good quality of food. In organic agriculture there is use of natural and environmental resources in such a way that it should not compromise with the future generation for availability of the resources.

4. **Principle of care:** Organic agriculture should be operate in a preventive and responsible way to protect the health and resources for the current and future generations and environment. Therefore farming in such a way that it is safe to health of human, animals and ecologically sound (figure 7.1).

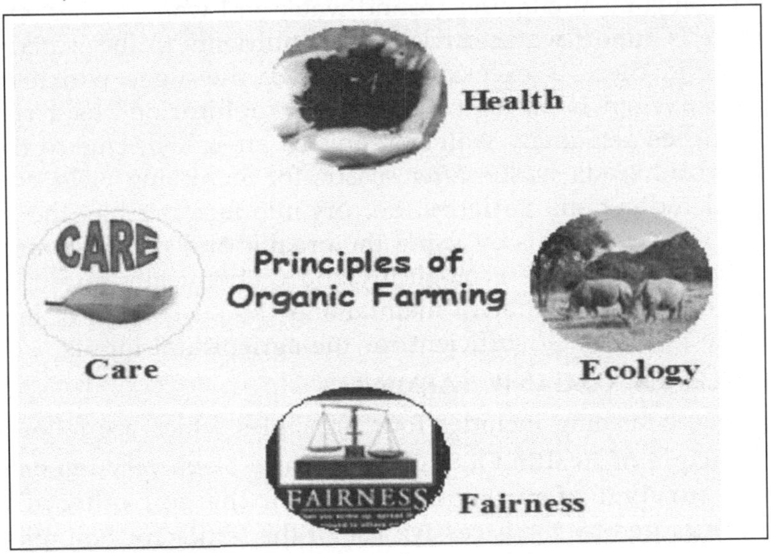

Fig. 7.1: Principles of organic farming

Source: http://agritech.tnau.ac.in/org_farm/orgfarm_principles.html

ORGANIC FARMING IN INDIA

Organic farming in India becoming popular day by day. Organic farming based on the natural sources for the crop production and yield benefit which helps to maintain healthy soil and provide healthy food for the peoples.

Farmers of India now realizing the importance of organic farming and its role for maintaining the sustainability in food production. There are three categories because of which organic farming is adopted by the farmers:

Category 1

Farmers which are living in those areas where the availability of the agricultural inputs is less or no availability of inputs. At those areas organic farming is a way of life. Organic farming has been practiced by the farmers since very long time or traditional way of doing farming.

Category 2

Farmer who realize the ill effects due the overuse of the agrochemicals and fertilizers to the soil and environment. As a result their crop productivity going down season after season which affects their economy and standard of living. All these farmers fall under this category.

Category 3

Under this category, farmers who willingly choose the organic farming to capture the market because organic products have very good market value.

- In India most of the farmers who adopt organic farming comes under category first but these farmers are not certified.
- Farmers comes under third category are the certified farmers.
- Second category farmers are both that is certified or non-certified.

There is the encouragement for the promotion of organic agriculture according to the 10th five -year plan by using the organic wastes, organic matter and integrated nutrient management practices (GOI, 2001). For the sustainability in agriculture and environment protection, 9th five-year plan also promoted the production of organic products in the spices and plantation crops by using bio inputs. There are many government departments and ministries for the encouragement of organic farming and responsible for providing certification to the farmers who grows organic crops in their farm only then they sold their produce as the organic products (Figure 7.2).

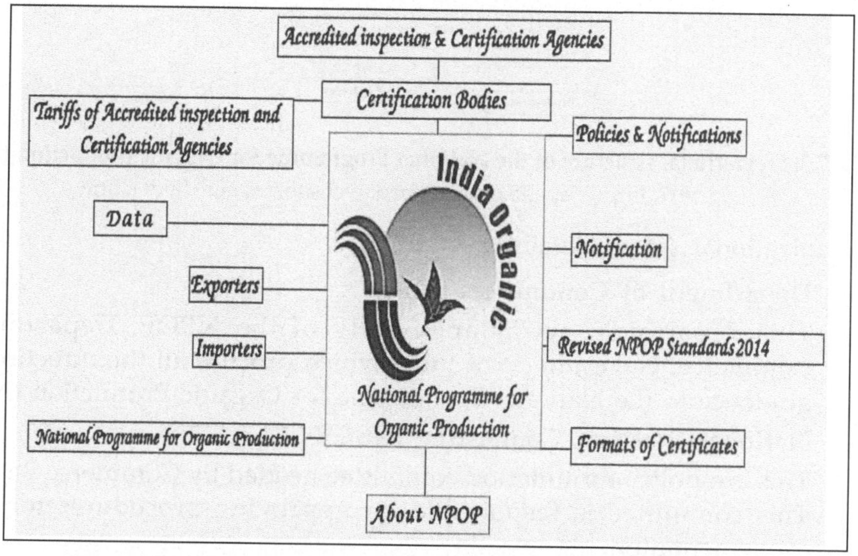

Fig. 7.2: National Programme for Organic Production (NPOP)

Source: http://apeda.gov.in/apedawebsite/organic/index.htm

The National programme for Organic Production (NPOP) procure the standards for organic production and also provides the criteria, procedure and systems for the accreditation of Certification body and National (India Organic) Logo. For controlling import and export of organic products the standards and procedures must be prepare according to the International Standards. Therefore, European Commission and Switzerland recognize the NPOP standards equal to their standards. United States Department of Agriculture (USDA) also recognize NPOP accreditation procedure as their equivalent.

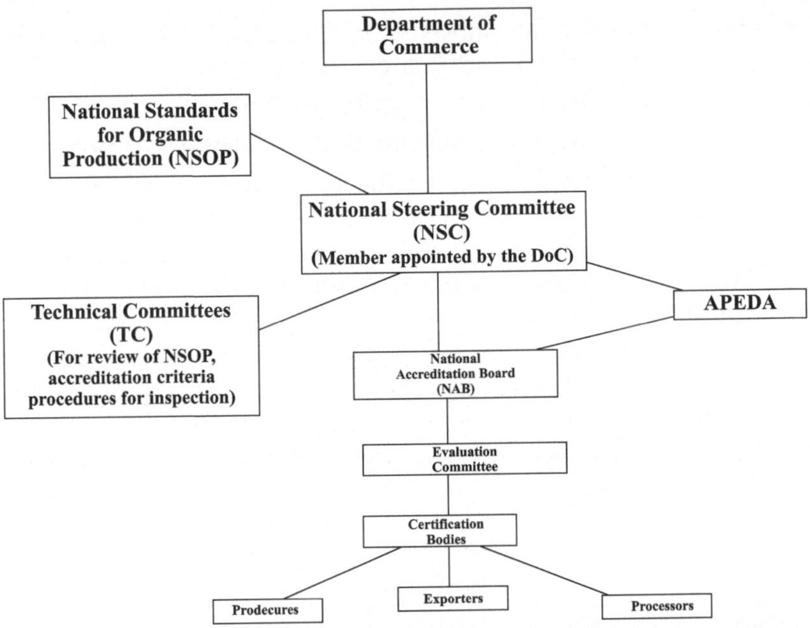

Fig. 7.3: Operational structure of the National Programme for Organic production (NPOP)
Source: http://apeda.gov.in/apedawebsite/organic/index.htm

Organizational set-up details:

(a) **Department of Commerce (DOC):**

This department act as apex body of the NPOP. Department of Commerce, Government of India which procure all the directions and guidance to the National Programme for Organic Production (NPOP).

(b) **National Steering Committee (NSC):**

This is a policy formulation committee headed by Commerce Secretary. This committee is responsible for approving procedures for NPOP implementation.

(c) National Accreditation Body (NAB):

This is constituted by the NSC and run by APEDA. This is responsible for formulating the procedures and guidelines for accreditation and assessment of the certification programme of certification bodies.

(d) Agricultural and Processed Food Products Export Development Authority (APEDA):

For the implementation of the NPOP, APEDA works as a Secretariat. There are following responsibilities of the APEDA:

(i) Assessment of the certification bodies.

(ii) If there is any complaint regarding organic products from importing country then APEDA has to be investigate it.

(iii) For inspection and certification, it provides guidelines to accredited certification bodies.

(e) Technical Committee:

This committee includes all the experts from different organizations and responsible for the formulation of any technical standards. If there is any need of changing in existing standards then they have the power to change it. They will also give advice to NSC regarding various issues persist in organic sector.

(f) Evaluation Committee:

This committee has the duty to evaluate the implementation of certification programme of Certification bodies and this committee is constitute by the NAB.

(g) Certification Bodies:

These are the agencies which are accredited by NAB under NPOP for certifying organic products.

Exports, production and area under organic farming in India:

Area: In India total area under organic certification process is 3.56 M ha (2017-18). Out of this total area 50% of area (1.78 M ha) is cultivable area and 50% of area includes wild harvest collection.

In India Madhya Pradesh covered largest area under organic certification and after MP there is Rajasthan, Maharashtra and Uttar Pradesh.

Sikkim has become first state in the country which covered all its cultivable area under organic certification. (> 76000 ha).

Production: In 2017-18 total production of certified organic products was 1.70 million MT which include oil seeds, cotton, sugarcane, cereals and millets, pulses, tea, medicinal plants, fruits, dry fruits, vegetables and coffee etc.

Madhya Pradesh is the largest producer of the organic products followed by Maharashtra, Karnataka, UP and Rajasthan and among all these crops oil seeds has the highest production.

Exports: In 2017-18 total export of organic products was4.58 lakh MT of about 3453.48 crore. India export organic products to USA, European Union, Canada, Australia, Israel, South Korea, Vietnam, New Zealand, Japan etc. Oil seeds (47.6%) export in larger amount among all the organic crops.

Major advantages of Organic farming:

1. **Poison free and nutritional food:**

   The organic food products are rich in minerals and vitamins and free from all the toxic chemicals which provide all the health benefit to the consumers.

2. **Lower cost of production of crops:**

   For the production of the organic products overall cost for production is low as compare to conventional farming because maximum of the inputs for crop production is available in the farm itself.

3. **Maintain soil health:**

   This is one of the most important advantage of the organic farming because all the inputs which we are applying are organic which have no negative effect on the soil microbes which helps in the soil nourishment.

4. **Less water pollution:**

   Organic farming avoids the water pollution which otherwise is major issue under conventional farming system because there is leaching of nitrate into the soil and contaminate the ground water when we overuse the application of nitrogenous fertilizers and there is also major problem of "Eutrophication" in the water bodies.

5. **Eco-friendly in nature:**

   There is no negative impact on the environment and does not cause any environmental pollution and helps in maintaining the biodiversity.

Problems faced by the Indian organic growers:

Indian Government and other agencies promote the organic farming nowadays and provide the subsidies and formulated the schemes for the organic farming even then farmers of India hesitate to adopt organic farming because of following reasons:

1. **Low crop yield:**

   For the establishment of organic farm,it requires two to three years. In the initial years there is loss of huge amount of yield which highly affects the economy of the farmers especially marginal and small farmers.

2. **Loss of quality as per standards:**

   There are some standards which have to be followed by the farmers for the organic crop production but most of the organic produce does not attain that quality which highly affects its marketing.

3. **No proper pest management practices:**

   For the organic farming, there are not much efficient organic pest management practices which is then responsible for the crop failure.

4. **Lack of quality seeds:**

   Indigenous varieties of seeds are very good for the organic farming but their availability in market is very low because maximum of the seed producing companies only concentrating on producing hybrid seeds which are highly responding to fertilizers and chemicals.

5. **Complex organic certification system:**

   This complexity in the certification system is one of the major constraint for the farmers and cost is also high for the marginal farmers.

CONCLUSION

Organic farming is very important for maintaining the sustainability in agriculture and protect the resources for the future generations. Because in conventional agriculture there is use of large amount of inputs and agrochemicals such as pesticides, fungicides and herbicides and other inorganic inputs which are very dangerous for the ecosystem and toxic to human health. So there is need of farming in such a way that it does not provide harm to humans and nature which can be possible by adopting organic farming. But most of the farmers does not want to adopt the organic farming because they are only bothered about the yield without much thinking about the negative impact on the environment by the conventional farming. So there must be some awareness programme both at farmers and consumer level for the importance of organic farming and health benefit by consuming organic products.

REFERENCES

Albert, H. (2000) An Agricultural Testament, Other India Press And Research Foundation for Science, Technology, and Ecology, Goa.

Barik, A.K. " Organic Farming in India : Present Status, Challenges and Technological Break through". Prof. and Head, Department of Agronomy, Palli Siksha Bhavana (Institute of Agriculture), Visva Bharati, Sriniketan, West Bengal.

Mamgain, Anuj. "Status, Importance, Prospects, and Vision of Organic Farming in India". Visva Bharati University.

Meena, R.S. " Organic Farming : Concept and Components". Asstt. Prof. (Entomology), KVK (SKRAU), Sri Ganganagar, Rajasthan.

http://apeda.gov.in/apedawebsite/organic/index.htm

Section III: Fertilizer

Pages: 115-137

Vermitechnology, Farm and Fertilizer

Edited by: **Dr. Ashok K. Rathoure; Dr. Pawan Kumar 'Bharti' and Dr. Jaswant Ray**

ISBN: 978-93-88854-38-2

Edition: **2020**

Published by: **Discovery Publishing House Pvt. Ltd., New Delhi (India)**

8

Biofertilizer – A Boon for Soil Health

M.R.A. Manimala

INTRODUCTION

One of the major concerns in today's world is the pollution and contamination of soil. The use of chemical fertilizers and pesticides has caused tremendous harm to the environment. An answer to this is the biofertilizer, an environmentally friendly fertilizer now used in most countries. Biofertilizers are organisms that enrich the nutrient quality of soil. The main sources of biofertilizers are bacteria, fungi, and cyanobacteria (blue-green algae). The most striking relationship that these have with plants is symbiosis, in which the partners derive benefits from each other. Plants have a number of relationships with fungi, bacteria, and algae, the most common of which are with mycorrhiza, rhizobium, and cyanophyceae. These are known to deliver a number of benefits including plant nutrition, disease resistance, and tolerance to adverse soil and climatic conditions. These techniques have proved to be successful biofertilizers that form a health relationship with the roots. Biofertilizers will help solve such problems as increased salinity of the soil and chemical run-offs from the agricultural fields.

Biofertilizers are microbial inoculants or carrier based preparations containing living or latent cells of efficient strains of nitrogen fixing, phosphate is solublizing and cellulose decomposing microorganisms intended for seed or soil application and designed to improve soil fertility and plant growth by increasing the number and biological activity of beneficial microorganisms in the soil (Gandora,1998). Organic fertilizers (manure,

Mother Terasa College of Agriculture, (Affiliated to Tamil Nadu Agricultural University) Mettusalai, Illuppur, Pudukkottai – 622 102, Tamilnadu (India)

compost, vermicompost) are also considered as Biofertilizers, which are rendered in available forms due to the interactions of microorganisms or their association with plants. Biofertilizers, thus include

(i) Symbiotic nitrogen fixers -*Rhizobium sp.*
(ii) Non-symbiotic, free living nitrogen fixers -*Azotobacter, Azospirillum*
(iii) Blue green algae inoculants -*Azolla-Anabaena*
(iv) Phosphate solubilizingmicroorganisms-*Bacillus,Pseudomonas,Penicillium, Aspergillus*
(v) Mycorrhiza
(vi) Cellulolytic microorganisms and
(vii) Organic fertilizers

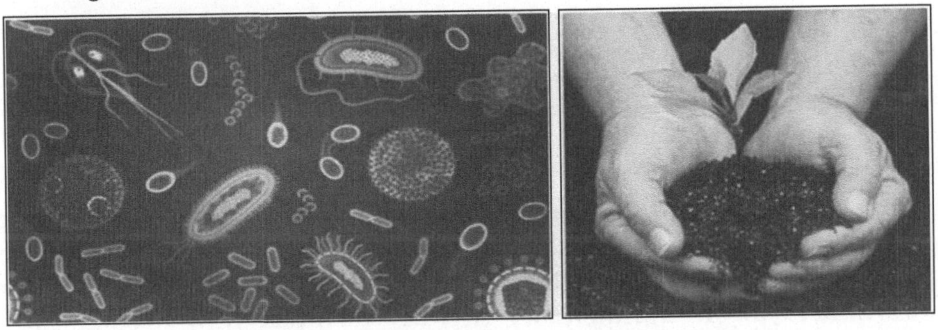

Fig. 8.1: Microorganism as biofertilizer

ROLE OF BIOFERTILIZERS IN SOIL FERTILITY AND AGRICULTURE

Biofertilizers are known to play a number of vital roles in soil fertility, crop productivity and production in agriculture as they are eco friendly and cannot at any cost replace chemical fertilizers that are indispensable for getting maximum crop yields. Some of the important functions or roles of Biofertilizers in agriculture are:

1. They supplement chemical fertilizers for meeting the integrated nutrient demand of the crops.
2. They can add 20-200 kg N/ha year (*eg. Rhizobium sp* 50-100 kg N/ha year; *Azospirillum, Azotobacter:* 20-40 kg N/ha /yr; Azolla: 40-80 kg N/ ha; BGA: 20-30 kg N/ha) under optimum soil conditions and thereby increases 15-25 percent of total crop yield.
3. They can at best minimize the use of chemical fertilizers not exceeding 40-50 kg N/ha under ideal agronomic and pest-free conditions.
4. Application of Biofertilizers results in increased mineral and water uptake, root development, vegetative growth and nitrogen fixation.
5. Some Biofertilizers (eg, *Rhizobium BGA, Azotobacter* sp) stimulate production of growth promoting substance like vitamin-B complex, Indole acetic acid (IAA) and Gibberellic acids etc.

6. Phosphate mobilizing or phosphorus solubilizing Biofertilizers/ microorganisms (bacteria, fungi, mycorrhiza etc.) converts insoluble soil phosphate into soluble forms by secreting several organic acids and under optimum conditions they can solubilize/mobilize about 30-50 kg P2O5/ha due to which crop yield may increase by 10 to 20%.
7. Mycorrhiza or VA-mycorrhiza (VAM fungi) when used as Biofertilizers enhance uptake of P, Zn, S and water, leading to uniform crop growth and increased yield and also enhance resistance to root diseases and improve hardiness of transplant stock.
8. They liberate growth promoting substances and vitamins and help to maintain soil fertility.
9. They act as antagonists and suppress the incidence of soil borne plant pathogens and thus, help in the bio-control of diseases.
10. Nitrogen fixing, phosphate mobilizing and cellulolytic microorganisms in bio-fertilizer enhance the availability of plant nutrients in the soil and thus, sustain the agricultural production and farming system.
11. They are cheaper, pollution free and renewable energy sources
12. They improve physical properties of soil, soil tilth and soil health in general.
13. They improve soil fertility and soil productivity.
14. Blue green algae like *Nostoc, Anabaena, and Scytonema* are often employed in the reclamation of alkaline soils.
15. Bio-inoculants containing cellulolytic and lignolytic microorganisms enhance the degradation/decomposition of organic matter in soil, as well as enhance the rate of decomposition in compost pit.
16. BGA plays a vital role in the nitrogen economy of rice fields in tropical regions.
17. *Azotobacter* inoculants when applied to many non-leguminous crop plants, promote seed germination and initial vigor of plants by producing growth promoting substances. (Lenart,2006)
18. *Azolla-Anabaena* grows profusely as a floating plant in the flooded rice fields and can fix 100-150 kg N/ha /year in approximately 40-60 tones of biomass produced.

Microbial Inoculants: 'Microbial inoculants' are carrier based preparations containing beneficial micro-organisms in a viable state, intended for seed or soil application, designed to improve soil fertility and help plant growth by increasing the number of desired micro-organisms in plant rhizosphere.In soil the activities of Nitrogen fixation, mobilisation of plant nutrients and degradation of ligno-cellulotic wastes are being carried out by a large number of micro-organisms. Artificially multiplied cultures of selected micro organisms augment the natural recycling of organic resources. There are different types of microbial inoculants.

Rhizobium: Legumes provide a protein – rich source of food, which is an essential part of the diet in many parts of the tropics. They play an important role in supplying those essential amino acids, particularly lysine that are not present in sufficient quantities in cereal crops. These leguminous plants in association with the soil bacterium, Rhizobium form root nodules and fix atmospheric nitrogen.

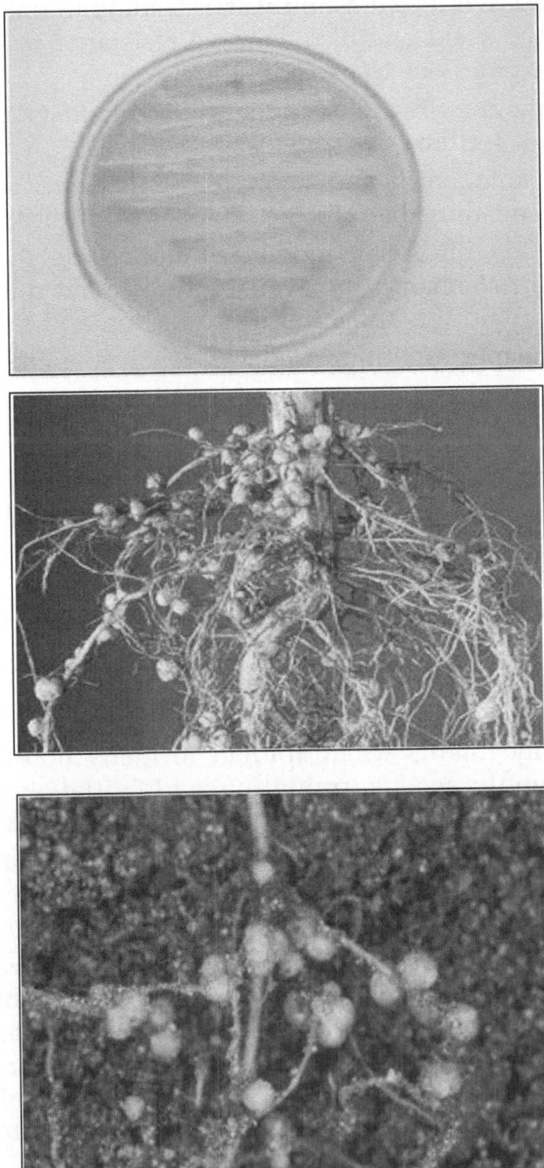

(A) (B) (C)

Fig. 8.2: ***Rhizobium leguminosarum*** **form root nodules in plants**

The rhizobia that form associations with the best know legumes have been characterized by nucleic acid sequence homologies as well as by the more traditional traits such as growth rates (fast and slow), acid production from carbohydrates, serology and legume associations. The success of these legume crops depends upon the efficient functioning of legume plant – Rhizobium symbiosis. The efficient functioning of nitrogen fixation under field conditions will contribute to improving the yield of legume crops. Yield can be influenced by several factors including the genotype of the plant, native rhizobial population, quality of rhizobial inoculant, and the environmental and ecological conditions in which legume crops are grown.

Rhizobium is a gram negative bacterium which inhabits the root nodules of most leguminous crops. Rhizobia are soil bacteria that fix N2 (diazotroph) after becoming established inside root nodules of legumes (Fabaceae). There are several different genera of rhizobia, all of them belong to the Rhizobiales, aprobably-monophyletic group of proteobacteria and they are soil bacteria characterized by their unique ability to infect root hairs of legumes and induce effective nitrogen fixing nodules to form the roots.

They are rod shaped living plants which exist only in the vegetative stage. Unlikemany other soil microorganisms, rhizobia produce nospores and they are aerobic and motile. Rhizobia (species of Rhizobium, Mesorhizobium, Bradyrhizobium,Azorhizobium, Allorhizobium and Sinorhizobium) form intimate symbiotic relationships with legumes byresponding chemotactically to flavonoid molecules released as signals by the legume host. These plants compounds induce the expression of nodulation (nod)genes in rhizobia, which in turn produce lipochitooligosaccharide (LCO) signals that trigger mitotic cell division in roots, leading to nodule formation [Matiru,2004].The legume-Rhizobium symbiosis is a typical example of mutualism. The Rhizobia, which are widely used in agricultural systems, are represented by 7 genera containing about 40 species. Although rhizobia naturally infect legumes as host plants, some Rhizobium strains can form symbiotic relationships with non-legumes species such as Parasponia (Trinick, 1979)

Cross inoculation groups of *Rhizobium* (CIG): It (CIG) refers the groups of leguminous plants that will develop effective nodules when inoculated with the rhizobia obtained from the nodules from any member of that legume group.

I. Rhizobium

1.	*Rhizobium leguminosarum*	**Cross inoculation groups of rhizobium**	**Host it can nodulate**
	bv. viceae	Pea	Peas, lentils, vicia
	bv. phaseoli	Bean	Phaseolus spp
	bv. trifoli	Clover	Trifolium spp
2.	*Rhizobium meliloti*	Alfalfa	Alfalfa, clover, fenugreek
3.	*Rhizobium loti*	Lotus	Trifoli, lupine
4.	*Rhizobium fredii*	Soybean	Soybean
5.	*Rhizobium spp*	Cowpea group	Vigna, Arachis, Cajanus, Dolichus, Sesbania, Acacia, Prosopis, green gram and blackgram
6.	*Rhizobium sp*	Chickpea group	Chickpea

II. Bradyrhizobium

B. japonicum	Soybean	Soybean
B. spp	Cowpea group	Cowpea group plants

III. Azorhizobium - Stem nodulating Nodulates *Sesbania rostrata.*

IV. Photorhizobia - Nodulants aeschynomene sp.

V. Sinorhizobium - Fast growing soybean nodulator

Azospirillum: *Azospirillum*, a free-living nitrogen-fixing bacteria closely associated with grasses. *Azospirillum* bacteria is a Gram negative motile bacteria belonging to the order Rhodospirillales, associated with roots of monocots, including important crops, such as wheat, corn and rice. Azospirillum contains 109/gm spores of Azospirillum species. This Azospirillum bacterium fixes the atmospheric nitrogen and makes it available to plants in non-symbiotic manner that can replace 50-90% of the nitrogen fertilizer required by plants. Azospirillum biofertilizer also secretes some fungicides, enzymes but in minute amount. Use of Azospirillum biofertilizer increases the crop production in large scale. We are engaged in manufacturing and marketing of Bio control agents comprise of different types of beneficial Bacterial, Fungal and Viral cultures. Azospirillum is mainly useful for monocot vegetables. (Chen, 2006)

Azospirillum is an eco-friendly liquid biological fertilizer formulation containing bacteria, Azospirillum which contain large amount of lipid granules, which enters the cortical cells of the root and fix up atmospheric nitrogen and also produces biologically active substances like vitamins, nicotinic acid, indole acetic acid, gibberellins etc and helps in better retention of flowers and enhances the plant growth.

(A) **(B)** **(C)**

Fig. 8.3 (A-C). ***Azospirillum*** **application in rice field**

Azotobacter: *Azotobacter* spp. are Gram negative, free-living, aerobic soil dwelling, oval or spherical bacteria that form thick-walled (Salhia,2013). There are around six species in the genus *Azotobacter (Martyniuk, 2003)* some of which are motile by means of peritrichous flagella, others are not. They are typically polymorphic and their size ranges from 2-10 µm long and 1-2 µm wide. The *Azotobacter* genus was discovered in 1901 by Dutch microbiologist and botanist Beijerinck *et al.* (founder of environmental microbiology). *Azotobacter chroococcum* is the first aerobic free-living nitrogen fixer.

These bacteria utilize atmospheric nitrogen gas for their cell protein synthesis. This cell protein is then mineralized in soil after the death of *Azotobacter* cells thereby contributing towards the nitrogen availability of the crop plants. *Azotobacter spp.* is sensitive to acidic pH, high salts, and temperature (Tchan, *1989). Azotobacter* has beneficial effects on crop growth and yield through, biosynthesis of biologically active substances, stimulation of rhizospheric microbes, producing phyopathogenic inhibitors. Modification of nutrient uptake and ultimately boosting biological nitrogen fixation. (Somers *et al.*, 2004)

Besides being quite expensive and making high cost of production, chemical fertilizers have adverse effect on soil health and microbial population. In such situation, biofertilizer can be the best alternative for enhancing soil fertility. Being economic and environmental friendly, biofertilizers can be used in crop production for better yield (Cocking, 2006). Similarly, microbial products are considered safer, self-replicating, target specific, which is regarded as major component of integrated nutrient management from soil sustainability perspective.

Azotobacter in Nutrient Cycling

Azotobacter makes availability of certain nutrients like Carbon, Nitrogen, Phosphorus and Sulphur through accelerating the mineralization of organic residues in soil and avoid uptake of heavy metals. *Azotobacter* can be an important alternative of chemical fertilizer because it provides nitrogen in the form of ammonia, nitrate and amino acids without situation of over dosage, which might be one of the possible alternatives of inorganic nitrogen source (eg. Urea). It also helps to sustain the plant growth and yield even in case of low phosphate content soil, as well as helps in uptake of macro and certain micro nutrients which facilitates better utilization of plant root exudates itself.

Role of *Azotobacter* in Growth Substances Production and Promotion

Besides, nitrogen fixation, *Azotobacter* produces, Thiamin, Riboflavin, Nicotine, Indol Acetic Acid and Gibberellins. When *Azotobacter* is applied to seeds, seed germination is improved to a considerable extent. Brakel and Hilger (1965) showed that *Azotobacter* produced Indol-3-Acetic Acid

(IAA) when tryptophan was added to the medium. Hennequin and Blachere (1966) found only small amounts of IAA in old cultures of *Azotobacter* to which no tryptophan was added.

Bacteria of the genus *Azotobacter* synthesize auxins, cytokinins, and GA-like substances, and these growth materials are the primary substance controlling the enhanced growth of tomato. (Azcorn and Barea, 1975). These hormonal substances, which originate from the rhizosphere or root surface, affect the growth of the closely associated higher plants. Eklund *et al.* (1970) demonstrated that the presence of *Azotobacter chroococcum* in the rhizosphere of tomato and cucumber is correlated with increased germination and growth of seedlings. Puertas and Gonzales (1999) report that dry weight of tomato plants inoculated with *Azotobacter chroococcum* and grown in phosphate-deficient soil was significantly greater than that of non inoculated plants. Phytohormones (auxin, cytokinin, gibberellin) can stimulate root development.

These responses suggest that *Azotobacter* probably influences the development of plants by producing growth-regulating substances. Therefore, *Azotobacter* spp. is often regarded as a member of "Plant Growth Promoting Rhizobacteria (PGPR)".It was also concluded that *Azotobacter* inoculants have a significant promoting effect on growth parameters like root, shoot length and dry mass of bamboo and maize seedlings in vitroand in pot experiments (Salhia, 2013). The dual inoculation of *A. chroococcum* and *P. indica* had beneficiary response on shoot length, root length, fresh shoot and root weight, dry shoot and root weight, and panicle number that affect growth of rice plant.

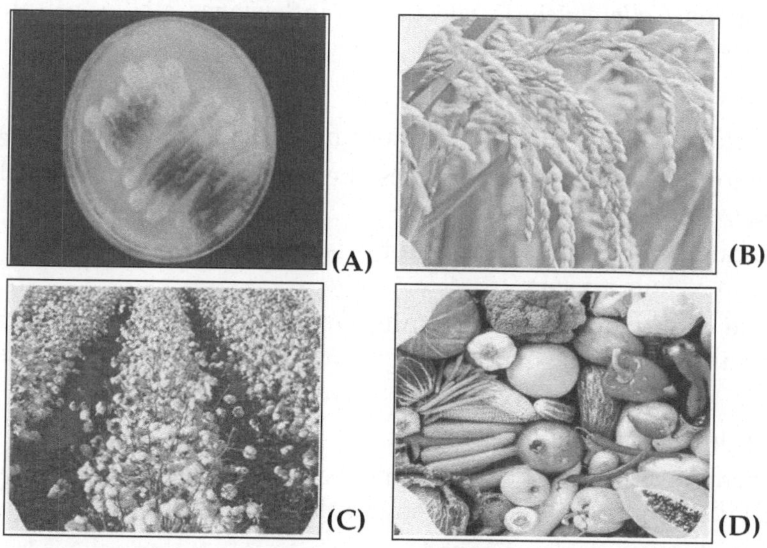

Fig. 8.4 (A-D). Application of *Azospirillum* biofertilizer in Vegetables, rice and cotton crop

Gluconoacetobacter

Gluconacetobacter diazotrophicus, an efficient nitrogen fixing diazotrophic bacterium is one among the endophytes studied as a model organism to evaluate the plant-bacterial interactions with non legumes (Cocking *et al.*, 2006). Although a number of diazotrophs have been isolated so far but G. diazotrophicus have conclusive proof for nitrogen fixation is available at present. G.diazotrophicus can grow in a wide range of conditions, such as low pH, high sucrose concentrations and high salt conditions. The bacterium is unique because it allows nitrogen fixation to remain active in nitrogen fertilized fields, unlike soybean innoculating Rhizobium bacteria which shut down when the soil is high in nitrogen. Compared to Rhizobium bacteria *G. diazotrophicus* is found to have multiple entry sites, such as stems and leaves, whereas Rhizobium that colonize legumes are limited to root nodules alone. The purpose of this review is divided into two broad sections; the first part comprising natural occurrence of G. diazotrophicus in different hosts is discussed. In this section, G. diazotrophicus isolation or association with sugarcane was elaborated. In addition, its occurrence in various crops, including coffee, pineapple, finger millet, rice, certain vegetables and other hosts like sugarcane mealybugs and arbuscular mycorrhiza (AM), was presented. The second major topic concerned is to appraise the multifaceted research conducted employing G. diazotrophicus to unravel various plant growth- promoting mechanisms. It comprises of N2- fixation and its inoculation effects, production of phytohormones such as indole acetic acid (IAA) and gibberellic acid (GA), in vitro solubilization of plant macro and micronutrients like P and Zn and biocontrol of the phytopathogens *Colletotrichum falcatum, Xanthomonas albilineans* and the nematode Meloidogyne incognita.

Salient features

- Acid tolerant nitrogen fixing bacterium associated with sugarcane.
- An endophytic organism colonizes the roots, stems, buds and leaves of sugarcane
- It is located in the apoplastic fluid of sugarcane stems and to a lesser extent in xylem vessels.
- Capable of growing and fixing nitrogen at 30% sucrose concentration and optimum sucrose concentration for better nitrogen fixation is 10%
- Growth and Nitrogen fixation observed even at pH 3. 0
- The optimum pH is 5.5
- An average of 200 kg N ha^{-1} would be fixed by using 30 per cent of the total sugar produced by a sugarcane crop.
- IAA production is also noticed

- Tolerant to higher level of combined nitrogen.
- Mode of entry is through mycorrhizae, mealy bug and mechanical injury of plant parts
- Exhibiting antibiotic resistance
- It is a member of alpha group of Proteobacteria
- In terms of 16s rDNA based phylogeny Gluconacetobacter clusters with the genera Rhodopila, Acidomonas, Acidiphilium and Gluconobacter
- In terms of nif H sequence, it is more related to Rhizobium sp. and Azospirillum brasilense than to other diazotrophs.

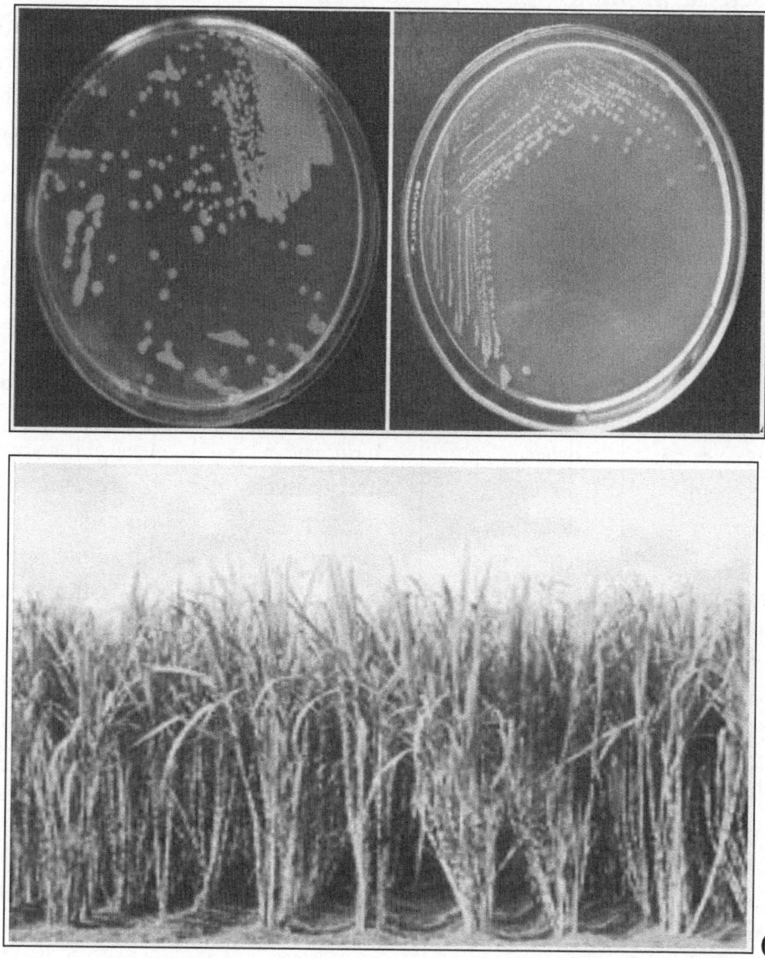

(A)

(B)

Fig. 8.5 (A-B): *Glucanoacetobacter diazotrophicus*-**biofertilizer for sugarcane**

Phosphobacteria

Phosphobacteria means microbial inoculants capable of solubilizing phosphate. Commonly used *Phosphobacteria* is Bacillus megaterium. Around 95-99% of the total soil phosphorus is insoluble which is directly not available to plants. Multiplies fast in the root zone. The P-solubilizers containing bacteria or fungi may convert isolable form of phosphate to soluble form by producing organic acids in general. About 15-25% of insoluble phosphate can be solubilized, saving chemical fertilizers significantly. *Phosphobacteria*can solubilize about 30 kg of insoluble source of phosphorus and making it available to plants. Application of phosphobacteria along with nitrogen fixing bacteria promotes growth and yield of the crops by 30%. A large fraction of soil microbial population can dissolve insoluble inorganic phosphates present in soils. In some soils this ability has been found to be present in as high as 8% of the total population. In addition to bacteria, actinomycetes belonging to the genera Micromonospora, Nocardia and Streptomyces have also been reported to solubilize insoluble phosphates. Thermophilic fungi which are normally not present in soil have been isolated from compost and characterised for solubilization of tricalcium phosphate and rock phosphate. Torula thermophila solubilized Mussoorie rock phosphate and utilized it as a sole P source efficiently.

Phosphate solubilising bacteria	Phosphate solubilizing cyanobacteria	Phosphate solubilizing actinomycetes	Phosphate solubilizing fungi and yeast
Achromobacter sp.	*Anabaena* sp.	*Actinomyces* sp.	*Aspergillus* spp.
Aerobacter sp.	*Calothrix*	Streptomyces	*A. awamorii*
Agrobacterium sp.	*Nostoc* sp.		*Mucor* sp.
Bacillus sp.	*Scytonema* sp.		*Penicillium* sp.
B.megaterium var. Phosphaticum	*Tolpothrix*		*Pythium* sp.
Escherichia sp.			*Fusarium* sp.
Pseudomonas sp.			*Rhizoctonia solani*
Xanthomonas sp.			*Helminthosporium* sp.

ORGANIC ACIDS AND P SOLUBILIZATION

The major microbiological means by which insoluble phosphorus compounds are mobilized is by the production of organic acid which is accompanied by the acidification of the medium. The organic and inorganic acids convert tricalcium phosphates to the di- and monobasic phosphates with the net result of an enhanced availability of the element to the plant. The type of organic acid produced and their amounts differ with different microorganisms. Tri- and di-carboxylic acids are more effective as compared to mono basic and aromatic acids. Aliphatic acids are also found to be more effective in P solubilization than phenolic acids and citric acid and fumaric acids has highest P-solubilizing ability.

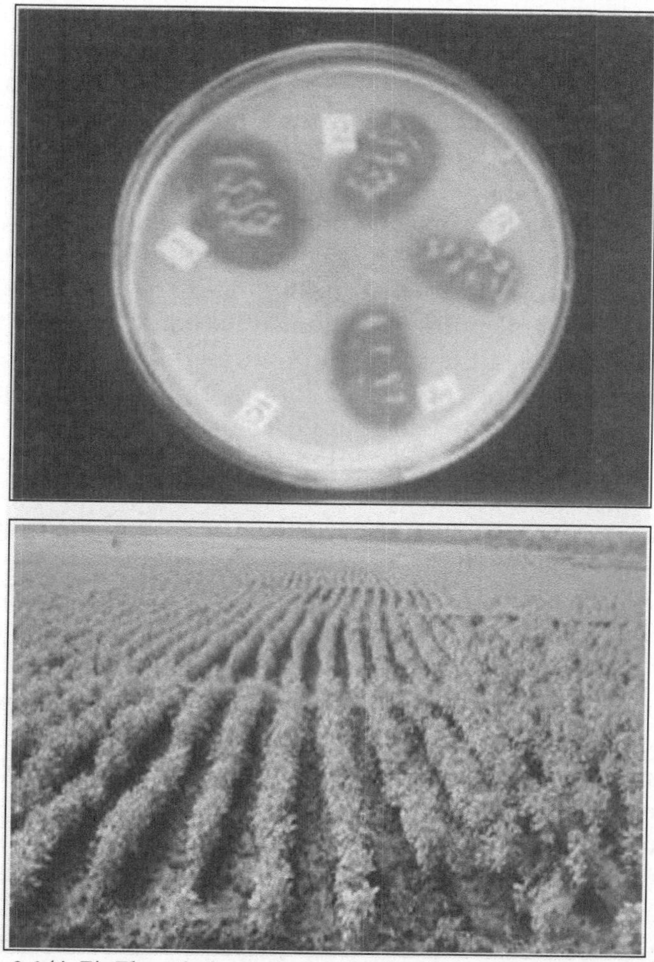

(A)

(B)

Fig. 8.6 (A-B). Phosphobacteria application in marigold (Horticultural crop)

ENZYMES AND P-SOLUBILIZATION

The liberation of P from organic phosphate compounds is mainly due to the action of enzymes of esterase type. PSM along with acid production, produces the phosphatase enzyme which cause the solubilization of P in aquatic environment. Besides these two mechanisms the production of chelating substances, H_2S, CO_2, mineral acids, siderophores are also involved in P solubilization by PSMs. In addition, the action of PSMs is not only due to the release of plant available phosphorus but also due to the production of biologically active substances like indole acetic acid, gibberellins, cytokinins production is also correlated with P solubilization.

MYCORRHIZA

Soil microorganisms such as arbuscular mycorrhizal fungi (AMF or AM fungi) represent a key link between plants and soil mineral nutrients. Thus, they are collecting growing interest as natural fertilizers. AMF are obligate symbionts, belonging to the phylum Glomeromycota (Schubler *et al.*, 2001), which form mutualistic symbioses with about 80% of land plant species, including several agricultural crops. They provide the host plant with mineral nutrients and water, in exchange for photosynthetic products (Smith and Read, 2008). The AMF mycelium that emerges from the root system can acquire nutrients from soil volumes that are inaccessible to roots (Smith *et al.*, 20012). Furthermore, fungal hyphae are much thinner than roots and are therefore able to penetrate smaller pores (Allen, 2011). Carbohydrates and mineral nutrients are then exchanged inside the roots across the interface between the plant and the fungus. AM fungal hyphae exclusively colonize the root cortex and form highly branched structures inside the cells, i.e., arbuscules, which are considered the functional site of nutrient exchange (Balestrini *et al.*, 2015). Thus, AMF can alleviate the limitation in plant growth caused by an inadequate nutrient supply (Nouri *et al.*, 2014). It has recently been suggested that, in natural environments, a non-mycorrhizal condition should be viewed as abnormal for the majority of species, although there is a marked diversity among AM fungal communities belowground, depending on plant species diversity, soil type, and season, or a combination of these factors (Smith and Smith, 2012).

In addition to an improved nutritional supply, AM interactions provide other benefits to plants, such as improved drought and salinity tolerance and disease resistance (Pozo and Azcón-Aguilar, 2007). Although several works have been devoted to studying the influence of AM symbiosis on the plant response to abiotic stress (such as drought, salinity, and flooding) in the last few years, the mechanisms responsible for the increased plant tolerance to stress have yet to be fully elucidated (Sánchez-Romera *et al.*, 2015). Metals such as Fe, Cu and Zn play essential roles in several subcellular compartments, but they constitute a highly reactive group of elements that are toxic at high concentrations. AM fungi are known to alleviate heavy metal toxicity in the host plants and to tolerate high metal concentrations in the soil. Metal transporters play a central role in heavy metal homeostasis. A Zn transporter has been identified in *Glomus intraradices* (*GintZnT1*)) and, more recently, through a genome-wide analysis of the recently published *Rhizophagus irregularis* (formely *Glomus intraradices* DAOM-197198) genome, several putative genes coding for Cu, Fe, and Zn transporters have been identified (Tamayo *et al.*, 2014). The next steps will involve the functional characterization of these transporters and the identification of their roles in the symbiosis.

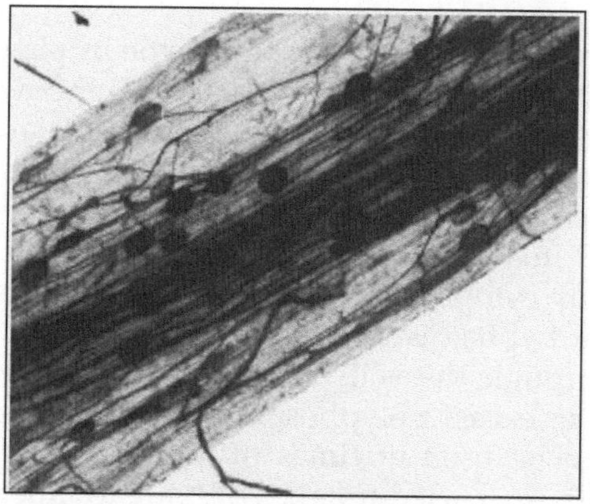

(A)

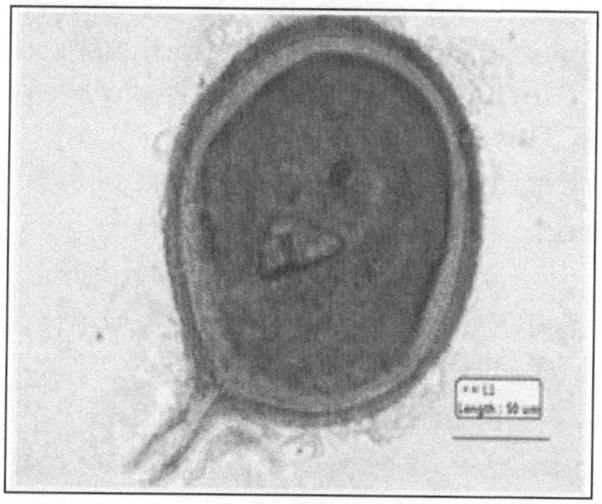

(B)

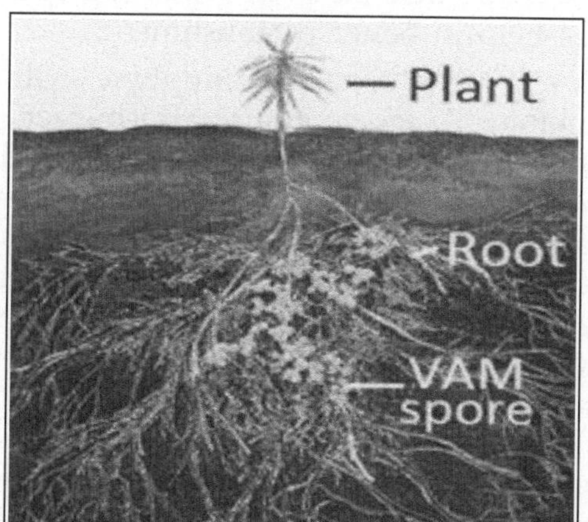

(C)

Fig. 8.7 (A-C): AM fungi spore and vesicles

P CONTRIBUTION

Phosphate transport by VAM is a key factor in plant nutrition. VAM can absorb several times soil P and have greater P inflow rates than roots. The fungal hyphae actually transport P over large distances into the root. The phosphate absorbed by VAM fungi from soil solution is accumulated in the vacuoles of the fungi as poly phosphate granules and this represents 16-40% of the total P in VAM fungi. The poly beta granules are propelled through the hyphae by cytoplasmic streaming to the arbuscules. The inflow rate through external hyphae is approximately thousand times faster than the diffusion rate through the soil pores. It is also important that when phosphate supply is in excess polyphosphate accumulates the nutrient as a storage pool that can be used at times of increasing demand to support stages of plant growth. Increased uptake of P due to inoculation with VAM fungi in various agricultural crops has been reported.The ability of mycorrhizal fungi to contribute to host nutrition is based on their status as soil-borne, beneficial fungi and therefore their capacity to gain access to soil derived nutrients. The mycelium produced by mycorrhizal fungi can:

- Survive as resting propagule in the absence of host
- Grow independently in soil
- Grow as symbiotic mycelium in soil (extra hyphal structure)
- Grow in close association with the roots (intracelluar hypae and arbuscles in VAM fungi)

FORM REPRODUCTIVE OR RESTING STRUCTURES

These fungi in addition to supplying P to the plant offer protection against root diseases. They also help in water uptake and overcoming transplant shock, thus help in better establishment.

Azolla: *Azolla* is a heterosporous pteridophyte, with seven species. It contains, as endosymbiont, *Anabaena azollae* Strasburger, a nitrogen fixing cyanobacterium (Nostocaceae family). *Azolla* is a green - floating water fern that floats in water and fixes atmospheric nitrogen in association with nitrogen fixing blue green alga *Anabaena azollae* (Lumpkin,1982). *Azolla* fronds consists of sporophyte with a floating rhizome and small overlapping bilobed leaves and roots. Rice growing areas in South East Asia and other third World countries have recently been evincing increased interest in the use of the symbiotic N_2 fixing water fern *Azolla* either as an alternate nitrogen source or as a supplement to commercial nitrogen fertilizers. *Azolla* is used as biofertilizer for wetland rice and it is known to contribute 40-60 kg N ha^{-1} per rice crop. The agronomic potential of *Azolla* is quite significant particularly for rice crop and it is widely used as biofertilizer for increasing rice yield. . The important factor in using *Azolla* as a biofertilizer for rice crop is its quick decomposition in soil and efficient availability of its nitrogen to rice. In tropical rice soil, the applied *Azolla* mineralizes rapidly and its nitrogen is made available to the rice crop in very short period. (Watanabe, 1982)

(A)

(B)

Fig. 8.8 (A-B): Mass production of AM fungi inside brick lined tank and its application in different crops

Azolla -*Anabaena* symbiosis

The eukaryotic water fern *Azolla* and the prokaryotic endosymbiont *Anabaena azollae* are actively involved in the symbiotic association and fix atmospheric nitrogen. The host plant *Azolla* provides the carbon source sucrose to the cyanobiont while the cyanobiont fix nitrogen and transfers to *Azolla* which in turn multiplies very rapidly. The cyanobiont is associated with dorsal lobes of the leaf from the onset of their development and is never in direct contact with the external environment and *A. azollae* is the only species found in symbiotic association with *Azolla*. The growth and development of the *Azolla* and the *Anabaena* are synchronous. *Azolla* shoot tips are supported above the water surface by the stem axes and a small colony of *Anabaena* filaments is associated with every apical merits. The heterocyst of the symbiont *Anabaena* is the site of nitrogen fixation, while vegetative cells are involved in photosynthesis. The total nitrogen requirement of the *Azolla* fronds is supplied by the cyanobiont. The ammonia from N_2 fixation by the cyanobiont is released into the leaf cavity and absorbed by the frond's ammonia assimilating enzymes. The growth rate of *Azolla* is very rapid so much so that it doubles its weight in a mere 2-3 days. Due to fast relative growth rate the biomass production is heavy in a given time and hence the biomass is exploited as biofertilizer for rice.

Fig. 8.9 (A-B): *Azolla* application in rice field as nitrogen fertilizer

SILICATE AND ZINC SOLUBILIZING BACTERIA (SSB)

Microorganisms are capable of degrading silicates and aluminum silicates. During the metabolism of microbes several organic acids are produced and these have a dual role in silicate weathering. They supply

H+ ions to the medium and promote hydrolysis and the organic acids like citric, oxalic acid, Keto acids and hydroxy carbolic acids which from complexes with cations promote their removal and retention in the medium in a dissolved state. The studies conducted with a *Bacillus* sp. isolated from the soil of granite crusher yard showed that the bacterium is capable of dissolving several silicate minerals under in vitro condition. The examination of anthrpogenic materials like cement, agro inputs like super phosphate and rock phosphate exhibited silicate solubilizing bacteria to a varying degree. The bacterial isolates made from different locations had varying degree of silicate solubilizing potential. Soil inoculation studies with selected isolate with red soil, clay soil, sand and hilly soil showed that the organisms multiplied in all types of soil and released more of silica and the available silica increased in soil and water. Rice responded well to application of organic sliceous residue like rice straw, rice husk and black ash @ 5 t/ha. Combining SSB with these residues further resulted in increased plant growth and grain yield. This enhancement is due to increased dissolution of silica and nutrients from the soil.

QUALITY CONTROL OF BIOFERTILIZERS

Quality of inoculants manufactured is one of the most important factors resulting in their success or failure and acceptance or rejection by the farmers. Basically quality means the presence of the right type of microorganism in active form and desired numbers. Quality has to be controlled at various stages of production, marketing and application.

Quality Control Measures (as per ISI Specifications)

1. Since, Biofertilizers contains live cells, care should be taken during their transportation and storage.
2. They should be kept in a cold place and not exposed to sunlight.
3. Biofertilizers for legumes are crop-specific; therefore, they must be used for the crop for which they are meant.
4. Biofertilizers when used under adverse soil conditions, appropriate remedial measures (liming and use of Gypsum) should be followed.
5. Biofertilizers must be carrier-based
6. Carrier material used should be in form of powder (75-106 micron size.
7. It should contain minimum of 10^8 viable cells of microorganisms/ gram of the carrier material on dry weight basis.
8. It should have a minimum period of six months expiry from date.
9. It should be tree from any contaminant/contamination with other microorganisms.

10. PH should be in the range of 6.0-7.5.
11. It should induce desired beneficial effects on all those crops, species/ cultivars listed on the packet before the expiry date.
12. It should be packed in 50-75 micron low density polythene packets

Stages requiring quality control

- During mother culture stage
- During carrier selection and standardisation
- During broth culture stage
- During mixing of broth with carrier
- During packing
- During storage
- Standards for quality testing

Bureau of Indian Standards (BIS) for carrier - based Biofertilizers

BIS have notified specifications for *Azotobacter* (ISI, 1979) and *Rhizobium* (ISI, 1986) long back for use of biofertilizer producersand suggested some modifications. The committee has also suggested specifications for phosphate solubilizing microorganisms and *Azospirillum.*

Indian Standard Specifications for different biofertilizers

Parameters	*Rhizobium*	*Azotobacter*	*Azospirillum*	PSM
Base	Carrier based	Carrier based	Carrier based	Carrier based
Cell No. at the time of manufacture	10^7	10^6	10^7	10^8
Contamination	Nil at 10^5 dilution	Nil at 10^5 dilution	Nil at 10^5 dilution	Nil at 10^6 dilution
Expiry period from date of manufacture	6 months	6 months	6 months	6 months
PH	6.5-7.5	6.5-7.5	6.5-7.5	6.5-7.5
Strain	Should be checked serologically	Nothing specific *A. chroococcum* sp. is mentioned	Nothing specific	Nothing specific
Carrier should pass through	150-212 micron IS sieve	106 micron IS sieve	106 micron IS sieve	106 micron IS sieve
Others	Nodulation test positive result in 50% or more dry matter than control	Minimum amount of N- fixation not less than 5 mg/g of sucrose utilized	Should produce white pellicle in NFB media at 10^7 dilution	Should show phosphate solubilizing zones of 12 mm in tricalcium phosphate medium at 10^5 dilution.

Constraints in Biofertilizer Technology (Rakesh Kumar *et al.*, 2017)

Though the biofertilizer technology is a low cost, eco-friendly technology, several constraints limit the application or implementation of the technology. The constraints may be:

- Technological constraints like unavailability of good quality carrier material and lack of qualified technical personnel in production units.
- Infrastructural constraints like lack of essential equipments, power supply, etc.
- Financial constraints like non-availability of sufficient funds and problems in getting bank loans.
- Environmental constraints like seasonal demand for biofertilizers, simultaneous cropping operations and short span of sowing/planting in a particular locality, etc.
- Human resources and quality constraints like lack of technically qualified staff in the production units, lack of suitable training on the production techniques.
- Unawareness on the benefits of the technology due to problem in adoption of the technology by the farmers due to different methods of inoculation, no visual difference in the crop growth immediately as that of inorganic fertilizers.
- Marketing constraints like non availability of right inoculant at the right place at the right time, lack of retail outlets or the market network for the producers.
- The different constraints in one way or the other affect the technique at production, or marketing or usage

CONCLUSION

Environmental stresses are becoming a major problem and as a detrimental consequence of the effect, productivity of crops is declining at an unprecedented rate. Our too much dependence on chemical fertilizers and pesticides to quench the huge demand of food by growing populations has encouraged the industries to produce life-threatening chemicals as a form of pesticides or fertilizers. These chemicals are not only hazardous for human consumption but also severely affect ecological balance in the environment. In this adverse situation, biofertilizer can act as a potent alternative that not only can feed the emerging population but also can save the agriculture from the severity of various environmental stresses. Biofertilizers being essential components of organic farming play a vital role in maintaining long term soil fertility and sustainability by fixing atmospheric di-nitrogen, mobilizing fixed macro and micro nutrients in the soil into forms available to plants. Currently there is a gap of ten million tons of plant nutrients between removal of crops and supply through chemical fertilizers. In context of both the cost and environmental impact of chemical fertilizers, excessive reliance on chemical fertilizers is not practicable in the long run because of the cost, both in domestic resources and foreign exchange involved in setting up of fertilizer plants and sustaining the production. In this context, biofertilizers would be the viable option for farmers to increase productivity per unit area.

REFERENCES

1. Allen M. F. 2011. Linking Water and Nutrients through the vadose zone: A Fungal Interface between the Soil and Plant Systems: Linking Water and Nutrients through the Vadose Zone: A Fungal Interface between the Soil and Plant Systems. J. Arid Land 3, 155-163.
2. Azcorn R, Barea JM. Synthesis of Auxins, Gibberellins and Cytokinins by Azotobacter Vinelandi and Azotobacter Beijerinckii related to Effects Produced on Tomato Plants. *Plant Soil*. 1975; 43: 609-619.
3. Balestrini R., Lumini E., Borriello R., Bianciotto V. 2015. Plant-soil Biota Interactions, in Soil Microbiology, Ecology and Biochemistry, ed Paul E. A., Editor. (London: Academic Press; Elsevier ;), 311-338.
4. Beijerinck MW. 1901. Ueber Oligonitophile Mikroben, Zentralblattfiir Bakteriologie, Parasitenkunde, Infektionskrankheiten and Hygiene. *Abteilung II.*; 7: 561-582.
5. Brakel J, Hilger F. Etude Qualitative et Quantitative de la synthese de substances de Nature auxinique par *Azotobacter chroococcum in vitro. Bull Inst Agron Stns Rech Gembloux*. 1965; 33: 469-487.
6. Chen J. 2006. *The Combined use of Chemical and Organic Fertilizers and/or Biofertilizer for Crop Growth and Soil Fertility*. International Workshop on Sustained Management of the Soil–Rhizosphere System for Efficient Crop Production and Fertilizer Use, Thailand;. p. 1-10.
7. Cocking, E.C., Stone, P.J. and Davey, M.R.2006. Intracellular Colonization of Roots of Arabidopsis and Crop Plants by Gluconacetobacter diazotrophicus. in vitro Cell Dev. Biol- Plant, 42: 74-82.
8. Eklund E. Secondary Effects of some *Pseudomonads* in the Rhizosphere of Peat Grown Cucumber Plant. In: Pharis RP, *et al*. Editors. *Hormonal Regulation of Development*. 1970; 3: p. 613
9. Gandora V, Gupta RD, Bhardwaj KKR.1998. Abundance of *Azotobacter* in Great Soil Groups of North-West Himalayas. *J Indian Soc Soil Sci*. 1998; 46(3): 379-383.
10. Hennequin JR, Blachere H. Recherches sur la synthese de phytohormones et de Composes phenoliques par *Azotobacter* et des bacteries de la rhizosphere. *Ann Inst Pasteur*. 1966; 3: 89-102.
11. ISI, 1979. Bureau of Indian Standards (BIS) for Carrier-based *Azotobacter* Biofertilizers.
12. ISI, 1986. Bureau of Indian Standards (BIS) for Carrier-based *Rhizobium* Biofertilizers.
13. Lenart A.2012. Occurance Characteristics and Genetic Diversity of *Azotobacter chroococcum* in Various Soils of Southern Poland. *Pol J Environ Stud*. 21(2): 415-424.
14. Lhuissier, F.G.P, de-Rujiter, N.C.A, Sieberer, B.J., Esseling, J.J. and A.M.C. Emons. 2001. Time of Cell Biological Events Evoked in Root Hairs by Rhizobium Nod Factors: State of the Art. Ann. Bot., 87: 289-302.

15. Lumpkin, T.A. and D.L. Plucknet.1982. *Azolla as a Green Manure: Use and Management in Crop Production*, Westview, Boulder, Colo, USA, 1982.
16. Martyniuk S, Martyniuk M. 2003. Occurrence of *Azotobacter* spp. in some Polish Soils. *Polish J Environ Stud.*; 12(3): 371-374.
17. Matiru, V.N.and Dakora, F.D. 2004. Potential use of Rhizobial Bacteria as Promoters of Plant Growth for Increased yield in Landraces of African Cereal Crops. Afr. J. Biotechnol., 3(1): 1-7.
18. Nouri E., Breuillin-Sessoms F., Feller U., Reinhardt D. 2014. Phosphorus and Nitrogen Regulate Arbuscular Mycorrhizal Symbiosis in Petunia Hybrida.
19. Puertas A, Gonzales LM. Aislamiento de cepasnativas de *Azotobacter chroococcum* en la provincial Granmayevaluacion de suactividadestimuladora en plantulas de tomate. *Cell Mol Life Sci*. 1999; 20: 5-7.
20. Pozo M.J., Azcón-Aguilar C. 2007. Unraveling Mycorrhiza-induced Resistance. Curr. Opin. Plant Biol. 10, 393-398.
21. Rakesh Kumar, Narendra Kumawat and Yogesh Kumar Sahu. 2017. Role of Biofertilizers in Agriculture. Popular kheti, vol. 5 (4): 63-66.
22. Salhia B. 2013. *The Effect of Azotobacter chrococcumas Nitrogen biofertilizer on the Growth and yield of Cucumis Sativus*. Deanery of Higher Education Faculty of Science, Master of Biological Sciences, Botany: The Islamic University Gaza.
23. Sánchez-Romera B., Ruiz-Lozano J.M., Zamarreño Á.M., García-Mina J.M., Aroca R. 2015. Arbuscular Mycorrhizal Symbiosis and Methyl jasmonate Avoid the Inhibition of Root Hydraulic Conductivity caused by Drought. Mycorrhiza.
24. Schubler A., Schwarzott D., Walker C. 2001. A New Fungal Phylum, the Glomeromycota: Phylogeny and Evolution. Mycol. Res. 105, 1413-1421.
25. Smith S.E., Smith F.A. 2012. Fresh Perspectives on the Roles of Arbuscular Mycorrhizal Fungi in Plant Nutrition and Growth. Mycologia 104, 1-13. Smith S.E., Smith F. A. (2012). Fresh Perspectives on the Roles of Arbuscular Mycorrhizal Fungi in Plant Nutrition and Growth. Mycologia 104, 1-13.
26. Somers E, Vanderleyden J, Srinivasan M. Rhizosphere Bacterial Signaling: A Love Parade Beneath our Feet. *Crit Rev Microbiol*. 2004; 30(4): 205-240.
27. Tamayo E., Gómez-Gallego T., Azcón-Aguilar C., Ferrol N. 2014. Genome-wide Analysis of Copper, Iron and Zinc Transporters in the Arbuscular Mycorrhizal Fungus *Rhizophagus irregularis*. Plant Traffic Transp. 5: 547.
28. Tchan YT, 1989. New PB. *Azotobacteraceae*. In: Holt JG, Williams, *et al*. Editors. *Bergey's Manual of Systematic Bacteriology Volume 1*. Baltimore, USA; p. 220-229.
29. Trinick. M.J.1979. Structures of Nitrogen Fixing Root Nodules Formed on *Parasponia andersonii* (Planch). Can. J. Microbiol. 25: 565-578. ISI, 1979. Bureau of Indian Standards (BIS) for Carrier - based *Azotobacter* Biofertilizers.
30. Watanabe, I.1982. "Azolla–*Anabaena symbiosis*–its Physiology and use in Tropical Agriculture," in *Microbiology of Tropical Soils and Plant Productivity*, Y.R. Dommergues and H.S. Diem,Eds., pp. 169-185, Martinus Nijhoff, The Ague, The Netherlands.

Pages: 138-166

Vermitechnology, Farm and Fertilizer
Edited by: Dr. Ashok K. Rathoure; Dr. Pawan Kumar 'Bharti' and Dr. Jaswant Ray
ISBN: 978-93-88854-38-2
Edition: **2020**
Published by: **Discovery Publishing House Pvt. Ltd., New Delhi (India)**

9

Use of Bio Fertilizers in Oilseed Crops
A Review

A.Solaimalai[1], M.Jayakumar[*], R. Kannan[2] and K.Baskar[1]

ABSTRACT

Bio-fertilizers have definite advantage over chemical fertilizers. Chemical fertilizers supply over nitrogen whereas bio-fertilizers provide in addition to nitrogen certain growth promoting substances like hormones, vitamins, amino acids etc. Crops have to be provided with chemical fertilizers repeatedly to replenish the loss of nitrogen utilized for crop growth. Bio-fertilizers application in agriculture will have greater impact on organic agriculture and also on the control of environmental pollution, soil health improvement and reduction in input use. Farmers try to increase yields of vegetable crops by mean of heavy nutrition's. The use of chemical nitrogen and phosphorus fertilizers at high levels had an adverse effect on the accumulation of NH_4+, NO_3-, NO_2- and PO_4- in vegetable product tissues. Therefore, clean agriculture recently depends upon using bio-fertilizers as well as organic in order to produce high yields with the best commodity quality without contamination and less accumulation with heavy metals.

INTRODUCTION

The application of high input technologies such as chemical fertilizers, pesticides, herbicides have improved the production but there is growing concern over the adverse effects of the use of chemicals on soil productivity

[1] **Agricultural Research Station, Tamil Nadu Agricultural University, Kovilpatti - 628 501, Tamil Nadu (India)**
[*] **Scientist, Regional Coffee Research Station, Coffee Board, Thandigudi - 624 216, Tamil Nadu (India)**
[2] **Department of Plant Pathology, Faculty of Agriculture, Annamalai University, Annamalai Nagar - 608 002, Tamil Nadu (India)**

andenvironment quality. Thus, integrated nutrient management has become an accepted strategy to bring about improvement in soil fertility and protecting the environment. This strategy utilizes a judicious combination of fertilizers, organic manures and bio-fertilizers. Bio fertilizer is a natural product carrying living microorganisms derived from the root or cultivated soil. So they don't have any ill effect on soil health and environment. Besides their role in atmospheric nitrogen fixation and phosphorous solubilisation, these also help in stimulating the plant growth hormones providing better nutrient uptake and increased tolerance towards drought and moisture stress. Asmall dose of bio-fertilizer is sufficient to produce desirable results because each gram of carrier of bio-fertilizers contains at least 10 million viable cells of a specific strain.

Bio-fertilizers means the product containing carrier base (solid or liquid) living microbial preparations which are agriculturally useful in terms of nitrogen fixation, phosphorus solubilization or nutrient mobilization toincrease the productivity of the soil and/or crop. These preparations in strict terms are called as microbial inoculants. Bio-fertilizers a cost effective renewable energy source play a crucial role in reducing the inorganic fertilizer level and at the same time increasing the crop yield besides maintaining the soil fertility. The replenishment of nutrients lost by crop removal through the use of chemical fertilizers alone is not advisable in the long run, since their continuous use, impaired the soil health and productivity. Bio-fertilizers can help in reducing the input of inorganic fertilizers for an extent of 25% for obtaining the same or higher yield. Bio-fertilizers are microbial preparations containing live or latent cells of specific microorganisms to apply to the seedor soil, so that the cells can multiply and bringing out the activities of nitrogen fixation or phosphate solubilization/mobilization in the root region or in association with theroot system of crop plants.

IMPORTANCE

Bio-fertilizer has been identified as an alternative to chemical fertilizer to increase soil fertility and crop production in sustainable farming. The use of bio-fertilizers effectively enriches the soil and cost less than chemical fertilizers, which harm the environment and deplete non-renewable energy sources. Bio-fertilizers have definite advantage over chemical fertilizers. Chemical fertilizers supply over nitrogen whereas bio-fertilizers provide in addition to nitrogen certain growth promoting substances like hormones, vitamins, amino acids etc. crops have to be provided with chemical fertilizers repeatedly to replenishthe loss of nitrogen utilized for crop growth. On the other hand bio-fertilizers supply the nitrogen continuously throughout the entire period of crop growth in the field under favourable conditions. Continuous use of chemical fertilizers adversely affects the soil structure whereas bio fertilizers when applied to soil improve the soil structure.The effects of chemical fertilizers are that they are toxic at higher doses. Bio-fertilizers, however, have no toxic effects.

Bio-fertilizers are commonly called as microbial inoculants which are capable of mobilizing important nutritional elements in the soil from non-usable to usable form by the crop plants through their biological processes. For the lastone-decade, bio-fertilizers are used extensively as an ecofriendly approach to minimize the use of chemical fertilizers, improve soil fertility status and for enhancementof crop production by their biological activity in the rhizosphere. Chemical fertilizers are expensive; they disturbthe equilibrium of agro-ecosystems and cause pollution tothe environment. Bio-fertilizers are commonly called as microbial inoculants which are capable of mobilizing important nutritional elements in the soil from non-usable tousable form by the crop plants through their biological. Chemical fertilizers are expensive; they disturb the equilibrium of agro-ecosystems and cause pollution to the environment. These problems may be avoided by the use of bio-fertilizers. The utilization of microbial products has several advantages over conventional chemicals for agricultural purposes:

- Microbial products are considered safer than many of the chemicals now in use.
- Neither toxic substances nor microbes themselves will be accumulated in the food chain.
- Self-replication of microbes circumvents the need for repeated application.
- Target organisms seldom develop resistance as is the case when chemical agents are used to eliminate the pests harmful to plant growth.
- Properly developed bio control agents are not considered harmful to ecological processes or the environment. The deleterious effects of chemical fertilizers are that they are toxic at higher doses. Many of these countries are attempting to farm marginal land that requires an input of nutrients. Current costs for chemical fertilizer are so high that farmers in many developing cannot afford them, and must find alternative nutrient inputs. But bio-fertilizers are no substitute for chemical fertilizers.

  Bio-fertilizers are known to make a number of contributions in agriculture.
- They supplement fertilizer supplies for meeting the nutrient needs of crops.
- They can add 20-200 kg N/ha (by fixation) underoptimum conditions and solubilize/mobilize 30-50 kgP_2O_5/ha.

- They liberate growth promoting substances and vitamins and help maintain soil fertility.
- They suppress the incidence of pathogens and control diseases.
- They increase crop yield by 10-15%, N-fixers reduce depletion of soil nutrients and provide sustainability to the farming system.
- They improve soil physical properties, tilth and soil health in general.

Microorganisms such as bacteria, fungi and actenomyces play a principle role in N fixation and Pavailability in soil which may increase the uptake of N and P through plant roots. These microorganisms could be grown under laboratory conditions and then applied to seeds, roots or directly to the soil. The aim of using N-biofertilizersis to increase soil content of free living bacteria such as; *Azotobacter sp., Azospirillum sp., Klebsiella sp.*and others which are expected to increase N- fixation in the soil. Of course symbiotic bacteria of genus *Rhizobium* is also considered as a good way of N- fixation in legumecrops.

Among the various nutrients, nitrogen is one of the key elements for higher productivity. Nitrogenous fertilizers and biological nitrogen fixation represents the major inputs of nitrogen for crops. Although improved technologies of fertilizer nitrogen production and increased efficiency of fertilizer use by plants could make more nitrogen available for the plants, alternate technologies are being sought toreduce the dependence of plants on fertilizer nitrogen. The nitrogen-fixing microorganisms like *Rhizobium, Azospirillum, Azotobacter, Azolla,* cyanobacteria etc. Fixesnearly 175 × 106 tonnes of N on the earth surface and it may be possible to meet a large part of nitrogen demand through proper manipulation of these organisms in crop production system. Use of efficient strains of bio-fertilizers are environment friendly, low cost agricultural inputs that have an important role in improving nutrient supply to crops but also reducing the cost of production (Kumar, 2013).

Benefits of using BNF (Biological nitrogen fixation)

Economics: BNF reduces costs of bio fertilizers production.

Environment: The use of inoculants as alternatives to Nfertilizer avoids problems of contamination of water resources from leaching and runoff of excess fertilizer.

Efficiency: Legume inoculants do not require high levels of energy for their production or distribution. Application onthe seed is simple compared to spreading fertilizer on the field.

Better yields: Inoculants increase legume crop yields inmany areas. BNF often improves the quality of dietary protein of legume seed even when yield increases are not detected.

Increased soil fertility: Through practices such as green manuring, crop rotations, and alley cropping, N fixing legumes can increase soil fertility, permeability, and organic matter to benefit non-legume crops.

Sustainability: Using BNF is part of the wise management of agricultural systems. The economic, environmental, and agronomic advantages of BNF make it a cornerstone of sustainable agricultural systems.

Azotobacter

Azotobacter represents the main group of heterotrophic free living nitrogen-fixing bacteria. They are Gram negative, large ovoid pleomorphic cells of 1.5-2.0 µm or more in diameter ranging from rods to coccoid cells. They occursingly, in paired or irregular clumps and sometime in chains of varying length. They do not produce endospores but formcysts. They are motile by peritrichous flagella or non-motile. *Azotobacter spp* is most specifically noted for their nitrogen fixing ability but they have also been noted for their ability to produce different growth hormones (IAA and other auxins, such as gibberellins and cytokinins), vitamins. *Azotobacter* is capable of converting nitrogento ammonia, which in turn is taken up by the plants. *Azotobacter sp* can also produce antifungal compounds to fight against many plant pathogens.

Azospirillum

They are called as associative endosymbiont on roots of grasses and similar types of plants. They are also known tofix atmospheric nitrogen and benefit host plants by supplying growth hormones and vitamins. Generally the nitrogen requirement of non-leguminous crops such as cereals, grasses and horticultural crops met partly from the activities of associative symbiotic bacteria – *Azospirillum*. *Azospirillum*is considered to be more efficient and it has been reported that *Azospirillum* inoculation increases the growth, nitrogen uptake and yield in number of crops.

Phosphobacteria

Microorganisms are also involved in the availability of phosphorus, the second most important nutrient required by crop plants. The phosphate solubilizing bacteria (PSB) solubilize the insoluble phosphates and make them available for crop plants in the rhizosphere region. Several soil bacteria and fungi notably species of *Pseudomonas, Bacillus, Penicillium* and *Aspergillus* etc. secrete organic acids and lower the *p*H in their vicinity to bring about solubilization of bound phosphates in soil. Increased in theyield of various crops were demonstrated due to inoculation of peat based cultures of phosphobacteria and saving up to 50 per cent of recommended level of P_2O_5 was observed in many experiments.

Vesicular Arbuscular Mycorrhiza (VAM)

Mycorrhiza is the mutualistic association between plantroots and fungal mycelia. Many graminaceous plants legumes and horticultural crops are highly susceptible toVAM colonization. The transfer of nutrients mainly phosphorus from the soil to the cells of the root cortex is mediated by intracellular obligate fungal endosymbiont of the genera *Glomus, Gigaspora, Acaulospora, Scleroscystis* and *Endogone* which possess vesicles for storage of nutrients and arbuscular for funneling these nutrients into the rootsystem. The mycorrhizal fungi mobilize phosphates andother micronutrients like zinc, boron and molybdenum from adjacent soil to the root system through hyphal network.

GROUNDNUT

Bio fertilizer management in groundnut Bio fertilizers are the source of microbial inoculants, which have brought hopes for many countries both economically and environmentally. Therefore, in developing countries like India, bio fertilizers can solve problems of high cost off fertilizers and thus can save the economy of the country (Gupta *et al.*, 2003). Due to intensive farming India is known as a heavy consumer of chemical fertilizers. The use of chemical fertilizers has been doubled during the last two decades. Thus the coincident application of organic manures and bio fertilizers is frequently recommended firstly for improving biological, physical and chemical properties of soil and secondary to get high and clean agricultural yield products free from undesirable high doses of heavy metals and other pollutants. Biofertilisation, in contrast to the use of chemical fertilizers, is receiving steadily increased attention and recognition from scientists because the microbial inoculants (including e.g. Rhizobium and mycorrhizal fungal inoculants) introduced into soil or plant culture enhances plant productivity directly or indirectly (Mahdi and Atabani, 1992). The highest dry matter production in application of both Rhizobium and phosphobacterium was due to the fact that it produced maximum shoot length, higher number of branches per plant and leaf area index (LAI) (Chetti *et al.*, 1995).

Rhizobium spp. inoculants have favourable effect on legumes like groundnut (Joshi *et al.*, 1989). Phosphobacterium and phosphate solubilizing bacteria able to convert the phosphate present in soil from unavailable to available form. It has indirect effect on nodulation which contribute to increase in yield of groundnut crop (Ghosh and Poi, 1998). In respect of individual bio-fertilizer inoculation, *Rhizobium* spp. seed treatment recorded superiority over PSB inoculation (More *et al.*, 2002; Zaltate and Padmani, 2009).

Seed inoculation with *Rhizobium* has increased the number of nodules, pods per plant, 100-seed weight and gave yields of 1.27 t seeds per ha in groundnut as compared to 1.11 without seed inoculation (Joshi *et al.*, 1989). Asha *et al.* (1996) observed that seed inoculation with *Pseudomonas striata or*

Paecilomyces fussisporus resulted in higher number of nodules plant^{-1}, dry weight of nodules plant^{-1}, protein content in kernels and haulm of groundnut over no inoculation. PSM have synergistic effect on the population of *Rhizobium* in the soil. Patel and Thakur (1997) recorded 8.23 per cent increase in groundnut yield due to *Rhizobium* inoculation compared to uninoculated control.

Baig *et al.* (2002) revealed that significant increase in the growth and yield of groundnut plants treated with *Rhizobium* + PGPR followed by PGPR alone both in field and pot trials. Panwar and Singh (2003) reported that seed inoculation with *Rhizobium* or phosphorus solubilizing microorganisms (PSM) marginally improved yield, but their combined use increased pod yield significantly. Both the organics, i.e. FYM and neem cake, significantly increased pod and haulm yields, but when half quantity of these organics was integrated with *Rhizobium* and PSM, the highest pod yield of 31.80 q/ha with FYM 5tonnes/ha + *Rhizobium* + PSM was obtained. Debasree Gupta (2007) reported that nodule number and weight per plant improved marginally with VAM and MRP treatments, but was much better in cases where FYM was applied. Growth parameters such as plant height, leaflet number and shoot dry weight showed a trend similar to each other. The improvement in all the parameters took place in the following order of the treatments: VAM + FYM (almost 30% over the control) > FYM > VAM+MRP (almost 14% over the control) > VAM > MRP > control. Pod number and weight per plant improved significantly over the control in FYM, VAM + MRP and VAM + FYM (45%, 35% and 50% over the control, respectively) treatments.

At Umiam (Meghalaya), Patel *et al.* (2002) observed that inoculation of *Rhizobium* increased the plant height, number of branches, dry biomass per plant and root length due to increased nitrogenase activities of nodules. Patra *et al.* (2008) observed that application of recommended dose of fertilizer along with inoculation of groundnut seeds with *Rhizobium* strain 1GR-6 or NRCG-9 significantly increased nodules/plant and nodule dry weight/plant at 40 and 80 days after sowing (DAS) during both the year (2004 and 2005) over control.

There was significant influence of nitrogen and *Rhizobium* inoculation on enhanced vegetative growth in terms of number of branches. But the correction studies confined negative association between plant height and number of branches (Edna Antomy *et al.*, 2000). Farmers practice was supplemented with *Rhizobium* inoculation significant increase dry pod yield was observed not only in the first year but during subsequent years under medium deep black soils of Maharashtra (Karmakar *et al.*, 2005).

In sandy loam soils of mid hill zone of Meghalaya, inoculation with *Rhizobium* culture resulted in improvement of pod yield of groundnut but higher values were obtained at dual inoculation of *Rhizobium* and phosphate solubilizing bacteria (Panwar *et al.*, 2002). At Union (Meghalaya), Patel *et al.*, 2002 reported a significant increase in pod yield, 100 pod weight and shelling per cent due to *Rhizobium* inoculation but as of pods/plant, pod weight plant-1 were at par with uninoculated treatment. Datta *et al.* (2014) carried out an experiment at the ICAR Research complex for NEH region, Lembucherra during *kharif* season for 3 consecutive year with 10 different combination of nutrient treatments and found that the inoculation of *Rhizobium* culture along with 50 kg P_2O_5 + 50 kg K_2O/ha showed 45% increment in pod yield (from 1.37 to 1.95 t/ha) over control.

The crop inoculated with bio fertilizers (*Rhizobium* + PSB) recorded significantly higher pod (1.74 t/ha) and haulm yields (3.64 t/ha) of groundnut over control in groundnut – rice cropping system at Deodhe (Maharastra) (Chavan *et al.*, 2014). Mohapatra and Dixit (2010) studied that inoculation with *Rhizobium* improved the nodulation that enhanced N fixation, activation of amino acids for synthesis of carbohydrate and consequently expressed in increase in number of pods/plant, 100 kernel weight and pod yield. Bandyopadhyay *et al.* (2011) reported that local strain of *Rhizobium* inoculation performed better (Rabi 2.22 tons/ha and pre-kharif 2.50 tons/ha) than foreign strain and control during both the season (2005 and 2006) of crop growth. Sharma *et al.* (2013) observed that application of *Rhizobium*, being at par with PSB and VAM, significantly increased number of pods per plant, kernels per pod, seed index, pod, haulm and biological yield and shelling percent over control.

Ram Chatra Singh *et al.* (2013) reported that the highest pod and haulm yield was recorded in *Rhizobium* which was 35.5 and 26.1 per cent higher over no inoculation. Singh *et al.* (2013) observed that maximum seed yield of 1713 kg/ha was recorded with combined inoculation with *Rhizobium* + PSM which was 5.67, 16.60 and 28.60% higher over *Rhizobium*, PSM and inoculated control respectively. Application of *Rhizobium* + PSM increased uptake of N, P, and Ca significantly over the control.Patra *et al.* (2008) found that RDF + *Rhizobium* inoculation with IGR -6 strain increased pod yield by 62% over control and 14.2% over RDF. Sharma *et al.* (2014) observed that the inoculation of *Rhizobium* recorded highest uptake of N, P and K to the tune of 25.5, 23.0 and 18.5 per cent over no inoculation but remained at par with PSB and VAM inoculation during kharif season.

Ola *et al.* (2013) reported that seed inoculation with *Rhizobium* recorded the higher N content and uptake than PSB and found significantly superior to control. Singh *et al.* (2011) reported that application of *Rhizobium* + PSM recorded higher net return of 22, 755/ha with benefit cost ratio of 1.49 followed by *Rhizobium*. Biofertilizers enriched vermicompost (E2 - E6) shows increased growth attributes, yield, protein and oil content than Co and E7. The organic fractions of flower waste vermicompost and the microorganisms in the bio fertilizers could be an alternative to chemical fertilizers to improving the growth and yield of groundnut (Senthil Kumar *et al.*, 2014).

Application of 50% RDF + 5 ton FYM/ha + *Rhizobium* + PSB to groundnut provided an alternate best option of nutrient management in groundnut - pigeon pea relay intercropping system (Poonia *et al.*, 2014). Seed inoculation with bio fertilizers (*Rhizobium* + PSM) significantly increased the plant height, nodules per plant, yield attributing characters and yield of groundnut. Manuring the crop with FYM 6 t/ha + *Rhizobium* + PSM gave significantly 40.19 and 35.96 per cent higher pod and haulm yields of groundnut, respectively over no manuring. Fertilizing the crop with vermicompost 2.0 t/ha + *Rhizobium* + PSM and FYM 3.0 t/ha + *Rhizobium* + PSM found equally effective and significantly superior to control in respect to growth parameters, yield attributes and yield of groundnut (Zalate *et al.*, 2009).

The crop inoculated with bio fertilizers (*Rhizobium* + phosphate-solubilizing bacteria) recorded significantly higher pod (1.74 t/ha) and haulm yields (3.64 t/ha) of groundnut and grain (5.34 t/ha) and straw yields (5.52 t/ha) of succeeding rice over the control. Inoculation of groundnut with bio fertilizers significantly increased N, P, K uptake by groundnut and succeeding rice (except N uptake by rice straw) as well as total N, P and K uptake (393.1 kg/ha), rice-grain equivalent yield (9.92 t/ha), net returns (66.8×103/ha) and benefit: cost ratio (2.01) in groundnut–rice cropping system over no inoculation (Chavan *et al.*, 2014).

At Latur (Maharashtra), seed treatment of dual inoculation of bio-fertilizers (*Rhizobium* + PSB) recorded higher growth and yield attributes, dry pod yield (2381 kg/ha) and haulm yield (3630 kg/ha) than either *Rhizobium* (2159 kg/ha) or PSB (1831 kg/ha) alone in summer groundnut crop (Patil *et al.*, 2014).

At Bhubaneswar (Orissa), integrated application of RDF, *Rhizobium*, FYM, lime and gypsum produced higher pod yield of 2292 kg/ha (Table 9.1). Supplementation of RDF + *Rhizobium* + FYM, RDF+ gypsum (250 kg ha^{-1}), RDF + *Rhizobium* + FYM+ Lime, RDF + *Rhizobium* + FYM+ Lime+ gypsum produced 16.82, 17.73, 26.26 and 39.16% higher pod yield respectively over RDF alone (Baruna Kumar, 2015).

At Junagadh (Gujarat), application of 100% RDF for both the crops recorded higher pigeon pea equivalent (PE) seed yield (2546 kg/ha) which was on par with 50% RDF + 5 ton FYM/ha + *Rhizobium* + PSB by producing 2350 kg/ha PE seed yield (Table 9.2). However, the reduction in chemical fertilizers up to 50% of RDF gave 7.7% less yield over 100% RDF application. Similarly, higher net return was recorded in 100% RDF to both the crops (Rs.64, 400/ha) than 50% RDF + 5 ton FYM/ha + *Rhizobium* + PSB (Rs. 59,300/ha). Application of 50% RDF + 5 ton FYM/ha + *Rhizobium* + PSB to groundnut provided an alternate best option of nutrient management in groundnut-pigeon pea relay intercropping system (Poonia *et al.*, 2014).

Table 9.1
Effect of integrated nutrient management practices on yield and oilcontent of summer groundnut

Treatment	Pod yield (kg /ha)	Haulm yield (kg /ha)	Harvest Index (%)	Oil content (%)	Oil yield (kg /ha)
RDF	1547	3272	30.23	43.9	440
RDF + *Rhizobium* (Seed inoculation)	1715	3389	33.58	44.8	501
RDF + *Rhizobium* + FYM	1924	3567	34.99	46.3	599
RDF + *Rhizobium* + FYM + Lime	2129	3794	37.15	48.4	741
RDF + *Rhizobium* + FYM + Lime + Gypsum	2292	4067	39.30	49.8	850
CD (5 %)	247	245	4.37	2.1	107

(Baruna Kumar, 2015). RDF: 20:40:40 kg NPK/ha, *Rhizobium*: Seed inoculation 20 g/kg of kernel, FYM: 10 t /ha, Lime: 0.2 LR, Gypsum: 250 kg /ha.Sesame

Imayavaramban *et al.* (2002) reported that the integrated nutrient supply with farmyard manure at 12.5 t/ha + recommended NPK of 35:23:23 kg/ha +*Azospirillum* seed inoculum favorably improved the varied yield attributes and yield of sesame. Sarala and Jagannatham (2002) in red loam soils of Tirupati reported that application of 60 kg N/ha to sesame produced seed yieldwhich was comparable to that of 45 kg N/ha + *Azospirillum.*

Jaishankar and Wahab (2005) reported that application ofrecommended dose of NPK + vermicompost at 5.0 t/ha + *Azospirillum* recorded higher yield components of sesame viz., number of capsules/plant and number of seeds/capsule. Duhoon *et al.* (2002) reported thatthe highest yield of sesame was recorded under 50% N through urea+ 50% N through FYM + 50% P with soil application of PSB at 500gm/ha + 100 % potash. Further Munji *et al.* (2010) reported that the combined application of RDF + FYM +*Azospirillum* showed the highest yield and yield component of sesame.Shaikh *et al.* (2010) reported that the seed weight per plant, seed andstalk yields and grain to stalk ratio were favourably influenced due to application of RDF+5 t FYM/ ha+5 t vermicompost /ha + seed treatment of *Azospirillum* and PSB followed by the application of 75% RDF + 5 t FYM/ha + 5 t vermicompost/ha + seed treatment of *Azospirillum* and PSB.

Gosh and Mohiuddin (2002) further reported that the use of bio fertilizers or growth regulator significantlyincreased the yield component such as number of capsules/plant and number of seeds/capsule. At Rahuri (Maharashtra), Deshmukh *et al.* (2010a) reported that the growth attributes like plant height and number of branches/plant, yield attribute like number of capsules/plant and test weight as well as yield were favorably influenced due to application of RDF + 5 t/ha each of FYM and vermicompost + seed treatment with *Azospirillum* and PSB and this treatment was significantly superior to all other treatments followed by 75 per cent RDF + 5 t/ha each of FYM and vermicompost + seed treatment with *Azospirillum* and PSB in summer sesame on clayey soil.

Table 9.2

Effect of different organic, inorganic and bio fertilizers on growth and yield attributes of groundnut and pigeon pea

Treatments	Groundnut				Pigeonpea			Pigeonpea seed equivalent yield (kg/ha)
	100 seed weight (g)	Shelling (%)	Pod yield (kg/ha)	Haulm yield (kg/ha)	Pods/ plant	Seed yield (kg/ha)	Stalk yield (kg/ha)	
100 % RDF for both crops	41.7	68.7	1299	1708	202.0	1501	1681	2546
FYM10 t/ha	41.1	67.3	1009	1428	150.6	1122	1334	1969
VC1 t/ha	41.4	68.1	991	1463	146.7	1075	1228	1900
50 % RDF + FYM 5 t/ha	41.3	69.6	1037	1475	131.3	1091	1289	1960
50 % RDF + VC1 t/ha	42.0	69.0	983	1414	144.8	1174	1372	1990
50 % RDF + FYM 5 t/ha + *Rhizobium* +PSB	42.0	69.1	1162	1632	180.2	1382	1520	2350
50 % RDF + FYM 1 t/aha + *Rhizobium* +PSB	41.5	67.6	1102	1631	170.0	1287	1439	2182
CD (5 %)	NS	NS	115.3	NS	32.6	168	173	198

Rhizobium @ 25 g/kg seed + PSB @ 30 g/kg seed.RDF: recommended doses of fertilizers for groundnut and pigeon pea are 12.5:25:00 and 25:50:00 kg NPK/ha.

Palaniappan *et al.* (1999) reported that seed inoculation with bio fertilizers (*Azospirillum* and phosphobacteria) significantly increased the plant height, number of branches/plant in sesame. Jaishankar and Wahab (2005) reported that seed inoculation with *Azospirillum* recorded the highest growth viz., plant height, leaf area index (LAI) and dry matter production of sesame. Deshumkh *et al.* (2010b) reported that growth attributes like plant height and number of branches per plant in summer sesame was favourably influenced due to seed inoculation with *Azospirillum.*

Palaniappan *et al.* (1999) reported that integrated application of farmyard manure at 10 t/ha and 100 % recommended dose of N and P and bio fertilizers (*Azospirillum* and phosphobacteria) significantly increased the number of capsules/plant and seed yield. Gosh and Mohiuddin (2002) reported that combined application of bio fertilizers and growth regulator improved all the yield and yield attributes and thus markedly increased grain and stalk yields. *Azospirillum* increases dry matter production and yields in sesame (Senthilkumar *et al.*, 2000). Application of *Azospirillum* increased protein yield of sesame (Thiruppathi *et al.*, 2001).Imayavaramban *et al.* (2002) reported that the *Azospirillum* seed inoculum favorably improved the varied yield attributes and yield of sesame. Researches on the nutrition of sesame in the tropics have shown significant yield increase due to inorganic and biofertilizers in India (Kalaiselvan *et al.*, 2002). Sarala and Jagannatham (2002) in red loam soils of Tirupati reported that application of 60 kg N/ha to sesame produced seed yield which was comparable to that of 45 kg N/ha + *Azospirillum.*

The combined application of inorganic and bio fertilizer might have increased the number of seeds per capsule, due to better absorption of applied nutrient by the plant system and increased photosynthetic activity and translocation of nutrients rapidly to the sink (Subramanian *et al.*, 1999; Paramasivam *et al.*, 2003).Integrated application of chemical fertilizer and biofertilizer supplied plant nutrients for a longer period and higher uptake of nutrients by sesame (Duhoon *et al.*, 2004).

Jaishankar and Wahab (2005) reported that seed inoculation with *Azospirillum* recorded higher yield components of sesame viz., number of capsules/plant and number of seeds/capsule. Munji *et al.* (2010) reported that seed inoculation with *Azospirillum* showed the highest yield and yield component of sesame. Shaikh *et al.* (2010) reported that the seed weight per plant, seed and stalk yields and grain to stalk ratio were favourably influenced due to seed treatment of *Azospirillum* and PSB.

Table 9.3

Number of seeds/plant, number of seeds/capsule, test weight, seed and straw yield of sesame as influenced by various treatments

Treatments	Seeds/ plant	Seeds/ capsule	Test weight (g)	Seed yield (kg/ ha)	Straw yield (kg/ha)
Fertilizer grades					
80% RDF	1513	36.54	2.69	529	1827
100% RDF	1867	38.77	2.70	648	2156
120% RDF	2026	40.34	2.71	701	2234
CD 5%	222	2.14	NS	57	177
Biofertilizers					
Azotobacter	1620	36.52	2.69	550	1839
PSB	1850	39.26	2.71	646	2159
Azotobacter+ PSB	1932	40.00	2.71	682	2219
CD 5%	222	2.14	NS	57	177

(Wayase *et al.*, 2014).RDF: 25:50:00 kg NPK/ha

At Latur (Maharashtra), higher number of seeds per plant, capsules per plant, test weight, seed yield, straw yield, biological yield and harvest index was recorded from 30:60:00 kg NPK/ha. Combined application of *Azotobacter* + PSB registered higher number of seeds per plant, capsules per plant, test weight, seed yield, straw yield, biological yield and harvest index (Wayase *et al.*, 2014).

The oil yield increased by 33.3%, while protein yield increased by 47.5% with treatment of halfdose of fertilizer along with LES 4 (*Pseudomonas aeruginosa*) bacterized seeds, as compared to full dose of fertilizers (Kumar *et al.*, 2009). Seed production of six sesame genotypes after seed inoculation with either *Azotobacter* or *Azosprillum* along with Phospho-bactrin and Potash solubilising bacteria in both cases, un-inoculated control was included for comparison. *Azotobacter* was able to produce seeds with either significantly higher or similar 1000 seed weight. Variation in performance of individual genotypes after different bio-fertilizer application indicated existence of genotype specific response for the parameters studied (Debnath *et al.*, 2007). Soil inoculation with micro-symbiontinocula (particularly *Azospirilium spp.*), may be suitable for improving sesame performance in the study areas, where soils are mostly very low in essential nutrients (particularly N) (Babajide and Fagbola, 2014).

SUNFLOWER

Application of PSB, *Bacillus* M-13 was able to mobilize P efficiently in the sunflower and enhanced the head diameter, 1000 seed weight, kernel ratio and oil content and led to seed and oil yield increase to 15 and 24.7 per cent respectively over no application. Higher seed yield of sunflower possible with 100 kg P_2O_5/ha fertilizer was achieved with about 50 kg P_2O_5/ha when used in conjunction with PSB (ZehraEkin., 2010).

Inoculation of bio fertilisers and sulphur has significant effect on yield and yield attributes of sunflower. However, PSB + VAM + *Azotobacter*, as well as application of sulphur @40 kg /ha may be considered as the best treatment for sunflower, with respect to height, total chlorophyll content, thalamus diameter, weight of thalamus, filled seeds capitulum^{-1} and 100 seed weight, grain yield, stalk yield, biological yield, harvest index and oil content (Patra *et al.*, 2013). The crop was fertilized with respective dose of NPK of 80:100:100 kg /ha. Results revealed that inoculation of bio fertilizers significantly affected plant height and total chlorophyll content. Bio fertilizers also significantly increased yield attributes, viz. thalamus diameter, weight of thalamus, filled seeds capitulum^{-1}, and 100 seed weight (g), as well as seed and biological yield and oil content. The bio fertilizers used as inoculum for seeds treatment of sunflower cv. Geza 1 were *Azospirillum* (nitrogen fixing bacteria, N.F.B.) and *Bacillus polymyxa* (phosphate dissolving bacteria, P.D.B.) and their mixture. Both bacterial inoculants and their mixture showed an increase in growth parameters, nutrients content and yield when compared to the control (fulldose of NPK chemical fertilization). The results revealed that bio fertilization treatments of *Azospirillum* + *Bacillus* plus 100% chemical fertilizers produced the highest values in all growth and yield parameterscompared with the control (Mostafa and AboBaker, 2010).

Bio fertilizer can increase the soil fertility, the seed yield and its oil content (Dhanasekar and Dhandapani, 2012). Higher stem girth was recorded with the 100 % N+ *Azospirillum* + *Azotobacter* which was significantly superior over all other treatments, except 75 % N + *Azospirillum* + *Azotobacter* (Keshta *et al.*, 2006; Javahery and Rokhzadi, 2011; Farnia and Moayedi, 2014; Farnia and Moayedi, 2015). Lower leaf area due to less number of leaves was found with control (Nandhagopal *et al.*, 2003; Mirparsa *et al.*, 2016; Shehata and El-Khawas, 2013). Patra *et al.* (2013) also reported that bio fertilizers helped in increasing plant height and leaf chlorophyll content of sunflower.

At Tehran (Iran), bio fertilizer improved plant productivity and quality in sunflower seed. Application of bio fertilizer decreased the saturated fatty acids (palmitic and stearic) and increased unsaturated fatty acids (linoleic acid and oleic acid) and oil content, compared with untreated plants (Akbari *et al.*, 2011). At Birbhum (West Bengal), inoculation of bio fertilizers significantly increased aerial biomass production, CGR, test weight, weight of thalamus, number of filled seeds per capitulum and as well as seed yield, biological yield and oil content. The combined inoculation of PSB + VAM + Azotobacter recorded higher seed yield (3225kg /ha) over Azotobacter, PSB + Azotobacter and VAM + Azotobacter inoculation (Pramanik and Bera, 2013).

Table 9.4

Effect of biofertilizer and different fertilizer levels on yield attributes of sunflower

Treatments	Seed yield (kg/ha)	Filled seeds/ plant	Unfilled seeds/ plant	Test weight (g)
Control	705	441	166	45.47
75% Nitrogen	1300	605	142	46.74
100% Nitrogen	1383	665	129	47.26
75% N + Azospirillum	1341	644	141	46.77
75% N + Azotobacter	1343	654	134	47.05
75% N + Azospirillum +Azotobacter	1784	774	102	49.05
100% N + Azospirillum	1667	714	127	48.16
100% N + Azotobacter	1699	742	124	48.32
100% N+Azospirillum + Azotobacter	1848	802	99	49.72
CD 5%	180	99	15	NS

(Khandekar *et al.*, 2018)

At Parbhani (Maharashtra), application of 100% N + *Azospirillum*+ *Azotobacter* recorded higher seed yield (1848 kg /ha) with net monetary return (Rs.34313) and B: C ratio (1.96) (Khandekar *et al.*, 2018).

SOYBEAN

Seed inoculation with *Rhizobium* has increased the number ofnodules, pods per plant, 100-seed weight and gave yields of 0.97 t/ha as compared to 0.88 t/hawithout seed inoculation (Joshi *et al.*, 1989). Pandzou *et al.* (1990) and Singh *et al.* (2007) noticed that inoculation of *Rhizobium*increased the seed yield from 21 to 41 per cent in soybean and there wasno significant difference between seed treatment and soil application. Phosphate solubilizing bacterium (PSB) has a capacity to render the insoluble soil phosphorus into plant available form because of their ability to secrete various organic acids (Gautam and Pant 2002; Mookherjee *et al.*, 2014).

Rhizobium RS-1 was significantly increased the N and K availability by 19.57 and 5.47 per cent over control due to increased nitrogen fixation with the *Rhizobium* inoculation (Dubey, 1998; Dubey, 2000; Meshram *et al.* 2005). Interaction effect of liquid *Brady rhizobium* and PSB increased the seed yield of soybean (Deshmukh, 2005). Govindan and Thirumurugan (2003) found any change in EC with the treatment of bio-inoculants in soybean.

Rhizobium culture @ 1.25 kg/188 kg seed/ha can be used as seed treatment. Cross inoculation group: *R. japonicum* slow growing type strain will form the root nodules in soybean crop andfixes nitrogen efficiently. Inoculation of soybean seedswith proper bacterial strains increased seed production by 70-75% (Simanungkalit *et al.*, 1996). The application of phosphate-solubilizing bacteria in soybean crop revealed that most examined traits were better than chemical fertilizer (Zarei *et al.*, 2012; Singh *et al.*, 2009). Soybean plants, as inoculated *Brady rhizobium japonicum* with plots appeared much greener (Thelenand Schulz, 2010). Some of the popular varieties of soybean (J.S-335, PK-1029, MACS-124 and LSB-1) in the statewere treated with commercially available *Brady rhizobium* bio fertilizer and compared with no *Brady rhizobium* inoculation plus recommended dose of N fertilizer and a Control without fertilizer and without *Brady rhizobium* inoculation. Different plant characteristics *viz.*, nodule number, nodule dry weight, plant dry weight and nitrogen content were determinedon 45 day old plants to identify nitrogen fixation responsive soybean variety among the soybean varieties. Among the popular four soybean varieties J.S-335, PK-1029, MACS-124 and LSB-1 used in potculture experiment conducted in the present study, variety J.S-335 showed significantly better response to *Brady rhizobium japonicum* biofertiizer treatment compared to other varieties (Naveen kumar *et al.*, 2010).

Sawarkar and Thakur (2001) found that nodule number and its weight/ plant, plant height, number of branches, number of pods andseed index has significantly improved with seed/soil inoculation of PSB in combination with chemical fertilizers. The yield was highest (1950 kg/ha) with the treatment of 100 per cent P_2O_5 and seed inoculation of PSB (2 kg/ha) followed by soil application + 100 per cent P_2O_5 (1867 kg/ha) compare to other treatments. Meshram *et al.* (2004) found that there was significant improvement in soil fertility status by co-inoculation of *Rhizobium* + PSBalong with chemical fertilizers in soybean. There was significant improvement in the amounts of available N, P_2O_5 and K_2O in all the bio fertilizer treated plots. Menaria and Pushpendra Singh (2004) observed that application of N40+P40+K20+S40 kg/ha have significantly increased the yield attributing characters in soybean. Seed inoculation with various inoculants viz., *rhizobium japonicum* and phosphate solubilizing bacteria and *Brady rhizobium japonicum* + phosphate solubilizing bacteria has significantly improved the seed and stover yield over control. Jain and Trivedi (2005) found that the combined application of *Rhizobium* and PSB resulted in higher seed yield, oil yield and protein content in soybean.

At Latur (Maharashtra), availability of nitrogen in soil was increased by seed inoculation with liquid 10ml of Brady rhizobium. Phosphorus availability in soil was improved by seed inoculation with liquid 10ml of PSB. However in later stages N uptake in soybean was increased significantly due to seed inoculation with 10ml of PSB. Organic carbon content in experimental soil was improved due to residual effect of soybean crop grown under liquid biofertilizers treatment (Raja and Takankhar, 2017).

Different components like bio fertilizers (Kumrawat *et al.*, 1997), phosphours and biofertilziers (Sharma and Namdeo, 1999; Thanki *et al.*, 2005) increased the yield of soybean. At Raipur (Chhattisgarh), maximum response in terms of seed yield of soybean was observed in treatment with application of 100 per cent RDF plus FYM (10 t/ha) plus zinc (5 kg/ ha) plus magnesium (10 kg/ha) plus rhizobium plus PSB (65% increase over control), which was at par with 100 per cent RDF, 50 per cent RDF plus FYM (10 t/ha) plus zinc (5 kg/ha) plus magnesium (10kg/ha), 50 per cent RDF plus FYM (5 t/ha) plus zinc (5kg/ha) plus magnesium (10 kg/ha) plus rhizobium plus PSB and 50 per cent RDF plus FYM (10 t/ha) (Joshi, 2003; Sonkar *et al.*, 2008).

Greater availability of nutrients with the application of microbial inoculants (R2 and psr) seems to have promoted various physiological activities in plant which are considered to be indispensable for proper growth and development (Krishna *et al.*, 1995; Umale *et al.*, 2002). At Latur (Maharashtra), 100% RDF + 10 t FYM+ 45 kg S/ha + Bio fertilizer recorded significantly higher number of flowers, pods and grains per plant but it was at par 50% RDF + 10 t FYM+ 45 kg S/ ha + Bio fertilizer with the highest grain 2731 kg/ha and straw 4111 kg/ha yield were recorded due to treatment 100% RDF + 10 t FYM+ 45 kg S/ha + Bio fertilizer followed by treatment 50% RDF + 10 t FYM+ 45 kg S/ha + Bio fertilizer under rainfed condition during *kharif* season (Ghodke *et al.*, 2018).

Table 9.5

Effect of integrated nutrient management on yield attributes and yield of soybean

Treatments	Pods/ Plant	Grains/ Plant	Grain yield (q/ha)	Straw yield (q/ha)
100% RDF	50.0	83.33	44.66	83.33
100% RDF + 10 t FYM/ha	51.66	108.3	57.00	108.3
50% RDF +10 t FYM/ha + Biofertilizer	47.33	99.33	52.33	99.33
100% RDF+10 t FYM/ha + Biofertilizer	54.0	111.3	59.66	111.3
100% RDF+ 45 Kg S/ha	41.66	87.66	50.66	87.66
50% RDF+10 t FYM/ha + 45 kg S/ha	50.00	102.3	55.0	102.3
100% RDF+45 kg S/ha + Biofertilizer	43.33	93.33	49.33	93.33
50% RDF+10t FYM/ha + 45 kg S/ha + Biofertilizer	57.0	117.6	63.00	117.6
50% RDF+10t FYM/ha + 45 kg S/ha + Biofertilizer	62.0	123.0	67.66	123.0
CD (5%)	7.80	9.80	6.74	9.80

(Ghodke *et al.*, 2018)

At Akola (Maharashtra), application of 50% N through glyricidia green manuring + 50% N through inorganics + bio fertilizers + 25 kg K/ha resulted in higher yield and nutrient uptake by soybeanover other INM practices (Satpute *et al.*, 2018).

SAFFLOWER

In Ilam (Iran), farmers can obtain the same safflower yield if they apply half of conventional consumption of nitrogen (60 kg N /ha) with bio-fertilizers. In this way, decreasing nitrogen fertilizer can be reduced the environment pollution and developed sustainable agriculture (Naseri and Mirzaei, 2010). Seed inoculation with *Azospirillum* alone resulted in enhanced growth in terms of plant height and other yield attributing characters and was on par with 50% recommended inorganic N application. Seed inoculation with *Azospirillum* both alone and in combination with 50% recommended inorganic N has resulted in on parseed yield with treatment supplied with 50% N and 100% inorganic nitrogen respectively. Interestingly, seed inoculation with *Azotobacter* did not cause any improvement in seed yield. This assumes that seed inoculation with *Azospirillum* could result in absolute saving of 50% of inorganic nitrogen (Sudhakar and Sudha Rani,

2010). Increasing uptake of NPK was observed with the increase in RDF level along with seed treatment with Azospirillum+ PSB (Naseri Rahim *et al.*, 2010).

Table 9.6

Effect of INM on yield and nutrient uptake by soybean

Treatments	Grain yield (kg/ha)	Straw yield (kg/ha)	Nutrient uptake (kg/ha)		
			N	P	K
Control	939	1352	52.79	10.15	10.15
100% RDF (30:75:00 NPK kg/ha)	1063	1707	72.35	13.50	13.50
100% RDF + biofertilizers	1083	1819	77.29	15.93	15.93
100% N through FYM + biofertilizers	1028	1574	62.72	12.64	12.64
100% RDF +25kg K /ha	1193	1871	84.21	17.29	17.29
100% N through FYM + biofertilizers + 25kg K /ha	1220	1894	87.84	19.48	19.48
50% N through green leaf manure + 50% N through inorganics	1042	1662	68.67	15.27	15.27
50% N through green leaf manure + 50% N through inorganics + biofertilizers	1179	1871	84.95	18.52	18.52
50% N through green leaf manure +50% N through inorganics+ biofertilizers + 25kg K/ha	1255	2039	96.04	21.19	21.19
CD 5%	184	344	10.64	1.91	1.91

(Satpute *et al.*, 2018)

At Parbhani (Mharashtra), Kadu and Ismail (2008) reported improvement in dry matter (3154 kg/ha) and seed yield (1230 kg /ha) of safflower with application of full RDF (60-40-0 kg NPK/ha) + vermicompost 5 t/ha + vermiwash spray + bio fertilizer + cow dung urine slurry as compared to RDF alone or organics alone on Vertisol. Hegde (1998) observed there was an increase seed yield upto (6.71 q/ ha) due to the 100% of recommended NPK through inorganic fertilizers and 100% N or P by the use of Azotobacter and phosphorus solubilising bacteria (PSB)in safflower based cropping systems.

At Solapur (Maharashtra), significantly higher seed yield (1189 kg/ha) of safflower was recorded under RDF (50:25:0 NPK kg/ha + chemical control). Application of FYM @ 5 t/ha + Bio fertilizer+ bio pesticide (Neem cake @ 200kg/ ha, *Trichoderma* seed treatment @ 5 g/kg seed + spray of NSKE 5%) and FYM alone @ 6.5 t/ha were at par with RDF (50:25:0 NPK kg/ha + chemical control). Numerically higher values of test weight

(5.87 g) were recorded under FYM @ 2.5 t/ha + bio fertilizer and FYM (equal to 50 kg N = 6.5 t/ha). Significantly higher uptake of nitrogen was recorded under RDF (50:25:0 NPK kg/ha) + chemical control and it was at par with FYM @ 5t/ha + bio fertilizer + bio pesticide in respect of P_2O_5 and K_2O (Naik *et al.*, 2007; Khadtare *et al.*, 2016).

Table 9.7

Yield and uptake of nutrients by safflower crop as influenced by various treatments

Treatments	Grain yield (q/ha)	Straw yield (q/ha)	Uptake of nutrients (kg /ha)		
			N	P	K
Control	15.95	45.20	55.88	7.62	71.32
75% RDF	19.97	68.18	81.70	11.70	125.66
75% RDF + Azospirillum + PSB	20.53	69.42	84.15	12.16	138.05
100% RDF	21.00	69.84	95.17	13.72	142.21
100% RDF + Azospirillum + PSB	23.00	84.68	112.02	16.99	173.88
125% RDF	21.68	76.24	100.60	14.67	156.50
125% RDF + Azospirillum + PSB	21.82	77.17	105.87	15.40	165.90
CD (5 %)	0.34	0.27	1.44	1.05	2.54

(Shillode *et al.*, 2016)

At Nagpur (Maharashtra), higher organic carbon (6.5 g/kg), available NPK (112.02, 16.99 and 173.88 kg/ha) and available Fe, Mn, Zn and Cu (7.26, 15.72 1.12 and 1.80 mg/kg respectively) were recorded in the treatment of 100 % RDF + Azospirillum + PSB. Application of 100% RDF + Azospirillum + PSB improved the yield and significantly increased the uptake of NPK by safflower (Shillode *et al.*, 2016)

INDIAN MUSTARD

Indian mustard crop also responds favorably to bio-fertilizers viz., *Azotobacter* (Azo) and phosphorus solubilizing bacteria (PSB) (Vyas, 2003).Bio-fertilizer with *Azotobacter* inoculation decreases the nitrogen requirement of crop (Chauhan *et al.*,1996).

At Kukma (Gujarat), the interaction between bio-fertilizers and N was foundto be significant. On an average Azosprillum increased seed yield by 27.1% over control, but this increase was 22.7% only incase of PSB. The crop receiving 30 kg N/ha and inoculated with bio fertilizer (Azosprillum) produced seed equivalent to the cropreceiving 60 kg N/ha (Vyas, 2005).

Phosphate solubilizing bacteria inoculants when applied to mustard promote seed germination and initial vigour of plants by producing growth promoting substances. Application of bio fertilizers results in increased mineral and water uptake, root development, vegetative growth and nitrogen fixation (Gangwal *et al.*, 2011).

Table 9.8

Effect of PSB on seed and straw yield of mustard

Treatments	Seed yield (kg/ha)	Straw yield (kg/ha)
PSB inoculation	18.14	47.04
Control	17.28	42.52
C.D (5 %)	0.39	1.12

(Solanki *et al.*, 2015)

At Chittorgarh (Rajasthan),the seed yield of 1814 and straw yield 4704 q /ha from plants emerging from bio fertilizer inoculated seeds recorded consistently and significantly greater than seed yield of 1727 and straw yield 4252 kg/ha in plants from bio fertilizer control (Solanki *et al.*, 2015 and Kumar and Kumar.,1994).

The maximum yield was obtained by the sulphur application @ 40 kg/ ha and by the source of biofertilizer (B1) @ *Azotobacter*/10 kg seed inoculates. The interaction between sulphur and biofertilizer was significant and the maximum increase in yield was obtained by applied sulphur @ 40 kg/ ha at bio fertilizer (B0, B1) 0 and 200 g *Azototobacter*/10 kg seed inoculate. The soil samples collected after harvest of mustard crop showed the slight decrease in pH and EC and increase in organic carbon, available nitrogen, phosphorus, potassium and sulphur was recorded by the application of sulphur and bio fertilizer applied alone orin conjunction with each other (Yadav *et al.*, 2010).

At Kolkata (West Bengal), significantly higher leaf area index (1.75 at 40 days after sowing; DAS), dry matter accumulation (1366.9 g/m^2 at 80 DAS) and higher number of siliquae/plant (118.3), number of seeds/siliqua (21.8), seed yield (1.90 t/ha), stover yield (3.86 t/ha) were recorded significantly (at 5% level) higher with poultry manure (PM) @2.5t/ha +50%RDF (Recommended Dose of Fertilizer *i.e.* 80:40:40 kg NPK/ha) + PSB (phosphate solubilizing bacteria) + AZ (*Azotobacter*) during both the years and on pooled basis. An average of 30.5% and 233% increase in seed yield by this treatment was recorded over sole application of RDF and control respectively. Integrated application of PM (2.5 t/ha) + 50% RDF + PSB + AZ recorded highest oil content (43.16%) and positive effect on soil fertility status. Higher benefit: cost ratios (2.26 and 2.4 respectively) were achieved from the use of 50% RDF + PM (2.5 t/ha) +PSB+AZ during winter season (Amrit Raj and Mallick (2017). Gudadhe *et al.* (2005) agreed beneficial role of bio fertilizer in improving yield components of Indian mustard.

Mookherjee *et al.* (2014) reported use of organic manure (like, farm yard manure) in combination with bio fertilizers and reduced dose of chemical fertilizers found to increase net return in yellow sarson.

Mustard and rapeseeds gave good response to *Azotobacter* growth and development, seed yield and oil yield. Incidence of some diseases of mustard and rapeseeds could be reduced by inoculating with *Azotobacter*. Better results were given when seeds were treated in combination with *Azotobacter* and N (Singh *et al.*, 2006). Farmers should be advised to mix Bio fertilizers to get benefits of thesynergistic effect on plant growth and ultimately on yield, but multi strains bio fertilizers may be avoided (Khan *et al.*, 2012). Sulphur @40 kg /ha and bio fertilizer @200 g *Azotobacter* per 10 kg seed inoculated (S2B1) treatment combination was the best treatment as compared toothers (Yadav and Thomas, 2010). Integrated use of biofertilizers, FYM with 40 kg of nitrogen gave seed yield equal to the 80 kg N/ha alone. Maximum seed yield was obtained in the use of higher doses of N fertilizer in conjunctions with bio fertilizers and FYM in both years (Singh *et al.*, 2014).

At Allahabad (Uttar Pradesh), Azotobacter + PSB + 30 kg/ ha N through inorganic Fertilizer + 30 kg/ ha N through organic manure poultry manure (PM) produced significantly higher plant height 75 Days (95.53 cm), number of branch/plant (8.37), dry weight (15.58 g). Significantly higher siliqua/plant (235.33), seed siliqua/plant (20.40), test weight (4.17 g), seed yield (1500 kg/ha), stover yield (3790 kg/ha), harvest index (28.36 %) and oil content (42.03%) was recorded in Azotobacter + PSB + 30 kg/ha N through inorganic Fertilizer + 30 kg/ha N through poultry manure (PM). Azotobacter + PSB + 30 kg/ha N through inorganic Fertilizer + 30 kg/ha N through poultry manure (PM) also recorded the higher gross return (67740/ ha), net return (33265/ha) and benefit cost ratio (1.96) (Saini *et al.*, 2017).

CONCLUSION

Effect of locally available organic manures, green manures and bio-fertilizers in different combinations improve growth and yield of vegetables which can improve the economics of cultivation of farmers. The potential nitrogen fixing biological systems like *Azospirillum*, phosphorus-solubilizing bacteria such as *Bacillus* and *Pseudomonas* and the vesicular arbuscular mycorrhizae plays a triggering role in nitrogen and phosphorus nutrition of horticultural crops under protected cultivation. Application of biological fertilizer greatly involved in the accumulation of soil enzymes, which directly reflects on soil fertility index. The effective utilization of bio-fertilizers for crops not only provide economic benefits to the farmers but also improves and maintain the soil fertility andsustainability in natural soil ecosystem.

REFERENCES

Akbari, P., Ghalavand, A., Modarres Sanavy, A.M. and M.A. Alikhani. 2011. Effect of Bio fertilizers, Nitrogen Fertilizer and Farmyard Manure on Grain yield and Seed Quality of Sunflower (*Helianthus annus*L.) Effect of Bio fertilizers, Nitrogen Fertilizer and Farmyard Manure on Grain yield and Seed Quality of Sunflower (*Helianthus annus*L.). Journal of Agricultural Technology, 7(1): 173-184.

Amrit Raj and R.B. Mallick. 2017. Effect of Integrated Nutrient Management on Growth, Productivity, Quality and Nutrient uptake of Irrigated Yellow Sarson (*Brassica campestris*L var. Yellow Sarson) in Older Alluvial Soil of West Bengal. *Journal of Applied and Natural Science,* 9 (3): 1411-1418.

Asha, C., D.D. Metha, B.B. Malavia and V.D. Khanpara.1996. Response of Groundnut (*Arachishypogaea)* to Farmyard Manure, Phosphorus and Phosphate-solubilizing Microorganism. *Indian J. Agron.,* 41(1): 172-174.

Babajide PA, Fagbola O. 2014. Growth, Yield and Nutrient Uptakes of Sesame (Sesamumindicum L.) as Influenced by Biofertilizer Inoculants. Int. J. Curr. Microbiol. App. Sci., 3(8): 859-867.

Baig, M.M.V., Mia Baig and S.M. Muley. 2002. Enhanced Growth of Groundnut by Plant Growth Promoting Rhizobacteria. *Int. Arachis News,* 22: 60-63.

Bandyopadhyay, S, L. Sharma, A.K. Roy and D. Gupta. 2011. Season wise Performance of Groundnut (*Arachishypogaea*) Cultivars as Influenced by Local and Foreign Strain of Rhizobium Inoculation, *Indian Journal of Agricultural Sciences,* 81(1): 60-66.

Baruna Kumar, B. 2015. Effect of Integrated Nutrient Management Practices in Summer Groundnut (*Arachishypogaea*L.).M.Sc (Agronomy) Thesis, Department of Agronomy, College of Agriculture, Orissa University of Agriculture and Technology, Bhubaneswar, Orissa.

Chauhan, O.R., Paroda, S. and Ram, M. 1996. Response of Indian Mustard *(Brassica juncea)* to Biofertilizers, Sulphur and Nitrogen Fertilization. *Indian Journal of Agronomy,* 41: 620-623.

Chavan, A.P, N.K. Jain and U.V. Mahadkar. 2014. Direct and Residual Effects of Fertilizers Biofertilizers on yield Nutrient uptake and Economics of Groundnut (*Arachishypogaea*)-rice (*Oryza sativa*) Cropping System. *Indian Journal of Agronomy,* 59 (1): 53-58.

Chavan, A.P., N.K. Jai and U.V. Mahadkar. 2014. Direct and Residual Effects of Fertilizers and Biofertilizers on yield, Nutrient uptake and Economics of Groundnut (Arachishypogaea)–rice (*Oryza sativa*) Cropping System. Indian Journal of Agronomy, 59 (1): 53-58.

Chetti, M.B., E. Antony, U.V. Mummigatti and M.B Dodamani. 1995. Role of Nitrogen and Rhizobium on Nitrogen Utilization Efficiency and Productivity Potential in Groundnut Genotypes. Farming Systems. 11(1-2): 209-216.

Datta, M., G.S. Yadav and S.Chakraborty. 2014. Integrated Nutrient Management in Groundnut (*Arachishypogaea*) in Sub-tropical Humid Climate of North-east India. *Indian Journal of Agronomy* 59(2): 322-326.

Debasree Gupta. 2007. Effect of VAM and Soil Amendments on the Nodulation, Growth and yield of Groundnut in Acid Lateritic Soil. *J. of Mycopathological Res.* 45(1): 51-53.

Debnath S, Moharana RL, Basu AK. 2007. Evaluation of Sesame (*Sesamum indicum* L.) Genotypes for its Seed Production Potential as Influenced by Biofertilizer. Journal of Crop and Weed, 3 (2):33-36.

Deshmukh, K.K., Khatik, S.K. and D.P. Dubey. 2005. Effect of Integrated use of Inorganic, Organic and Bio fertilizers on Production, Nutrient Availability and Economic Feasibility of Soybean Grown on Soil of Claymore Plateau and Satpura Hills. *J. Soils and Crops,* 15 (1): 21-25.

Deshmukh, S.S., A.A. Saikh, M.M. Desai and R.S. Kamble. 2010b. Effect of Integrated Nutrient Management on yield Sesamum (*Sesamum indicum L.*). *J. Maharastra agric. Univ.,* 35(3): 453-455.

Deshumkh, S.S., A.A. Shaikh and M.M. Desai. 2010 a. Influence of Integrated Nutrient Management on Growth and yield Contributing Characters of Summer Sesame. *Journal of Maharashtra Agricultural Universities,* 35(1): 3-6.

Dhanasekar, R. and Dhandapani, R. 2012. Effect of Biofertilizers on the Growth of *Helianthus annuus. International Journal of Plant, Animal and Environmental Sciences,* 2(4).

Dubey, S.K. 2000. Effectiveness of Rock Phosphate and Super Phosphate Amended with Phosphate Solubilizing Microorganism in Soybean Grown in Vertisols. J. Indian Soc. Soil Sci., 48(1): 71-75.

Dubey, S.K. 1998. Response of Soybean (*Glycine max*) to Bio fertilizers with and without Nitrogen, Phosphorus and Potassium on Swell-shrink Soil. *Indian J. Agron.,* 43 (3): 546-549.

Duhoon, S.S., A. Jyotishi, M.R. Deshmukh and N.B. Singh. 2004. Optimization of Sesame Production through Bio-natural Inputs. In: International Crop Science Congress. September 2004. Available from www.cropscience.org.au/icsc.2004.

Duhoon, S.S., M.R. Deskmukh, H.C. Jain and U. Goswami. 2002. Integrated Nutrient Management in Sesame for Kymore Plateau Zone of Madhya Pradesh. Journal of Oilseeds Research, 19: 73-75.

Edna Antony, M.B. Doddaman, A.R. Alagavadi and M.B. Chetti. 2000. Response of Groundnut Genotypes to Nitrogen Level, and Inoculation. *Annals of Agricultural Research,* 21(2): 311-313.

Farnia A. and Moayedi M. 2014. Effect of Phosphate and Nitrogene Bio fertilizers on yield, yield Components, Oil and Protein in Sunflower (*helianthus annus* L.). *Bull. Env. Pharmacol. Life Sci.,* 3: 110-117.

Farnia A. and Moayedi M. 2015. Study on some Morphological Characteristics and Phonological Stages of Sunflower (*Heliantus annuus* L.) under Application of Bio-fertilizers. *International Journal of Biosciences,* 6(5), 317-323.

Gangwal, T.V., Patel, M.V. and Jadav, N.J. 2011. Effect of Phosphorus, Sulphur and Hosphate Solubilising Bacteria on yield, Nutrient uptake and Soil Fertility after Harvest of Mustard. Indian J. Fertilizer 7: 32-40.

Gautam, P. and Pant, L. M. 2002. Effect of co inoculation of Pseudomonas Species and Brady rhizobium japonicum on Nitrogen and Phosphorus Availability to Soybean (Glycine max). Indian J. Agric. Sci., 72(4): 248-251.

Ghodke, P.D., M.A. Jagannath and V.J. Takankhar. 2018. Effect of Integrated Nutrient Management on Growth and yield of Soybean (*Glycine max* L. Meril). International Journal of Chemical Studies, 6(4): 264-266.

Ghosh, D.C. and M. Mohiuddin. 2002. Response of Summer Sesame (*Sesamum indicum* L.) to Biofertilizers and Growth Regulator. *Agricultural Science Digest,* 20(2): 90-92.

Gosh, G. and S.C. Poi. 1998. Response of r*hizobium,* Phosphorus Solubilizing Bacteria and Mycorrhizal, Organisms on some Legume Crops. *Env. Ecol.,* 16 (3): 607-610.

Govindan, K. and Thirumurugan. 2003. Effect of Rhizobium and PSMS in Soybean. J. Maharashtra Agric. Univ., 28(1): 54-60.

Gudadhe, N.N., Mankar, P.S., Khawale, V.S. and Don-garkar, K.P. 2005. Effect of Biofertilizers on Growth and yield of Mustard (*Brassica junceaL.*). *Journal of Soils and Crops,* 15(1): 160-162.

Gupta, R.K., S. Kaushik, P. Sharma and V.K. Jain. 2003. Biofertilizers: An Ecofriendly Alternative to Chemical Fertilizers. Environmental Challenges of the 21st Century, APH Publishing Corporation, New Delhi, pp 275-287. Hameed Ansari A, SM Qayym, M Usman Usmani Khail (1993). Impact of Row Spacing and NPK Fertilizer Levels on the Growth, Seed yield and Oil Content in Pea Nut. Oil crops Newsletter, 10: 50-53.

Hedge, D.M. 1998. Integrated Nutrient Management for Production Sustainability of Oilseeds. J. of Oilseeds Res. 15(1): 1-17.

Imayavaramban, V, K.Thanunathan, R. Singaravel and G. Manickam. 2002. Studies on the Influence of Integrated Nutrient Management on Growth, yield Parameters and Seed yield of Sesame (*Sesamum indicum* L.). Crop Research, 24 (2): 309-313.

Jain, P.C. and S.K. Trivedi. 2005. Response of Soybean to Phosphorus Biofertilizers. *Legume Res.*, 28(1): 30-33.

Jaishankar, S. and K.Wahab. 2005. Effect of Integrated Nutrient Management on the Growth, yield Components and yield of Sesame. Sesame and Safflower Newsletter, 20: 732.

Javahery M. and Rokhzadi A. 2011. Effects of Biofertilizer Application on Phenology and Growth of Sunflower (*Helianthus annuus* L.) Cultivars. *J. Basic. Appl. Sci. Res.,* 1(11) 2336-2338.

Joshi, M.N. 2003. Effect of Varying Levels of Irrigation, Phosphorus and Bio-fertilizers on Summer Soybean (Glycine max. (L.) Merril) under South Gujarat Condition. M.Sc (Agri.) Thesis, Submitted to GAU. Navsari.

Joshi, S.S., P.V. Thorve and K.T. Nagre. 1989. Effect of *Rhizobium* and Nitrogen on the yield and Quality of Groundnut and Soybean. *PKV Res. J.,* 13(2): 152-155.

Joshi, S.S., Thorve, P.V. and Nagre, K.T. 1989. Effect of *Rhizobium* and Nitrogen on the yield and Quality of Groundnut and Soybean. *P.K.V. Res. J.,* 13(2): 152-154.

Kadu, P.S. and Ismail, S. 2008. Impact of Organics and Bio fertilizers on yield, Quality and uptake of Major Nutrients by Safflower Grown on Vertisols. Annals of Plant Physiology. 22 (2): 214-216.

Kalaiselvan P., K. Subramaniyan and T.N Balasubramaniyan. 2002. Effect of Application of N and K on the Growth, yield Attributes and yields of Sesame. Sesame and Safflower Newsletter, 17: 62-65.

Karmakar, S., B.N. Mittra and B.C. Ghosh. 2005. Effect of Different Organic Materials with Flyash in Integrated Plant Nutrient System for Groundnut (*Arachis hypogaea* L.). *Indian Journal of Agronomy,* 50(2): 152-155.

Keshta, M.M., Rizk, T.Y. and Abdou, E.T. 2006. Sunflower Response to Mineral Nitrogen, Organic and Bio-fertilizers under Two Different Levels of Salinity. *Proc. 17th International Sunflower Conference, Córdoba, Spain.*

Khadtare, S.V., S.K. Shinde andV.M. Toradmal. 2016. Yield Attributes and Nutrient uptake of Organic Safflower (*Carthamus tinctorius* L.) in Drylands of Maharashtra. International Journal of Agricultural Sciences, 12(2): 314-318.

Khan TA, Mazid M, da Silva JA, Mohammad F, Khan MN. 2012. Role of NO-mediated H_2O_2 Signaling under Abiotic Stress (Heavy metal)-induced Oxidative Stress in Plants: An Overview. Funct Plant Sci Biotech., 25: 27-31.

Khandekar, S.D., A.K. Ghotmukale, A.S. Dambale and S.B. Suryawanshi. 2018. Response of *Kharif* Sunflower to Biofertilizers and Different Fertilizer Levels. *International J. Curr. Microbiol. App. Sci*, 6: 1558-1563.

Krishna KG, Rao KL, Kumar AR, Sreelatha P. 1995. Response of Soybean to Hydrogen, Phospnorus and Rhizobium. Journal of Maharashtra Agriculture University. 1995; 20(2): 246-248.

Kumar, V. and V.Kumar. 1994. Effect of *Azotobacter chroococum* on Indian Mustard Grown in Different Soil Environments. Crop Res., Hisar. 7(3): 446-450.

Kumar, A. 2013. Development of a Liquid Biofertilizer with Indigenous Microbial Strains of Himachal Pradesh. Available on http://shodhganga.inflibnet.ac.in Access on Dated 27th October, 2014.

Kumar, S., P. Pandey and D.K. Maheshwari. 2009. Reduction in Dose of Chemical Fertilizers and Growth Enhancement of Sesame (Sesamumindicum L.) with Application of Rhizospheric Competent Pseudomonas Aeruginosa LES4. European Journal of Soil Biology, 45 (4): 334 - 340.

Kumrawat, B., J.M. Dighe, R.A. Sharma and G.V. Katti. 1997. Respose of Soybean to Bio-fertilizer in Black Clay Soils. Crop Research, 14: 209-14.

Mahdi, A.A. and I.M.A. Atabani. 1992. Response of Bradyrhizobium inoculated Soybean and Lablab Bean to Inoculation with Vesicular Mycorrhizae. Experimental Agric., 28: 399-407.

Menaria, B.L. and Pushpendra Singh. 2004. Effect of Chemical and Biofertilizers on yield Attributing Characters and yield of Soybean *Legume Res.*, 27(3): 231-232.

Meshram,S.U., Pande, S.S., Shanware, A.S., Kamdi, R.R. and Tajane, V.S. 2005. Efficacy of Biofertilizers Integrated with Chemical Fertilizers *in-vivo* in Soybean. *Bio Fertilizer Newsletter*/July (2005).

Meshram, S.U., S.S. Pande, A.S. Shanware, R.R. Kamdi and V.S. Tajane. 2004. Efficacy of Bio Fertilizers Integrated with Chemical Fertilizers in-vivo in Soybean. *Biofert. Newsletter*, pp. 7-9.

Mirparsa T, Ganjali HR and Dahmardeh M. 2016. The Effect of Bio fertilizers on yield and yield Components of Sunflower Oil Seed and Nut. *Inter J Agriculture Bio sci.*, 5(1): 46-49.

Mohapatra, A.K.B and L. Dixit. 2010. Integrated Nutrient Management in Rainy Season Groundnut (*Arachis hypogaea*). *Indian Journal of Agronomy*, 55(2): 123-127.

Mookherjee, S., Malik, G.C., Bandyopadhyay, S. and Mitra, B. 2014. The Productivity of *Brassica rapa*var. Yellow Sarson as Influenced by Integrated Nutrient Management Practices and Seed Priming in Eastern Indian Sub-himalayan Plains. *SAARC Journal of Agriculture* 12(1): 106-116.

More, K.A., C.B. Gaikwad and D.V. Dahat. 2002. Effect of N, P, *Rhizobium* and Phosphate Solubilizing Bacteria on Groundnut. *J. Maharashtra Agric. Univ.*, 27(2): 202-204.

Mostafa GG and AA. AboBaker. 2010. Effect of Bioand Chemical Fertilization on Growth of Sunflower (Helianthus annuus L.) at South Valley Area. Asian Journal of Crop Science, 2 (3): 137-146.

Munji, R., H.B. Babalad, B.H.P. Kumara and V. Pushpa. 2010. Effect of Organics and Fermented Organics on Growth, yield and yield Component of Sesame. *Advance Research Journal of Crop Improvement*, 1(2): 97-102.

Naik, R., A.S. Halepyati and B.T. Pujar. 2007. Effect of Organic Manures and Fertilizer Levels on Growth, yield Components and yield of Safflower (*Carthamus tinctorius* L.). *Karnataka J. Agric. Sci.*, 20(4): 835-836.

Nandhagopal, A., Subramanian, K.S., Jayakumar, R. and Balasubramanian, A. 2003. Integrated Nutrient Management for Hybrid Sunflower (*Helianthus annus*L.). *Madras Agric. J.*, 90(1-3): 66-73.

Naseri R, Mirzaei A. 2010. Response of Yield and Yield Components of Safflower (Carthamustinctorius L.) To Seed Inoculation with Azotobacter and azospirillum and Different Nitrogen Levels under Dry Land Conditions. American-Eurasian J. Agric. & Environ. Sci., 9 (4): 445-449.

Naseri Rahim, Mirzaei Amir and Vazan Saied. 2010. Response of Yield and Yield Components of Safflower (Carthamus tinctorius L.) to Seed Inoculation with Azotobacter and Azospirillum and Different Nitrogen Levels under Dry Land Condition. World Applied Sci. J., 11(10), 1287-1291.

Naveen Kumar R, 2010. Isolation and Characterization of Rhizobia for Soybean from Adilabad District. M.Sc Thesis, ANGRAU, Hyderabad.

Ola, B.L, B.L. Pareek, R.S. Yadav, A.C. Shivran and O.P. Sharma. 2013. Influence of Integrated Nutrient Management on Productivity and Quality of Groundnut in Western Rajasthan, *Annals of Agricultural Research New series*. 34(2): 156-159.

Palaniappan, S.P., A. Jeyabal, and S. Chelliah.1999. Evaluation of Integrated Nutrient Management in Summer Sesame (*Sesamum indicum*L.). *Sesame and Safflower Newsletter,* 14: 33-36.

Pandzou, J., P. Beunard and M.H. Saint. 1990. Inoculation of Soybean in Congo. *Agronomic. Tropicale,* 45: 199-204.

Panwar, A.S. and Singh, N.P. 2003. Effects of Conjunctive use of Phosphorus and Bio-organics on Growth and yield of Groundnut (*Arachis hypogaea).Indian J. of Agron.*,48(3): 214-216.

Panwar, A.S, N.P.S Singh, D.C. Saxena and V.K. Hazarika. 2002. Nutrient Management in Groundnut (*Arachis hypogaea*) in Mid Hills of Meghalaya. *Extended Summaries, 2nd International Agronomy Congress,* New Delhi, 1: 277-278.

Paramasivam, V., V.K. Ravichandran, P.K. Venkatesan and V. Manoharan. 2003. Nutrient Management for Seed yield Maximization in Sesame (*Sesamum indicum*L.). *Sesame-and-Safflower- Newslett.*, (18): 61-63.

Patel, D.P., G.C. Munda and N.P.Singh. 2002. Response of Groundnut (*ArachishypogaeaL.*) to Rhizobium and PSM Inoculation in the Acid Soils of Meghalaya. Journal of Oilseeds Research, 19(2): 245-246.

Patel, S.R. and D.S. Thakur.1997. Influence of Phosphorous and *Rhizobium* on yield Attributes, yield and Nutrient uptake of Groundnut (*Arachis hypogaea*L.). *J. Oil seeds Res,* 14(2): 189-193.

Patil, R.S., K.R. Swati, N.K. Kalegore and P.R. Dadgale. 2014. Effect of Inorganic and Bio-fertilizers on Growth and yield of Summer Groundnut. *Adv. Res. J. Crop Improv.*,5 (1): 23-25.

Patra, P, B.K. Pati, G.K. Ghosh, Mura SS and A. Saha. 2013. Effect of Bio fertilizers and Sulphur on Growth, Yield, and Oil Content of Hybrid Sunflower (Helianthus annuus. L) In a Typical Lateritic Soil. 2: Scientific Reports, 2 (1):1-5.

Patra, P., Pati, B.K., Ghosh, G.K., Mura, S.S., Saha, A. 2013. Effect of Bio fertilizers and Sulphur on Growth, yield, and Oil Content of Hybrid Sunflower (*Helianthus annuus.*L) in a Typical Lateritic Soil. 2: 603 doi:10.4172/scientificreports. 603 Page.

Patra, R.K., A.K. Patra, K. Pradhan and R.N. Nayak.2008. Response of Groundnut (*Arachis hypogaea*L.) to Rhizobium and Phosphobacterium Inoculation. *Journal of Research. Orissa Univ.* Agric, Tech., 26 (2) 43-47.

Poonia, T.C., A.D. Raj and M.S. Pithia. 2014. Effect of Organic, Inorganic and Biofertilizers on Productivity and Economics of Groundnut-pigeonpea Relay Intercropping System in *vertisols* of Gujarat. Journal of Experimental Biology and Agricultural Sciences, 2 (6): 560-566.

Pramanik, K. and A.K. Bera. 2013. Effect of Biofertilizers and Phytohormone on Growth, Productivity and Quality of Sunflower (*Helianthus annuus.* L). Journal of Crop and Weed, 9(2): 122-127.

Raja, D. and V.G. Takankhar. 2017. Effect of Liquid Bio fertilizers (*Brady rhizobium* and PSB) on Availability of Nutrients and Soil Chemical Properties of Soybean (*Glycine max* L.). *International J. Pure App. Biosci.*, 5 (5): 88-96.

Ram Chatra Singh, H.B., R.B. Patel, H. Singh and G. Kumar. 2013. Effect of Various Nutrient Sources on Productivity and Economics of Groundnut (*Arachishypogaea*L.). *Annals of Agricultural Research,* 34(2): 176-178.

Saini, L.B., P.J. George and S.S. Bhadana. 2017. Effect of Nitrogen Management and Biofertilizers on Growth and Yield of Rapeseed (*Brassica campestris* var. toria). *Int. J. Curr. Microbiol. App. Sci* 6(8): 2652-2658.

Sarala, N.V. and A. Jagannatham. 2002. Effect of Nitrogen and *Azospirillum* on yield Attributes and yield of Sesame under Rainfed Conditions. *Journal of Oilseeds Research,* 19(1):125-126.

Satpute, U.V., V.V. Gabhane, D.V Mali and M.B Nagdeve. 2018. Impact of Integrated Application of Mineral Fertilizer and Glyricidia Green Leaf Manuring on yield and Nutrient uptake by Soybean in Vertisols. Journal of Pharmacognosy and Phytochemistry, 7(1): 1110-1113.

Sawarkar, S.D. and N.S. Thakur. 2001. Effect of Fertilizer and Phosphorus Solubilizing Bacteria on the yield of Soybean (*Glycine max* L. Merr.). *J. Oilseeds Res.*, 18(2): 198-200.

Senthil Kumar, D., P. Satheesh Kumar, V. Uthaya Kumar and G. Anbuganapathi. 2014. Influence of Bio fertilizer Mixed Flower Waste Vermicompost on the Growth, yield and Quality of Groundnut (*Arachis hypogea*). World Applied Sciences Journal. 31 (10): 1715-1721.

Senthilkumar, R., V. Imayavaramban, K. Thanunathan and G. Manickam. 2000. Effect of intra-row Spacing and Different Levels of Nitrogen in Combination with *Azospirillum* Inoculation on Growth and yield of Sesamum. Research on Crops 1(3), 351-354.

Shaikh, A.A. Desai, M.M. Shinde, S.B. and Tambe, A.D. 2010. Yield of Summer Sesame (*Sesamumindicum*L.) as Influenced by Nutrient Management. *International Journal of Agricultural Sciences,* 6 (1): 144-146.

Sharma S, Jat NL, Puniya MM, Shivran AC and Choudhury S. 2014. Fertility Levels and Bio fertilizers on Nutrient Concentrations, uptake and Quality of Groundnut. *Annals of Agricultural Research, New Series,* 35 (1): 71-74.

Sharma, K.N and K.N. Namdeo. 1999. Effect of Bio-fertilizers and Phosphorus on Growth and yield of Soybean. Crop Research, 17: 160-3.

Sharma, S., N.L. Jat, A.C. Shivran, S. Choudhary, M.M. Puniya and R.L. Jeetarwal. 2013. Effect of Fertility Levels of Bio fertilizers on yield and Economics of Groundnut, *Annals of Agricultural Research,* 34 (4): 353-356.

Shehata, M.M. and El-Khawas, S. A. 2013. Effect of Two Bio fertilizers on Growth Parameters, yield Characters, Nitrogenous Components, Nucleic Acids Content, Minerals, Oil Content, Protein Profiles and DNA Banding Pattern of Sunflower (*Helianthus annus*L. cv. Vedock) yield. *Pakistan Journal of Biological Sciences,* 6(14): 1257-1268.

Shillode, G.U. D.S. Patil, S.D. Patil and S.R. Joshi. 2016. Soil Properties and yield of Safflower as Influenced by Different Fertilizers. Research Journal of Agriculture and Forestry Sciences, 4(2): 13-16.

Simanungkalit, R.D.M., R.I. Roughley, R.D. Hastuti, A. Indrasumunar and E. Pratiwii. 1996. Inoculation of Soybean with Selected Strains of Brady Rhizobium Japonicum can Increase yield on Acid Soils in Indonesia. Soil Bio. Biochem., 28 (2): 251-259.

Singh MS, Dutta S. 2006. Mustard and Rapeseed Response to Azotobacter-A review. Agricultural Reviews, 27 (3): 232-234.

Singh SR, Nasar GR, Singh U. 2007. Productivity and Nutrient uptake of Soybean (*Glycine max*.) as Influenced by Bio inoculants and Farm yard Manure under Rainfed Condition. Indian J. Agron., 52(4): 325-329.

Singh SR, Singh U, Singh JK. 2009. Effect of Bio inoculants and FYM on Growth, yield and Quality of Soybean (*Glycine max*) under Rainfed Conditions of Kashmir Valley. Ann. Agric. New Series, 30 (3 & 4): 87-90.

Singh, G.P., P.L. Singh and A.S. Panwar. 2011. Response of Groundnut (*Arachis hypogaea*) to Biofertilizer, Organic and Inorganic Sources of Nutrient in North East India. *Legume Research*, 34(3): 196-201.

Singh, G.P., P.L. Singh and A.S. Panwar. 2013. Seed yield Quality and Nutrient Uptake of Groundnut (*Arachishypogaea*) as Affected by Integrated Nutrient Management in mid hill Attitude of Meghalaya, India, *Legume Research*, 36 (2): 147-152.

Singh, R., A.K. Singh and P. Kumar. 2014. Performance of Indian Mustard (*Brassica juncia L.*) in Response to Integrated Nutrient Management. Journal of Agri. Search, 6 (1): 34-38.

Solanki, R.L., S.Mahendra., S.K.Sharma, H.S.Purohit and V. Arvind. 2015. Effect of Different Level of Phosphorus, Sulphur and PSB on the yield of Indian Mustard (*Brassica juncea*L.) and Soil Properties and Available Macronutrients. Scholarly Journal of Agricultural Science Vol. 5(9), pp. 305-310.

Sonkar, T., R. Lakpale and S.S. Tuteja. 2008. Productivity of Soybean (*Glycine max* L. Merrill) as Influenced by Integrated Nutrient Management Practices under Vertisols of Chhattisgarh Plains. Soybean Research, 6: 81-84.

Subramanian, K., P. Sridhar and N. Arulmozhi. 1999. Response of Sesame to Sulphur and Micronutrients with and without Farmyard Manure under Irrigated Condition. *Indian J. Agron.*, 44 (4): 826-829.

Sudhakar C, Sudha Rani C. 2010. Effect of Inclusion of Biofertilizers as part of INM on yield and Economics of Safflower (*Carthamus tinctorius* L). 7th International Safflower Conference, P: 122-126.

Thanki, J.D., M.N. Joshi and V.M. Patel. 2005. Effect of Irrigation, Phosphorus and Bio fertilizer on Growth and yield of Summer Soybean (Glycine max L. Merrill) under South Gujarat Condition. Journal of Oilseeds Research, 22: 373-5.

Thelen, K. and T. Schulz. 2010. Soybean Facts. http//web/.msue.msu.edu/soybean.

Thiruppathi, M., K. Thanunathan, M. Ganapathy, M. Prakash and V. Imayavaramban. 2001. Nutrient uptake and Quality Characters of Sesame (*Sesamum indicum*L.) as Influenced by Micronutrient, Bio fertilizer and Phytohormones. Sesame and Safflower Newsletter, 16: 195.

Umale SM, Thosar VR, Chrey AB, Chimate AN. 2002. Growth Response of Soybean to P Solubilizing Bacteria and Phosphorus Level. Journal of Soils and Crops. 2002; 12(2): 258-261.

Vyas, S.P. 2005. Interactive Effects of Nitrogen and Bio-fertilizers on Indian Mustard. Annals of Arid Zone, 44(2): 147-150.

Wayase, K.P., B.D. Thakur and M.D. Bhalekar. 2014. Influence of Chemical Fertilizer and Bio Fertilizer Application on Yield Contributing Characters of Sesame. World Journal of Agricultural Sciences 10 (3): 91-94.

Yadav HK, Thomas T and Khajuria V. 2010. Effect of Different Levels of Sulphur and Bio fertilizer on the yield of Indian Mustard (*Brassica juncea* L.) and Soil Properties. Journal of Agricultural Physics, 10 (1): 61-65.

Yyas, S.P. 2003. Efficacy of Bio fertilizer on *Brassica* Genotypes in Arid Gujarat. *Fertilizer News,* 48*:* 49-51.

Zalate, P.Y. and D.R. Padmani 2009. Effect of Organic Manure and Bio fertilizers on yield, Harvest Index, Shelling Percentage and Quality of Kharif Groundnut (*Arachis hypogeae*L.). 5 (2): 417-419.

Zaltate, P.Y. and Padmani, D.R. 2009. Effect of Organic Manure and Biofertilizers on Growth and yield Attributing Characters of *Kharif* Groundnut. *Internat. J. agric. Sci.,* 5(2): 343-345.

Zarei, I., Y. Sohrabi, G. Reza, A. Heidari Jalilian and K. Mohammadi. 2012. Effects of Biofertilizers on Grain yield and Protein Content of Two Soybean (Glycine max L.) Cultivars. African Journal of Biotechnology, 11 (27): 7028-7037.

ZehraEkin. 2010. Performance of Phosphate Solubilizing Bacteria for Improving Growth and yield of Sunflower (*Helianthus annuus*L.) in the Presence of Phosphorus Fertilizer. *Afr. J. Biotechnol.,* 9(25): 3794-3800.

Index

❐ ❐ ❐ ❐ ❐ ❐